D1436439

To

THOMAS PYLES, with respect and affection.

WOODCUT OF THE KNIGHT
by Richard Pynson, c. 1490

artistic ambivalence
in chaucer's knight's tale

by

PAUL T. THURSTON Howell III

UNIVERSITY OF FLORIDA PRESS

Gainesville • 1968

A University of Florida Press Book

DESIGNED BY STANLEY D. HARRIS

*Library of Congress
Catalog Card No. 68-24367*

PRINTED FOR THE PUBLISHER BY
STORTER PRINTING COMPANY, INCORPORATED
GAINESVILLE, FLORIDA

preface

THE PRINCIPAL PROBLEM embodied in this book was first presented to me by Thomas Pyles, whose communications of his own perceptions of Chaucer's humor and satire in *The Knight's Tale* were largely responsible for my desire to undertake this study. Throughout its course he has been unfailingly generous with his professional help and advice. Earlier, as my master in Chaucerian studies, he was patient beyond measure as a mentor and guide.

The approach to humor and satire I adopted in this study grew out of conversations with James Willard Oliver, to whom I owe an intellectual debt far greater than I can ever repay. I am particularly grateful to Herschel H. Elliott for his detailed criticism of the entire manuscript and for his invaluable help in those portions which deal with logical analysis. Stephen F. Fogle's suggestions have been especially valuable in clarifying what I believe is the most important aspect of the relationship between Boccaccio's *Teseida* and *The Knight's Tale*. Lalia P. Boone's criticism of my analyses of the metrical romances has been most welcome. I am indebted to C. A. Robertson for his painstaking reading of the manuscript and thoughtful suggestions. I have freely drawn upon Professor Robert A. Pratt's carefully executed English summaries of Boccaccio's *Teseida*, and supplemented substantial segments of them. Paola Boezi Langford's advice and assistance in translating

portions of the *Teseida* have been most helpful; the linear translations in Chapters VI and VII are entirely hers.

I have freely drawn upon the advice and suggestions of an
unidentified reader to whom I offer here my sincere thanks. Also,
to Chaucerians past and present I gratefully acknowledge enormous indebtedness.

Less tangibly, much of the most significant creative experience
I have undergone in the final preparation of this work evolved
from what I consider to be the total personal context of Michel-
angelo's "La Notte." One can acknowledge and try to comprehend,
but gratitude is perhaps superfluous.

This work could not have been accomplished without the steadfast faith and constant encouragement of my wife.

PAUL T. THURSTON

Gainesville, Florida

contents

introduction

M Y PURPOSE IN THIS STUDY is to demonstrate that *The Knight's Tale* may be interpreted from a point of view very different from that which has been so ably reiterated in various related forms by many generations of critics. It has long been considered a shining example of the medieval metrical romance—a tale of courtly love and chivalric warring on the grandest scale, replete with knightly valor and a lovely heroine. This is both the traditional and the still prevailing interpretation; it has been so authoritatively demonstrated that there is no need in this examination for extensive documentation of either its existence or the evidence upon which it is based. My concern with this entire body of critical work is limited to acknowledging the tenor of Chaucerian thought it represents and to pointing out certain of its difficulties from the standpoint of a *total* critical assessment of *The Knight's Tale*.

Accordingly, a second point of view is presented and examined in some detail here—that for the sophisticated reader *The Knight's Tale* is a work of art satirizing the hallowed institutions of the chivalric tradition and their literary and supposed societal foundations. I most emphatically do not insist that the poem is unadulterated satire, but rather that it may be interpreted on two levels, determined by the kind of audience reading it. Thus for the more literal-minded it idealizes the faded age of chivalry and embodies in graceful quantity the traditional elements of the metrical romance. But for the more realistic, Chaucer's treatment of these elements of medieval romance, as opposed to their seemingly copious presence in the work, becomes extremely significant. Herein, then, lies Chaucer's artistic ambivalence: a glowing tale of chivalry for the one kind of reader and a satire of cherished chivalric traditions as well as the literary forms in which they are celebrated for the more sophisticated reader. Since the former interpretation enjoys almost universal and exclusive scholarly sanction, it is my intention to demonstrate the existence and significance of the poem's pervasive satire and humor.

The point of view concerning Chaucer's satirical intent embodied throughout this book is that what is conveyed is germane, whether or not it is intentionally conveyed. I make no attempt to demonstrate Chaucer's literary purposes in terms of empirical proof, whatever my personal convictions may be.

The scope of my examination, then, is limited to an extension of earlier scholarly contributions to our knowledge of *The Knight's Tale* by the addition of a new dimension to our appreciation of it; there is no attempt to differ fundamentally from many of the Chaucerian critics of the past. It is further limited to the establishment of this new dimension of appreciation in terms of the modern reader. That it might have been at least equally obvious to a reader of comparable literary sophistication in Chaucer's own day need not for present purposes be insisted upon. Finally, there are certain implications in this investigation for future work in Chaucerian studies. These will be considered in the concluding chapter.

I have begun the study with a synthesis of the traditional critical view of *The Knight's Tale*. This is followed by a discussion of Chaucerian humor, including analyses of passages from Chaucer's works upon which there is a substantial measure of scholarly agreement as to their humorous and satirical content. The final area of examination is a detailed consideration of the poem's four books and an assessment of its love complex, partly in terms of the conclusions derived from the preceding portions of the essay.

I

the traditional point of view

NTIL RELATIVELY RECENTLY there has been a surprising lack of disagreement among critics as to the fundamental nature of *The Knight's Tale*. Indeed, despite the fact that it is widely acknowledged as one of the best known and most frequently read works of Chaucer, the body of critical material specifically devoted to it is comparatively small. There are several explanations which may account for this.

In the first place, it is patently somewhat difficult for the student reading *The Knight's Tale* for the first time to actually "test" prior critical authority. The notes in his text will characterize the work as medieval romance and additional critical opinion, with few exceptions, supports such a characterization. Furthermore, the work *is*, in one very well documented view, a metrical romance in terms of its external characteristics. There is no strikingly apparent reason for most readers to perceive its other dimensions at the first sitting, if their only critical background is this authoritatively documented traditional point of view.

If the age of chivalry was already fading into the gossamer of "used-to-be" in Chaucer's time—indeed, it always was in the past—*The Knight's Tale* must have been dated, at least in some respects, for some members of its contemporary audience. For later audiences it has inevitably become more dated. The fuzziness of much of the characterization, so atypical of most of Chaucer's creative

1

work, emphasizes the datedness by indirectly removing attention from the characters to the long extinct codes and rites of chivalry. The student is perhaps inclined, then, as he progresses in Chaucerian studies, to view *The Knight's Tale* as an example of Chaucer's genius in a genre which is primarily of historical interest. He therefore goes on to the "modernity" and "presence" of the Human Comedy in much of the rest of Chaucer's poetry, where he finds that stimulating controversy and critical potentialities are much more apparent than in *The Knight's Tale*.

Also, in part, the relatively small amount of criticism and analysis of *The Knight's Tale* may be accounted for by the kind of critical investigations undertaken in the late nineteenth and early twentieth centuries. The invaluable work of such masters as Skeat, Furnivall, Manly, and Ten Brink, to name but four, was primarily directed toward philological and bibliographical research, and only secondarily toward textual criticism more or less directly related to their findings in these areas.

Finally, because the detailed descriptions have emphasized the paraphernalia of metrical romance, the genre of *The Knight's Tale* appears straightforward. It would seem evident, then, that all these factors have given rise to the established or traditional interpretation, which I shall treat here in terms of some of the critical problems it fails to resolve. An analysis with a fresh, unprejudiced approach will demonstrate the subtlety underlying the poem and establish the grounds for an additional, satirical interpretative dimension.

Even if space permitted, no useful purpose could be served by the mere chronological cataloguing of centuries of critical opinion on *The Knight's Tale*. I have therefore selected from the quantity of material available that which satisfies two related criteria. First, it is typical of the traditional point of view and, second, it is the product of authoritative and influential critics and hence is representative of the most widely accepted interpretations from 1700 to the present. Much of this criticism reflects the difficulties involved in accepting the traditional view of the poem as a totally serious work in the romance genre.

One of the most renowned critical statements on *The Knight's Tale* is that of Dryden: "I prefer in our Countryman [Chaucer], far above all his other Stories, the Noble Poem of *Palamon* and *Arcite*, which is of the Epique kind, and perhaps not much inferior to the

Ilias or the *Aeneis*: the story is more pleasing than either of them, the Manners as perfect, the Diction as poetical, the Learning as deep and various; and the Disposition full as artful: only it includes a greater length of time; as taking up seven years at least; but Aristotle has left undecided the Duration of the Action; which yet is easily reduc'd to the compass of a year, by a Narration of what preceded the Return of Palamon to Athens."[1]* One of the points of interest in this statement is Dryden's pronouncing the poem an epic. Possibly he was in part influenced by the epic form of the *Teseida*, which he recognized as Chaucer's source. The importance of the term is that it emphasizes the highly serious nature of his interpretation.

Dryden found the work a "Noble Poem," then, comparable in several ways to the *Iliad* and the *Aeneid*, surely two of the most seriously heroic works in Western literature. He was so impressed with these aspects of *The Knight's Tale* that he even made an attempt—if a rather lame one—to find a means of bringing it more nearly within what he apparently intuited to be an Aristotelian "duration," Aristotle having failed to be specific in this matter. The fact remains, however, that of the poem's four books, no less than two are devoted to the events which take place prior to the return of Palamon to Athens. Hence, although Dryden's interest was sufficiently aroused to move him to consider the problem, he did not attach to it the same kind of significance I am concerned with here, since he considered the work solely as one of high seriousness.

Basically, Dryden's comments form an accurate summation of the traditional interpretation of the poem, expressed in neo-classical terms. Until very recently, this literal, serious approach has been the prevailing one, with modifications which can be accounted for by the critical tastes of the literary periods concerned. During the Romantic period, for example, more detailed analysis of a clearly aesthetic nature made its appearance. Scott exemplified this kind of criticism: "The work of Chaucer cannot, however, be termed a translation [from the *Teseida*]; on the contrary, the tale has acquired its most beautiful passages under the hand of the English bard. He abridged the prolix, and enlarged the poetical, parts of the work; compressed the whole into one concise and interesting tale; and left us an example of a beautiful heroic poem."[2] Here

*Notes citing sources begin on page 233.

again *The Knight's Tale* is pronounced a serious heroic work in the most uncompromising terms. Most readers today, whatever their background in medieval literature, would hardly refer to it as "concise," however interesting they might find it. Even considered as a serious work in the metrical romance genre, it is not lacking in verbosity.

Another characteristic example of the nineteenth-century Romantic criticism of the poem is this brief comment of Hazlitt's: "The death of Arcite is the more affecting, as it comes after triumph and victory, after the pomp of sacrifice, the solemnities of prayer, the celebration of the gorgeous rites of chivalry."[3] This touches the very core of Chaucer's art in the poem: his great powers of description so lavishly expended upon the spectacles of medieval pageantry and his sense of the dramatic, which is so obviously characteristic of almost all his poetry. But what lies behind this "celebration of the gorgeous rites of chivalry"? It is a contest of arms on an almost incredible scale of grandeur for a girl who speaks but once throughout the entire affair, and at that only to indicate her total indifference to the outcome of the struggle. She is not in love with either combatant and supposedly does not wish to marry; she is simply resigned to her fate. Surely this is carrying chivalric rites and courtly love convention beyond considerations of form and genre. The death of Arcite, upon careful analysis, does not appear as completely moving as Hazlitt implies. Indeed, some aspects of Arcite's death are certainly facetious, as Professor Baum has recently insisted.[4]

Few men have contributed as greatly to medieval studies over so many years as Skeat, Manly, Ten Brink, and Furnivall. They exemplified in ideals and accomplishment the finest in late nineteenth-century and early twentieth-century Chaucer criticism. We have them to thank for authoritative texts, much of the present-day understanding of Chaucer's language, and, through some of their distinguished students, the wide interest and consequent great accomplishments in Chaucer studies today. Manly had this to say about *The Knight's Tale*:

Boccaccio's *Teseide* is a fine example of the courtly epic. It is full of brilliant and elaborate descriptions of sieges, and social functions, and of long and eloquent speeches. Partly by eliminating these features, and partly by confining his narrative strictly to the love story of Palamon and Arcite, Chaucer has reduced the length of the poem to about one-fifth the original, has simplified its structure, and given it the qualities of a metrical romance instead of those of a courtly epic. The interest in Boccaccio's poem lay chiefly in its rich elaboration; that of Chaucer's lies chiefly in dramatic situation. The characters are, with the exception of Theseus, drawn in simple outline. This is doubtless due, not to any lack of development of Chaucer's power of characterization, but to the requirements of the story itself. Emelye has necessarily no individuality, not so much because of her youth, but because she is merely the prize for which the two noble kinsmen contend. They in their turn are necessarily so much alike that the reader is as little able to choose between them as was Emelye herself.[5]

This is a later version of the traditional point of view and is representative of the interpretations of Manly's most authoritative contemporaries. There has been little disagreement with this view, and the few differences that exist are more concerned with matters of detail than fundamentals. For instance, Professor Marckwardt disagrees with Manly's opinion concerning the characterization of Palamon and Arcite. He finds Arcite less active and more realistic than Palamon, as well as intellectually superior to him. Palamon, he maintains, is more emotional and idealistic but less able than Arcite to express himself clearly. Fairchild, however, has expressed almost the opposite point of view of the two royal Thebans. For him, the fault of Arcite is that he is "too completely devoted to the Active Life" while "the fault of Palamon . . . lies in excessive devotion to the Contemplative Life." In the end, Palamon becomes what a man should be—"a working dreamer."[6] Such differences of detail do not affect the interpretation of the poem as a serious metrical romance when they are considered singly, however important they may be intrinsically. When they are considered cumulatively, however, one's doubt that the traditional point of view is the only possible interpretation becomes acute.

Another, more far-reaching difference of opinion has arisen more recently. This finds its expression in what might be called the philosophical point of view. It is perhaps best articulated by Professor Lumiansky, who holds that *The Knight's Tale* is in fact a philosophical poem, illustrating in its events the tenets of Boethian thought, of which Chaucer had such a thorough knowledge. Accordingly, the poem as romance becomes a kind of peg on which to hang philosophical clothing.[7] In point of fact, there seems to be no reason why the work cannot still be a metrical romance. Each metrical romance implies or expresses a philosophy of life—that of the age of chivalry—no less systematic and broad in scope than Boethian philosophy. If Chaucer blended another philosophical dimension into *The Knight's Tale* in combination with that of the chivalric age, it becomes a richer work but scarcely one of another genre. In any case, such factors still do not alter the fundamental assumption of the traditional point of view, that the work is entirely serious.

Robert Kilburn Root had a somewhat more subjective approach to *The Knight's Tale*: "If we are to read the Knight's Tale in the spirit in which Chaucer conceived it, we must give ourselves up to the spirit of romance; we must not look for subtle characterization, nor for strict probability of action; we must delight in the fair shows of things, and not ask too many questions. Chaucer can be realistic enough when he so elects; but here he has chosen otherwise." Concerning Emelye, "Chaucer wisely kept her a vision and a name, letting us realize her character only in its effect upon others."[8] Certainly if one accepts the traditional point of view, Root's advice is at first glance thoroughly sound as well as charmingly persuasive, for it is a truism that works in the metrical romance genre do not lend themselves readily to divulge "sensible answers to sensible questions." This might seem especially apparent to the modern reader who has not been initiated into the labyrinthine ideals of the chivalric age. But even to the reader who has such a background, Root's admonition is difficult to resist, for if one compares *The Knight's Tale* to several of the monuments of the metrical romance genre, using basic criteria, one discovers that the poem eludes "sensible" analysis far more completely than can be accounted for by "the spirit of romance." Certainly many of its external characteristics—style, medieval pageantry, knightly combat, courtly love, and the like—are indeed found in the romance, but this need not dull our critical acumen or prevent us from seeing beyond appearances.

If the metrical romance genre requires us to practice especially diligently Coleridge's "willing suspension of disbelief," we may still assess such a work in "sensible" terms. If we take as our major premise the view that metrical romances cannot be appreciated except by taking "delight in the fair shows of things" and similar subjective approaches, Root's comments are sound. But such a major premise is unsound in at least one important respect, since more empirical approaches to an appreciation of the genre are possible.

One of Root's comments on *The Canterbury Tales* seems to be a striking instance of the operation of environmental influences: "It would have been perfectly possible to give a true picture of the varied humanity which made up the Canterbury pilgrimage, without suffering those churls [the Miller and the Reeve] to tell their 'cherles tales,' which no sophistry can elevate to true art." Evaluative judgments galore have been proffered on such opinions as this one, and I have no intention of joining the fray. It is perhaps sufficient to state that while there are still adherents to such a view, few critics today would insist that the presence of salaciousness in a work precludes its being true art. This seems quite clearly an example of changing societal values and emphasizes the difference between the values of some members of Root's generation and those of some of our own.

But analogically such a view as Root's on the "cherles tales" is not greatly different from the traditional point of view of *The Knight's Tale*. If Root's and similar views marked the prevailing attitude toward *The Miller's Tale* and *The Reeve's Tale* and became the traditional point of view concerning these works, the situation would be very much like that of *The Knight's Tale* and what has become the traditional point of view toward it. For, if a work is salacious, there would be little more to be said—it is classified and its critical fate settled. And what of *The Knight's Tale*? According to the traditional interpretation it is a metrical romance, and beyond elaboration of the time-honored external characteristics of the genre appearing in the poem, there is little to be said—it has been classified and its critical fate settled until someone *does* ask "too many questions."

Another aspect of the traditional point of view is illustrated in William George Dodd's remark, which summarizes his discussion of the principal difference between the *Teseida* and *The Knight's Tale*: "The total result is that which Chaucer was doubtless aiming at: namely to heighten the impression that the love passion of the two heroes was not only earnest but absolutely genuine."[9] Dodd's main concern is courtly love. Most critics agree upon the nature of these aspects of the poem, and it is often cited, together with *Troilus and Criseyde* and the translation of portions of *The Romaunt of the Rose*, as an example of Chaucer's treatment of this medieval convention, so fraught with chivalric codified rules and rites.

Coulton, too, was concerned with those aspects of the poem relating to courtly love: "Emelye is, within her limits, as beautiful and touching a figure as any in poetry; but her limits are those of a figure in a stained glass window, compared with a portrait of Titian's." He concludes that "tacit assumption of the chivalric love code comes out clearly in *The Knight's Tale*."[10] One of the most influential American students of English literary history, George Lyman Kittredge, also subscribed to the traditional point of view. In a discussion of *The Canterbury Tales* he writes of the Miller thrusting himself forward in his drunkenness "to tell a story as soon as the Knight has finished his romance of Palamon and Arcite."[11]

These three critics reflect the traditional point of view in the humorlessness of their approach, but the questions which arise here hinge upon the nature of courtly love. Taking at face value the many statements by various authorities, we encounter grave difficulties when we cite *The Knight's Tale* as an example of this erotic ideology.

Root in his discussion of courtly love says that marriage has no part in it.[12] Dodd and Lewis concur.[13] Indeed, the consensus of renowned scholars in this matter approaches unanimity. There is also the concept of secrecy in courtly love affairs; Root, representative of critical views on the subject, insists that "this irreconcilable conflict of standards that a love which is not only right and proper but ideally noble should if known become the height of dishonor, marks the essential artificiality of the whole code of courtly love."[14] What, then, of the public nature of the love contest in *The Knight's Tale*? What, too, of the marriage of Palamon and Emelye? There are, of course, other views of courtly love—D. W. Robertson, Jr.'s, for example—pertinent aspects of which will be considered later. But, as we shall discover, the difficulties remain.

Among contemporary critics, the traditional view still prevails, although much more interest is being shown in and emphasis placed upon the humorous passages of the poem. Professor Baum particularly has gone very far in this direction, but he has not attempted, as I am here doing, to add an entire humorous-satirical dimension to the appreciation of the work. Patch and

Tatlock both found at least one satirical aspect of *The Knight's Tale,* dependent principally upon characterization. Before considering these relatively bolder views, representative recent adherents to the more conservative aspects of the traditional point of view will be cited.

Professor Shelly is typical:

The Knight's Tale is a romance—the finest metrical romance we have in English. It is a tale of chivalry and romantic love. . . . The poem is out-and-out romantic.

As is to be expected in a romance, the characters of the *Knight's Tale* are less clearly drawn than are those of the other tales.

Palamon and Arcite are a bit blurred. They are not like the vivid, individualized characters of Chaucer's more realistic stories. They are conventional knightly lovers of medieval romance.[15]

This is clearly a reiteration of long held critical opinion, displaying the usual concern with the vagueness of characterization.

John Speirs also restates the traditional point of view and extends it as far as any critic has attempted to date, with the possible exception of Professor Muscatine: "Chaucer transforms Boccaccio's full-scale Italian epic into an English courtly romance. The heyday of medieval romance was over by Chaucer's day; yet this late romance, which is appropriately assigned to the old fashioned 'verray parfit gentil knight,' is the perfect flower of the tradition in English." Further, "How little separates the world of courtly romance from the world of courtly allegory the celebrated garden scene in the first part of the Knight's Tale reminds us."[16] The statement that the work as a chivalric romance is "the perfect flower of the tradition in English" is a very strong position to take under any circumstances. In view of the discrepancies concerning Chaucer's treatment of the external elements of the metrical romance, one wonders whether such a position can be made tenable even with careful qualification. Yet Professor Speirs does not qualify the statement or furnish a specific basis for it. For the present, the importance of this material is the re-emphasis of the fundamental seriousness of the poem, in accordance with the traditional view.

While Professor Brewer is by no means insensitive to some of the humor of *The Knight's Tale*, his opinion of the poem as a whole is perhaps most representatively expressed as follows: "Chaucer, untouched by the arrogance of the New Learning, saw better than Boccaccio what the [*Teseida*] material was worth, borrowed much description and the central plot and turned the whole thing [from an epic] back into Romance." And finally, "Chaucer hardly descends from the rather rarefied atmosphere to suggest the daily intercourse of common life."[17] These statements reflect the views of several critics concerning the *Teseida*—that the material scarcely justified the epic genre.[18]

More detailed consideration will be given to characteristics of the metrical romance; it is perhaps sufficient to observe here that one of them, very much evident in *The Knight's Tale*, makes Professor Brewer's position difficult to defend. This is the fact that most medieval romances contain lovely lyric passages, often of some length, which tend to create the "rarefied atmosphere" of which Professor Brewer writes, but which are often followed by brief, curt closings or transitions of almost brutal realism. For example, in *The Squire of Low Degree*, immediately following the protracted, loving monologue of the king's daughter addressed to the poor squire on the other side of the bedroom door, comes this bloody transition:

> Ryght as they talked thus in fere,
> Theyr enemyes approched nere and nere,
> Foure and thyrty armed bryght
> The steward had arayed hym to fyght.
> The steward was ordeyned to spy
> And for to take them vtterly.
> He wende to death he should haue gone;
> He felled seuen men agaynst hym one;
> Whan he had them to grounde brought,
> The stewarde at hym full sadly fought.
> So harde they smote together tho,
> The stewardes throte he cut in two,
> And sone he fell downe to the grounde
> As a traitour vntrewe, with many a wound.
> The squyer sone in armes they hente,
> And of they dyd his good garmente,
> And on the stewarde they it dyd,
> And sone his body therin th[e]y hydde,
> And with their swordes his face they share,

That she should not knowe what he ware;
They cast hym at her chambre dore,
The stewarde that was styffe and store.[19]

In contrast to the loose construction of this poem, a much more concise example can be found in *Sir Gawayne and the Grene Knight*. After more than four hundred lines which set the elaborately genteel banquet scene firmly in the reader's mind, the flowers of chivalry witness Sir Gawain prepare in minute detail for the mighty stroke. Finally, with the descent of the ax, the climax of this part of the poem is reached and over with very shortly:

Let hit doun lyȝtly lyȝt on þe naked,
Þat þe scharp of þe schalk schyndered þe bones,
And schrank þurȝ þe schyire grece, and scade hit in
        twynne,
Þat þe bit of þe broun stel bot on þe grounde.
Þe fayre hede fro þe halce hit to þe erþe,
Þat fele hit foyned wyth her fete, þere hit forth roled;
Þet blod brayd fro þe body, þat blykked on þe grene;
And nawþer faltered ne fel þe freke neuer þe helder,
Bot styþly he start forth vpon styf schonkes,
And runyschly he raȝt out, þere as renkkeȝ stoden,
Laȝt to his lufly hed, and lyft hit vp sone;
And syþen boȝeȝ to his blonk, þe brydel he cachcheȝ,
Steppeȝ into stelbawe and strydeȝ alofte,
And his hede by þe here in his honde haldeȝ;[20]

A third instance, even more striking in its economy, is in *Sir Orfeo*. The Queen lies in desperate but mysterious torment, to the despair of the devoted Orfeo. After some forty lines of catalogued woe, Orfeo's denouement is bluntly accomplished by the Queen:

'Allas, mi lord Sir Orfeo!
Seþþen we first to-gider were
Ones wroþ neuer we nere,
Bot euer ich haue y-loued þe
As mi liif, & so þou me;
Ac now we mot delen ato
— Do þi best, for y mot go.'[21]

Some of the rhetorical devices, so dear to the heart of the medieval writer of romance and presumably to his medieval audience, can become in the hands of a great artist a two-edged literary tool: serious or satiric. Since these or other devices are sometimes employed by Chaucer in accumulating great masses of detail concerning matters which appear trivial in relation to the main points at issue in the poem, a close analysis from the stand-point of possible artistic ambivalence seems a necessity. The effect of this technique in *The Knight's Tale,* in keeping with the external characteristics of the romance, is habitually to bring an emotional, "rarefied" atmosphere crashing back to earth by very economical means. But frequently, as I shall demonstrate, its effect is also humorous.

One of the most carefully worked out analyses of *The Knight's Tale* to appear in recent years is that of Charles Muscatine. While he adheres to the prevailing view of *The Knight's Tale* as funda-mentally serious, he has specifically substantiated his position with vigor and skill. He states, "Few of us will be willing to accept the notion that in the context of the *Canterbury Tales,* this *noble storie* . . . contains anything which is more than incidentally satirical." For him, Professor Baum's suggestions of pervading satire suffer "by the same kind of fallacy that may be inherent in those of his predecessors: that of seeking distinctions in what may not be meant as distinct, of seeking realism of action (or of characteriza-tion), for instance, in a poem not written under the assumption of realism of method." While agreeing with Root that Chaucer chose not to be "realistic" in *The Knight's Tale,* he finds that Root's subjective view generally shares the narrowness which character-izes both the traditional interpretation and Baum's approach.

Professor Muscatine suggests that the poem "is essentially neither a story, nor a static picture, but a poetic pageant and that all its materials are organized and contributory to a complex design expressing the nature of the noble life." He maintains that Theseus is the central figure of the poem and that there is an "obvious correspondence between the quality of the descriptions and the position of Theseus." Theseus is representative of "the highest chivalric conceptions of nobility."

Structurally, Professor Muscatine finds *The Knight's Tale* char-acterized by symmetry, which he defines as "a high degree of regularity and order among the parts." Its unity is "not unity in itself, but *unity through regularity.*" He goes on to demonstrate how the rich description does much to further the story but points out that a good deal of it far exceeds the story's demands. Finally, "Its grouping and action rather than existing for any great interest in themselves, seem constantly to point to a non-representational, metaphorical method."[22]

The most important conclusion Professor Muscatine draws from his very careful analysis is that the nature of the noble life's struggle is to successfully create order out of chaos, as reflected primarily by Theseus. This interpretation has been revised and amplified by Professor Underwood.[23] Clearly, such a view reflects the seriousness and tragedy long held by traditional critics to be the only important characteristics of the poem's subject matter and Chaucer's treatment of it.

Professor Muscatine's comment on the satirical aspects of the poem I must reserve for more detailed consideration, pending accumulation of evidence which can be brought to bear. I agree with his criticism of Professor Baum's suggestions, which occurred specifically in an early rather brief publication in which limitations of time and space may have prevented him from presenting the substantiation his suggestions needed.[24] At any rate, while Professor Baum's comments on *The Knight's Tale* certainly imply or suggest pervading satire, his published examinations of the poem have not been comprehensive enough to justify commitment in place of suggestions.

I also agree that *The Knight's Tale* does indeed exhaustively express "the nature of the noble life," as well as the concept of "order out of chaos." But it is the manner of this exhaustive treatment—in part, the effect of the excess—and not merely the existence of this material which is equally germane to a comprehensive interpretation. If Theseus is the ideal chivalric figure, what can be said of Palamon and Arcite? Surely a central trait of Theseus' character is thoroughgoing realism, which is conspicuously absent in Palamon and Arcite. If Theseus' realistic dealings with the characters and events of the poem are not inimical to the chivalric way of life, one would expect him to have far more in common with the two young men in this area. Instead he forms a marked contrast to them. Yet, as Professor Muscatine also points out, he is the central authority determining the course of events. Palamon and Arcite are the literal interpreters of chivalric ideals at the expense of their physical welfare. Professor Muscatine maintains that Theseus finds this "both laughable and admirable."

While I fail to discern admiration for Palamon and Arcite's pre-
dicament in Theseus, his attitude toward it is certainly humorous.
It is Theseus, as I shall subsequently demonstrate, who uses the
literal chivalric idealism of the two young men and translates it
into action within the framework of his environment, not as an
idealist but as a practical man of affairs. He is, then, a realist,
but not necessarily to the exclusion of ideals. However, Palamon
and Arcite are, to all external appearances, idealists without regard for mere matters of practicality. It is to *their* "grouping and
action" that Professor Muscatine's "metaphorical method" applies—
although only in part. This basic difference of outlook suggests
that from the traditional point of view, Palamon and Arcite are the
ideal chivalric figures and not Theseus.

There are additional difficulties in Professor Muscatine's analysis. Although he finds elements of balance among the characters
and action, he does not sufficiently account for Emelye's "flatness"
of character, for surely she does not fit in with any notion of
symmetry of structure. The rich descriptions far in excess of the
poem's demands also fail to substantiate fully an argument for
symmetry, and to view Theseus at the apex of a kind of hierarchy
of chivalric nobility to the exclusion of his more earthy qualities
seems to me an incomplete interpretation, rather than an example
of symmetry. In my opinion, Muscatine's examination of *The
Knight's Tale* also shares "the narrowness which characterized both
the traditional interpretation and Baum's approach," although to a
lesser degree than any other critic's work.

Of the less conservative relatively recent commentaries on the
poem, Patch's brief but rather detailed study seems the most prob-
lematical. It is quite apparent that he considered the work outside
the romance genre.

It [*The Knight's Tale*] is a tragedy, is it not, in which the youthful characters introduce the saving presence of humor? What then
of the *Teseide* and Chaucer's transformation of that poem for the
purposes of his Knight? This Italian *magnum opus* . . . according to
Mr. Ker . . . becomes . . . "a complete and perfect version of a medieval romance, worked out with all the resources of Chaucer's
literary study and reflection. . . ." Here, we may suppose, is his most
nearly perfect expression of the romantic spirit.

But when we stop to think of the nature of true romance, as it
has endeared itself to readers . . . does this observation seem quite

satisfactory? . . . let us remember the obvious fact that for critical purposes at least it is hardly profitable to classify as romance every sort of literary production in the Middle Ages which will not fit in with the religious, didactic, dramatic, or satiric writings. . . . The characteristic which marks romance, I think, and defines its quality is rather a primary appeal, through the nature or manipulation of the subject matter, to the imagination.

This material has been quoted at some length because of its disagreement with one fundamental aspect of the traditional view: Patch's conclusion based upon this reasoning is that "this quality hardly predominates in the *Knight's Tale*"—and that it is not a medieval romance.[25]

If one accepts Patch's "characteristic which marks romance . . . and defines its quality," it is evident that romance becomes defined only in terms of the degree of subjectivity of opinion. Such criteria are surely inadequate; the metrical romance genre has other, less intangible characteristics which lend themselves to more discrete demonstration. Patch's dictum fails to take these external characteristics into account, or perhaps disposes of them by the implied assumption that his single, sweeping, subjective measuring stick outweighs more empirical measures. Certainly most would agree that something like "a primary appeal, through the nature and manipulation of the subject matter, to the imagination" is found in romance. It is too imprecise by far, however, to become the sole criterion of judgment, just as its degree of predominance may be very difficult to assess. Hence, while I agree that *The Knight's Tale* is not a metrical romance (except in terms of external characteristics), the grounds for this conclusion are very different from those of Patch. Yet, while he obviously does not share the widely held view that *The Knight's Tale* is a metrical romance, his pronouncement of the poem as a tragedy "in which the youthful characters introduce the saving presence of humor" is in keeping with the traditional approach to the work.

In a relatively recent discussion of the poem, Professor Baum has much to say concerning its genre, substance, and interpretation. For instance, "The setting, the figures, the situations are all *romantic* to the last degree. That the combination of these elements is somewhat artificial does not lessen their attractiveness. But that their effect is mainly decorative and picturesque should be recognized fully and made the starting point of a sound criticism; and the additional elements which enthusiastic readers have discovered in the poem, the characterization of Palamon and Arcite and the profound moral significance, should be regarded with caution." In some respects, this approach is close to my own, so far as the establishment of a second or satiric interpretation is concerned. But the "additional elements" and the romantic elements as artificialities seem far too lightly dismissed by Professor Baum.

He accounts, in part, for the artificiality of the romantic elements in the following: "The background of chivalry, which Chaucer himself saw as passing, is described with a clear sense of its departing splendor, with exaggerated emphasis on the variety of armor, and the overcolored accessories of Lygurge and Emetreus. The grand tournament and the knightly virtues are represented with that slight artificiality of conscious revival, or deliberate retention, which he himself witnessed only a few years later, in the two tournaments at Smithfield, a pageantry which suited admirably the romantic remoteness of ancient Thebes and Athens, touched, like that of Malory for us, with the nostalgia for a glory that was slipping away."

Professor Baum seems intent upon avoiding commitment to a critical view of *The Knight's Tale* as a whole, contenting himself with pointing the way toward a critical "starting point." He comes closest to committing himself with his statement that the poem is a work with "a serious subject with opportunities for his [Chaucer's] natural proclivity towards the lighter vein." He is very much concerned, however, with inconsistencies of style, humor, and the like, and terms it "an imperfect poem, and early work."[26] Although Professor Baum is here more conservative, in my opinion, than in his earlier suggestions, it is difficult and perhaps unfair to categorize him as an adherent to the traditional point of view. It may be more accurate to attribute to him awareness of the problems involved in accepting the traditional view, even though at the time of writing he was not prepared to undertake a full-scale investigation with the approach he recommends.

Tatlock quite clearly agreed with the traditional view but with some modification with respect to the humor in the poem: "*The Knight's Tale* takes over the romantic narrative of the *Teseide*, and is pure romance. . . . But none of his works is more thoroughly Chaucerian. . . . Amusing touches, delicate ridicule . . . abound throughout his works, and by one who knows him and his day are constantly and unmistakably to be found or at least suspected, and constantly add to the delightfulness of his in general more serious works. It is a grievous mistake not to see touches even in the *Parson's Tale*. Chaucer's personality is one of the most marked and individual in literary history. What has been said is very true of the *Knight's Tale*." In one respect, however, Tatlock is strongly at odds with many adherents to the traditional view: "It [*The Knight's Tale*] is full of ideal romantic love, not of artificial 'courtly love.' "[27] He presents this statement as an assertion and does not enlarge upon it or furnish the grounds upon which it is based.

In his edition of the complete works, F. N. Robinson specifically denies the possibility of a humorous or satirical interpretation: "Only about a third of the English poem is actually translated from the Italian, and some of its most memorable features—the description of the temples, the account of the tournament, the passages of philosophical reflection—are in large part independent of the *Teseida*. By adapting both action and setting to the life of his time Chaucer made the tale more real and vivid. Its pervading humor, too, he greatly heightened, so that some critics have been led, unjustifiably, to pronounce the *Knight's Tale* a satire on chivalry or courtly love." For Professor Robinson, as for many other adherents to the traditional point of view, the poem is "a specimen of chivalric romance," a classification qualified by the statement that "it combines the traditions of medieval romance and classical epic, although the ancient type is more apparent in the title and structure of the Italian original."[28]

Like Tatlock's assertion concerning the courtly love aspects of the work, Robinson's regarding satire is not enlarged upon, and the specific grounds upon which it is based are not furnished. One would like to know who "some critics" were who have thought the poem a satire. The opinion was first published in 1933 in Robinson's first edition. Possibly Baum's "Characterization in the *Knight's Tale*"[29] was one source. Other possibilities include some early work of Tatlock[30] and J. R. Hulbert's "What was Chaucer's Aim in the Knight's Tale?"[31] None of these, however, seems to me likely; Tatlock somewhat conservatively takes note of a "tone" of levity and satire and possible ridicule of courtly love. Professor Hulbert says these qualities seem to him "clear in the speeches of Theseus, notably lines 944 ff." He also suggests, "Perhaps Chaucer in the *Knight's Tale* was becoming somewhat tired of courtly

love." None of these positions seems clearly enough defined or sufficiently comprehensive to warrant Professor Robinson's statement.

As is true of other editions which reflect in their editors' comments the traditional point of view, Professor Robinson's notes on
aesthetic or expository criticism were written with the presupposi-
tion that *The Knight's Tale* is basically serious with only isolated
satirical or humorous passages. In fact, there is in published form
no detailed critical examination of the poem from any other
interpretive standpoint.

The opinions of these representative authorities, then, comprise
this brief résumé of the traditional point of view. Clearly, critics
who embrace this view hold that *The Knight's Tale* is primarily a
serious work, and most of them find it a metrical or chivalric
romance permeated with the codified ideals of courtly love. Some
have found aspects of style, characterization, form, and the like
which have caused them concern in unqualifiedly classifying *The
Knight's Tale*. A few have been sufficiently concerned with various
humorous or satiric elements to emphasize them almost to the
point of questioning the basic seriousness of the work, which is the
most fundamental tenet of the traditional point of view. But the
cumulative effect of these differences in interpretation is by no
means sufficient to warrant total abandonment of the traditional
point of view. Of the authorities cited, none, with the possible
exception of Baum, is inclined to reject the fundamental basis of
this view.

My treatment of the problem of the traditional view and its
accumulated difficulties or inconsistencies is expressed hypotheti-
cally in the following:

(1) If *The Knight's Tale* has the external character of a serious
work of the metrical romance genre, and

(2) if, after thorough analysis, many of its most important
characteristics, permeating the entire work, prove atypical of the
genre and are also of a humorous or satirical nature, or both, then

(3) the critical view that the poem is a serious work of metrical
romance genre must be amplified to account for those contradictory characteristics, and to permit its interpretation as a serious
romance for the conventional reader, a satire for the more perceptive (and, it may be said, more sophisticated) reader.

In keeping with this argument, who can deny that Chaucer may
not have had both types of reader in mind?

The remainder of the investigation will document my attempts to demonstrate the truth of this hypothesis. The first portion of it has already been dealt with in part. The traditional view holds in broad outline that *The Knight's Tale* is a serious work of metrical romance genre. This is one side of the valence and is so well known that further development of it is unnecessary. But some of the very same characteristics which seem to identify the poem in terms of genre will be seen to be in fact atypical of the form, as Chaucer develops them in the course of the poem. For this reason, then, these characteristics are termed external. Their existence and, up to a point, the correctness of the interpretation given to them by the more literal-minded I do not deny. But their total effect is quite different from their apparent, more immediate effect, and the assessment of this total effect is a principal subject of this essay.

II

chaucerian humor and satire

I T SEEMS TO ME that any comprehensive view of Chaucer's art must involve for many of us a fairly rigorous assessment of our concepts of humor. Through the ages Western man has tended to judge virtually all literary humor in terms of tacit or explicit acceptance of the inferior role assigned to the "comic" as opposed to the "tragic" in classical aesthetics. Indeed, it would be difficult to exaggerate the influence on historical and analytical literary criticism of what may be described as Aristotelian pronouncements. Few authoritative critics of any era have disagreed with the notion that all art should be functionally concerned with the articulation of truths about humanity which have meaningful applications in time, place, and person beyond their specific treatment in any given work—that is, some form of the universality concept of *The Poetics* has become virtually inseparable from the concept of literary art itself.

If we are in something like a state of agreement on the concept of universality, however, it must be conceded that even in classical literary thought the Aristotelian concept of humor has not been consistently held. Thus, for example, whether we concern ourselves with Aristophanes or Shakespeare, we must conclude that humor as a form of art obviously communicates profound human verities by its own uniquely convincing means. An exploration of some of these

20

means should help clarify the fundamental tenets underlying this examination of *The Knight's Tale*.

Frequently man undergoes a species of projection when he interprets what he reads as humorous or satirical. Often with regard to humor and almost always with regard to satire, he must go beyond the literal, immediate meaning of the language symbols and project additional or alternative interpretations upon them. In this sense he becomes a kind of creator of the satire, however slight his contribution may be. Granted the fundamental condition that we share relevant varieties of environmental experience with our audience, we should be able to communicate our projective activities in literature which result in humorous or satiric interpretations as effectively as those involving the literal level of language interpretation. But we all realize that the effectiveness of the communication may be greatly enhanced or weakened by various predispositions which may direct our projective processes toward or away from perception of humor or satire in a given work. This could apply to "original" creative interpretations that we attempt to convey to others as well as to others' attempts to share their perceptions with us. For that matter, this kind of operation presumably takes place in any area of literary interpretation where the literal meaning of the language symbols is transcended—hence the "discovery" since the advent of Freud of sometimes bizarre sexual or scatological content in literature, of which James Lorimer Holliday's *Mr. Carlyle, My Patient* is an extreme case in point.

Certainly one hazard in such projective perception is the possibility of "reading" humor or satire unjustifiably into a work of literature. Even viewed in their most favorable light, a priori opinions can easily permit us to distort a general appreciation of what we read, however they may enrich certain aspects of that appreciation. Thus, when we perceive satire or humor in a work, we ought to have assurance that our total view of the work itself is not being selectively affected by such predispositions. At least two processes can operate effectively against this.

Subjectively there is the matter of communicability itself, and even this may rest upon somewhat empirical foundations. For if we cannot communicate our "creative" interpretation of satire and humor to others, it must remain solely an appreciation of our own, the validity of which depends upon the degree of integrity of methodology and sincerity of effort we apply to justify it. But the communication of our perception depends upon others' projective processes resulting in similar creative issue through the stimulation of our own findings.

Something very like this, then, accounts for much of the critic's function and influence in aesthetics. Often we "see" what the critic "sees" after it has been pointed out by him; almost all sensitive people have had their aesthetic experiences enriched by the communication of creative interpretation. But it is essential that the creative process be experienced, even though it may not be "original" in the same sense that the critic's was: the recipients must be genuine communicants—they must really "see" by virtue of *their* projective processes.

A second, more empirical process can operate against the possibility of "reading" humor or satire unjustifiably into a work of literature. It consists of ascertaining characteristic properties of the humor and satire of a given author inclusive enough to apply to all his works, yet rigorous enough to be acceptable to the educated, perceptive reader. Primarily the assumption must be made that humor and satire can be dealt with on the basis of the transmission of linguistic symbols which have, within reasonable bounds, a common meaning for the highly literate individual. Self-evident as this seems, such an assumption in practice can be very hazardous, for it is often subject to misunderstandings of which we are hardly aware.

To deal with qualities essentially projective in nature, it is usually necessary to employ broadly connotative linguistic symbols. Misunderstandings arise because of the richness in variation of symbolic connotation from individual to individual. Our projective processes are called upon to play an ever increasing part, inevitably influenced by mind-sets as the degree of abstraction becomes greater. While this circumstance lends itself to imprecise measurement only, we have but to observe man reacting to emotional phenomena referred to by such symbols as *love, hate,* or *fear,* to demonstrate that enormous interpretive variations exist in this highly abstract symbolic realm. Such a symbol as *run,* however, while it may be highly connotative in its meaning for many of us, would normally give rise to a far less differentiated series of interpretations. Bold would he be, truly, who would maintain that typical definitions of *love, hate,* or *fear* adequately express even a fraction of the possible connotative interpretations of these symbols at their most abstract levels of meaning. The same situation obtains with humor and satire—especially with humor—although the interpretive variations of these symbols at their most abstract may be considerably less extreme than the preceding examples.

Frequently meanings transmitted in the abstract, then, are not similar meanings. Informed readers of such works as *The Knight's Tale*, where much of the humor and satire is not obvious, but highly and subtly connotative, will find individual differences in interpretation in degree and kind almost inevitable. Demonstrating the perception of literary humor and satire must depend upon projection and connotative recognition of the specific situation via the language symbols used to describe it, if it is to be dealt with from the standpoint of even a limited sharing of identifiable properties. I have attempted to take these factors into account in devising the methodology used here.

We must also assume, finally, that humor and satire as they appear in the works of a single author do possess identifiable common properties. The soundness of this assumption depends upon the author concerned, in my opinion, although it is implicit in many studies. Certainly in Chaucerian criticism we are constantly confronted with such phrases as "Chaucerian humor" and "Chaucerian satire," which indicate an underlying assumption of the existence of at least some characteristic properties. It should be sufficient, then, that fine critical work supports this assumption so far as Chaucer's works are concerned.

It is now possible to outline a method by which characteristic properties of Chaucerian humor and satire can be determined, beginning with accepted notions of humor and satire as a basis for detailed exploration. Using the principle of the communication of creative interpretation discussed above, I shall cite passages from Chaucer's works which have been considered humorous and/or satirical by relatively unchallenged authority. Because of this widespread agreement, I consider these passages (some of which are from *The Knight's Tale* itself) established as examples of Chaucer's humor and satire. They will be analyzed to discover common grounds for describing them as humorous or satiric. These characteristic properties in turn will serve as criteria for determining the pervasiveness of humor and satire in *The Knight's Tale*.

These properties, accordingly, will have been directly derived from material by the same author which has been reasonably well established as humor or satire or both. Therefore, the connotative aspects of the language symbols employed, even on multiple levels of abstraction, will have their roots established in material which has yielded similar results through the projective processes of many critics.

Humor is generally agreed to be the quality which makes a person, thing, or situation funny, or the ability to perceive what is laugh-provoking. In the *OED* Lowell's neat summation appears: "Humor in its first analysis is a perception of the incongruous." Humor in literature presumably results from a combining of incongruities, emerging with apparent spontaneity from the author's treatment of his material, and our own perception of the consequent illustration of human absurdity. Satire, on the other hand, is the exposure of vice or folly by means of humor, including irony and sarcasm. Using these comments as points of departure, I shall attempt to identify in passages from Chaucer's works established as humorous or satiric just what constitutes the incongruity, ridicule, and so on. The problem is to analyze the effects of these passages in a causal manner. That is, if an effect is humorous or satirical, in what way does one perceive the humor or satire— what makes it what it is?

I have failed to cite such notions of humor and satire as those of Bergson, Kirnan, Meredith, and earlier, Hazlitt, neither as a result of disagreement with their work nor in the belief that my own treatment is the only possible one. Indeed, for much of what is here I am manifestly indebted to them and others. The theses of incongruity, irony, and sarcasm are fairly commonly accepted and the most suitable for my purposes in this study. The problem is not to determine what characteristics in the human personality make man laugh or to propose a total theory of laughter in aesthetics or merely to derive a descriptive *definition* of humor or satire in a given artist's work. Instead it is to determine characteristic properties of Chaucerian humor and satire in terms of criteria which can be expressed more unequivocally than in the approximations of theories or definitions. Thus, if most of us would agree, for example, that the thesis of incongruity is one widely accepted theory of humor, its significance in specific literary passages must be decided before any real progress can be made.

The first passage to be considered is in Book II of *The Knight's Tale.* It is Theseus' well-known extended statement broadly concerned with the follies of the servants of love. None of several passages which reveal Theseus' character as he appears throughout the poem is as enlightening as these lines and the context in which they appear. In terms of the Knight's idealism, he is portrayed as the man of affairs with the qualities of military grandeur and political judgment tempered with mercy which are traditionally associated with the great rulers of history. In this passage and its immediate context these qualities are presented in a new light by Chaucer, and a new dimension to Theseus' character appears: he becomes a human being, subject to at least some of the same failings as other human beings. Chaucer accomplishes the transition in some one hundred and fifty lines, of which these are the most germane:

> And shortly, whan his ire is thus agoon,
> He gan to looken up with eyen lighte,
> And spak thise same wordes al on highte:
>   "The god of love, a, *benedicite*!
> How myghty and how greet a lord is he!
> Ayeyns his myght ther gayneth none obstacles.
> He may be cleped a god for his myracles;
> For he kan maken, at his owene gyse,
> Of everich herte as that hym list divyse.
> Lo heere this Arcite and this Palamoun,
> That quitly weren out of my prisoun,
> And myghte han lyved in Thebes roially,
> And witen I am hir mortal enemy,
> And that hir deth lith in my myght also;
> And yet hath love, maugree hir eyen two,
> Broght hem hyder bothe for to dye.
> Now looketh, is nat that an heigh folye?
> Who may been a fool, but if he love?
> Bihoold, for Goddes sake that sit above,
> Se how they blede! be they noght wel arrayed?
> Thus hath hir lord, the god of love, ypayed
> Hir wages and hir fees for hir servyse!
> And yet they wenen for to been ful wyse
> That serven love, for aught that may bifalle.
> But this is yet the beste game of alle,
> That she for whom they han this jolitee
> Kan hem therfore as muche thank as me.
> She woot namoore of al this hoote fare,
> By God, than woot a cokkow or an hare!

> But all moot ben assayed, hoot and coold;
> A man moot ben a fool, or yong or oold, —
> I woot it by myself ful yore agon,
> For in my tyme a servant was I oon.
> And therfore, syn I knowe of loves peyne,
> And woot hou soore it kan a man distreyne,
> As he that hath ben caught ofte in his laas,
> I yow foryeve al hoolly this trespaas,
> At requeste of the queene, that kneleth heere,
> And eek of Emelye, my suster deere.
> And ye shul bothe anon unto me swere
> That nevere mo ye shal my contree dere,
> Ne make werre upon me nyght ne day,
> But been my freendes in al that ye may.
> I yow foryeve this trespas every deel."[1]   (1782-1825)

No critic disagrees with Robinson's view that the passage is basically humorous: "In Boccaccio, Theseus refers to the madness . . . of the lovers, and admits that he himself has been foolish because of love. . . . But the humorousness, even flippancy, of tone is Chaucer's."[2] Before further discussion of the passage itself, it will be informative to consider briefly its immediate context and setting and cite some short substantiating passages.

Accordingly Theseus, together with Ypolita, Emelye, a number of noble ladies, and presumably others in his hunting party, has discovered Palamon and Arcite warring fiercely with one another in the supposed privacy of the grove. Palamon extravagantly outlines the situation for Theseus, identifying first Arcite and then himself. Arcite, he says, deserves to be dead because he has been banished from the land on penalty of death, yet has tricked Theseus by posing as Philostrate and has become Theseus' squire —he is Theseus' mortal foe. This is accurate enough and more than enough to seal Arcite's fate, as Palamon well knows. He now identifies himself, however, in a most peculiar manner: "That I am thilke woful Palamoun/ That hath thy prisoun broken wikkedly./ I am thy mortal foo" (1734-36).

Now, considering Palamon's situation as a whole in the light of the customs of the period, an obvious and insistent question arises, notwithstanding Root's admonition. For even if one accepts Palamon as "woful" as a result of his current situation with relation to his prospects with Emelye and impending death, one may well ask why he proclaims himself as *wickedly* breaking out of jail? Arcite was released with the specific condition that he was banished from Athens on penalty of death. The outcome of Arcite's adventures is predictable, and Palamon's emotional statement that Arcite deserves death is not illogical if one leaves out of consideration the trifling facts that Arcite is his best friend, his cousin, and his sworn brother! But ignoring these matters for the present, it is important that Palamon himself has not been released; he has been imprisoned for life as a political danger of no mean importance. Morally, from his own standpoint, he would be expected to escape from the most idealistic patriotic motives. It may be posited that Palamon is in such a state of hopeless ardor over Emelye that his desire for his and Arcite's deaths adheres to a kind of emotional logic in the cultural perspective of chivalry. From such a point of view, every line of Palamon's address to Theseus is an accurate and cogent contribution to the facts of the situation, except for this brief complex culminating in his insistence that he "hath thy prisoun broken wikkedly." Hence it cannot reasonably be maintained that his emotional state, even stretched to the extreme lengths I have proposed, accounts for this single, isolated incongruity.

Nonetheless, this seems to me the most conservative interpretation warrantable of this incongruity—that it is an inconsistency arising from Palamon's emotional state. But by far a more likely interpretation is that the "woful" bears an intensifying relationship to the next line. That is, Palamon is a miserable, wretched, or woeful creature at least partly *because* he "wikkedly" broke out of prison. This is strongly supported by the grammatical structure, and the logical meaning resulting therefrom, of an entire complex of lines. There is a separation of concepts structurally emphasized not by a full stop, but by a following parallel construction:

> For sith the day is come that I shal dye,
> I make pleynly my confessioun
> That I am thilke woful Palamoun
> That hath thy prisoun broken wikkedly.
> I am thy mortal foo, and it am I
> That loveth so hoote Emelye the brighte
> That I wol dye present in hir sighte.   (1732-38)

Thus Palamon's condition resulting from his love for Emelye is clearly separated from his "wicked" act of breaking out of prison.

Also, that he is Theseus' mortal foe has been established far earlier in the poem. Logically, therefore, the prison break presumably merely adds a modicum of substantiation to a mortal enmity of which Theseus is amply aware, as well as unnecessarily accounting for Palamon's presence in the grove. But the "wikkedly" militates against logic in this specific context. There is simply no reasonable cause for Palamon to use such a term; yet plainly the prison break and mortal enmity *should* have a close logical connection.

It is clear, then, that "wikkedly" is an incongruity from a logical point of view. It has no business being in the passage in terms of relevance or meaningfulness compared to the content of the poem as a whole. Also, it is the one concept in the passage which cannot be accounted for in terms of the specific situation. Yet, in view of the immediate complex of lines in which it appears, its presence is not accidental. Finally, there is no question of manuscript inaccuracy here.[3] The preceding line seems obviously designed to complement "That hath thy prisoun broken wikkedly." As I have pointed out, the line immediately following, in terms of relationship of meaning, would be perfectly reasonable and appropriate were it not for "wikkedly." The total effect, then, is created by an *emphasis* upon the line containing "wikkedly." Its incongruity is accordingly emphasized since it is the only obviously inharmonious element in the entire address of Palamon. "I am thy mortal foo" should apparently be the culminative statement which the preceding line should support and prepare for. "I am thy mortal foo" does not quite "belong" with the preceding line, because of "wikkedly"; the connection is not quite made, hence emphasis on the "wikkedly."

"I am thy mortal foo" also has the effect of a kind of false repetition of the preceding line; one assumes that it will enlarge and clarify the "wikkedly," but it seems almost to belie it. Thus it has the effect of inviting attention back to the preceding line, since the apparent logical connection misfires, even though it does so very subtly.

By the end of this discussion the reader should be able to judge for himself whether or not this concept is in effect humorous according to characteristic properties derived from examples of Chaucer's work which are widely considered humorous by critics. For the present, it has been examined in terms of its incongruity. That is, its incongruity has been shown to derive from logical irrelevance in terms of its immediate context and the broader content of the plot, the structure of the language in which it is couched, and the emphasis placed upon it as a result of these two factors. It is incongruous in that it conveys a meaning which is plainly out of harmony with its specific and total surroundings, and our attention is directed to this "false" meaning by a "false" repetition which has the *apparent* purpose of dissolving or explaining the incongruity but which in fact emphasizes it.

Concerning the possibility of the concept as satire, it is clearly ironical that Palamon, despite the accuracy of his statements up to this point in his address, attributes to an act of his a moral character which is certainly inappropriate. One would expect Palamon to view his escape from prison as a laudable act, not a wicked one. There is no indication anywhere in the poem that Palamon, in keeping with the chivalric tradition, fought against Theseus for any but the highest motives. Sentenced to dwell perpetually in prison without ransom, he would only be doing his duty to escape, quite apart from personal motives. There is no reason to suppose that his political affiliations have changed in favor of Theseus. Moreover, Palamon is certainly sincere as he expresses this concept.

If this is satire, the effect is achieved by irony, which in turn is utilized to expose this aspect of Palamon's analysis of himself as fallacious. He has committed idealistic folly in describing his act as wicked. Thus the irony lies in his describing or attributing to his act a quality which is the opposite of what would be appropriate; further, he directs the irony against himself. It is not bitter satire nor is it employed to expose evil or vice, but instead it depicts its subject as a fool within its particular frame of reference. Palamon is erring on the side of idealism, but the harm done is to himself and its effect is comic rather than bitter because of its incongruity. These, then, are the grounds for considering the possibility that this brief passage is both humorous and satirical.

Just a dozen lines farther on is another passage which may be significant in the same way:

> The queene anon, for verray wommanhede,
> Gan for to wepe, and so dide Emelye,
> And alle the ladyes in the compaignye.
> Greet pitee was it, as it thoughte hem alle,
> That evere swich a chaunce sholde falle;

For gentil men they were of greet estaat,
And no thyng but for love was this debaat;   (1748-54)

Here, again, both incongruity and irony appear, but possibly
with more far-reaching significance than that which is evident in
Palamon's address. Very clearly, the effect of the first few lines is
cumulative: first the Queen, the epitome of proper womanliness,
begins to weep, followed by Emelye and finally all the women in
the company. Then a full stop, with the succeeding lines apparently
enlarging and explaining the reasons for their sorrow. Finally, in
the culminating lines, which ostensibly account for this extreme
grief, one is met with incongruity and irony. Moreover, in this
passage the incongruity plays its role on a far broader stage than in
the previous passage considered, and the irony has wider implications.

This passage, too, may be both humorous and satirical, for the
same reasons and with the same conditions applying as in the brief
passage from Palamon's address. A colleague warns me that there
is nothing in the least incongruous in "gentil" ladies weeping over
"gentil" men in combat—that the sensitivity of noble souls is a basic
fact of the aristocratic ideal. This is certainly true of the ideal as it
appears in literature and no doubt has been true in practice at
times, but the appropriateness of the response to the stimulus may
still be assessed. We have here what may be interpreted from
one point of view as satiric comment on the literary ideal. That it
has occurred in practice (very possibly as a result of the influence
of the literary models) makes it not one whit more appropriate
as genuinely experienced emotion. Its existence within the chivalric
ideal is not the point at issue; instead my discussion is intended
to be an assessment of this aspect of the ideal itself.

The grounds for this heart-rending display of grief in these
gentlest of female breasts, then, are first that such misfortune
should fall to the lot of the *rank* of men Arcite and Palamon
represent: "For gentil men they were of greet estaat." It is interesting to recall Chaucer's direct characterization of the Knight in
the *General Prologue*: "He was a verray, parfit gentil knyght."
Now, "gentil" has no single, precise synonym in modern English,
just as in modern French its English equivalent must depend upon
its context. In the *Prologue* the relatively rich detail of the context
implies that the word is used in its most inclusive sense—gentility

of birth, behavior, and character, based upon the knowledge of the narrator which in turn is presented to the reader. Here, however, this is not the case. The women have no personal knowledge of Arcite's and Palamon's characters; indeed, Theseus soon points out that Emelye knows no more of the two rivals' "hoote fare" than "a cokkow or an hare!" Further, "gentil" is coupled with "of greet estaat" so that its meaning here seems, with almost overwhelming probability, merely gentle birth. Thus, the first "reason" presented for this womanly concern for two young men attempting to hack each other to pieces, battling ankle deep in gore, and now about to be put to death for their political ideals, is that this should happen to lads of gentle birth and high rank.

Palamon's insistence that he "wikkedly" escaped from jail and, somewhat more logically, his cogent reasons for Arcite's deserved death at Theseus' hands negate any but the more conservative interpretation of "gentil." One point of view might be that the two incongruities in the two passages concerned are subtly but directly related to each other in that each invites attention to the other. I prefer the view that each is a part of a larger whole and in this sense is related to the other. The point is minor in any case, since the incongruity in this instance is far broader in scope than that in Palamon's address.

Many difficulties arise if one takes the women's view in these lines literally—that is, as truly representing genuine grief on the parts of genuine people, on the grounds that the two young men were objects of pity because of their rank. It is futile to expect consistency in every phase of a major poet's art, perhaps, but Chaucer's concern for the simple man of unexalted rank, living high ideals in thought and deed, is both too sincere and too patent to be ignored. In the *Prologue*, for example, it is particularly evident in his treatment of the Parson and the Plowman. While my concern here is not to demonstrate purposiveness in Chaucerian humor, this major inconsistency in a very basic concept is an important incongruity. The fact that the Knight is reciting the tale does not erase the incongruity—his noble naïveté does not in the slightest interfere with Theseus' occasionally earthy realism, for instance. The total effect is one of glaring incongruity, both in its immediate context and in the larger framework of Chaucer's work as a whole.

Another possible interpretation of "gentil" is that it may be a kind of double entendre—an equivocation of its more refined meaning. Thus, if it is understood to refer to the acts of Arcite and Palamon, that is, their bloody fighting, it is being used in its most limited sense and the effect is clearly comical in its unsubtle incongruity.

The final line of the quoted portion of this passage, "And no thyng but for love was this debaat," I interpret to mean in modern English, "And for not a single thing but love." This merely maintains the enormous importance accorded to love throughout the poem and is therefore logical in terms of context. One might expect an explanation of the incongruity in the preceding line despite the parallel construction; the expected does not occur and the incongruity stands out the more for it. Therefore this passage, too, having built up to a culminative explanation, very casually— almost innocently—effects instead a pronounced incongruity which is emphasized rather than enlarged upon or explained by its immediately following line or any other part of its context.

From the standpoint of possible satire, irony is clearly involved. One of the more traditional sources of grief in Western culture is the death of the young or at least the death of men during their years of physical prime, from whatever cause. (By this point in the poem, although Chaucer does not make it very clear, Palamon and Arcite are surely mature men from the medieval point of view, whatever their ages might have been at the beginning of the poem.) Hence the effect of "For gentil men they were of greet estaat" is possibly satirical, since it is primarily irony which, in its inappropriateness, constitutes the emotionally fallacious grounds for this display of grief originating in the supposedly tender hearts of the women. We might expect almost any grounds for this grief connected with the general theme of tragic, premature mortality or possibly fratricide, but certainly not the mere condition of high rank. The other reason given, that all this contention and strife is for love alone, is accorded equal structural importance, and the possible satirical relationship between the two lines is very interesting. If the first reason given is satirical and of equal importance in the immediate context as compared to the second reason, just how seriously can one take the second reason, even though it may appear to be in earnest?

The inappropriateness of the first reason, which constitutes its irony and is perhaps not unmixed with a gentle yet telling sarcastic effect, is very subtle in at least one sense—the more so when it is considered in the context of both reasons. For the literal reader, what may be conveyed is that in the all-powerful, idealistic code of courtly love, women can be moved to "natural" grief in a situation like this only if as a primary condition the individuals involved are of noble rank. The second reason, literally interpreted, is also well within the provisions of courtly love. But the second reason also merges smoothly and without perceptible inconsistency into a far broader, more universal social and cultural convention: surely it is tragic for two men in love to be facing death as a result of a situation ostensibly brought about by love. The "natural" grief ("natural" because the queen, Emelye, and the other women are weeping "for verray wommanhede") is given a most "unnatural" ground in the first reason and a far more natural ground in the second. Yet the two reasons are related in an external sense, since both appear to be derived from the chivalric tradition. Both are given equal importance in the structural and semantic contexts. The irony here is relatively subtle in its effect.

If this passage is satirical, its effect is very far-reaching because it displays one aspect of ideal, courtly womanhood as shallowly artificial in its reflection of courtly convention. It goes far beyond an individual and involves a whole class of supposedly admirable women by depicting them as incapable of normal grief in the presence of tragedy as a result of the social conventions and principles by which they live. It therefore exposes both the women and these aspects of their society as hollow examples of an essentially literary code so far removed from genuine emotional feeling and expression as to be ridiculous—perhaps even a parody of what is usually considered noble, human compassion.

By way of summary, this passage, if it is satire, also achieves its effect through irony. The irony is not openly bitter but is blended with sarcasm and may be slightly cynical as well. Here the narrator describes the situation and we discover no direct accusation or direct value judgments in a literal sense. It does not depict its subjects (the women and the aspect of the aristocratic code they reflect here) as evil or vicious or even worthy of reproof, but certainly ridiculous in the light of common sense and reality. Here, too, the effect is comic rather than bitter because of its incongruity. These are the grounds for considering the possibility that this passage is both humorous and satirical, pending the completion of this discussion.

I have considered these two passages here because, if indeed they are humorous or satiric or both, they bear a close relationship to Theseus' address, aside from their necessary furtherance of the plot. They are fully consistent with the flippancy and bluff earthiness with which Theseus treats matters that have been handled extremely delicately up to this point in the poem. If, then, these passages are humorous or satirical, part of their significance lies in the inference that much of Theseus' address is not an isolated example of humor for humor's sake.

Returning to the immediate context of his address, one is aware that Theseus must solve a many-faceted problem, part of which is stated and part of which one must gather from the events so far unfolded in the poem. Having delivered his edict of death as the lot of Palamon and Arcite, he is met by prolonged and, we may suppose, noisy "grief" on the parts of the women. The Knight tells us that this serves to cool his ire and allow his reason to come into play, and part of the humorous results are in the passage quoted. Theseus shows the understanding of a reasonable man for Palamon's escape from prison and sees the irrationality of love as the cause of the younger men's alleged transgressions. But he has an unstated political situation of no mean proportions to resolve. These young men, sworn enemies, are of sufficient rank and, presumably, sufficient influence to justify his earlier treatment of them as genuine political threats to his power. Therefore he would probably wish to solve the main parts of his problem by pacifying the women, extending mercy to the two men, and at the same time rendering the men harmless politically. The first and in some ways the most significant step in this solution is taken in this address.

Chaucer devotes the first few lines of the passage to a review of the power of the god of love (1785-90). By way of illustrating this power, Theseus cites the cases of Arcite and Palamon, indicating that the most primitive use of reason ("maugree hir eyen two") would have resulted in their leading royal lives in Thebes rather than their being in their present state. Love has prevented this use of reason, and has "Broght hem hyder bothe for to dye." He concludes, in two pungent lines: "Now looketh, is nat that an heigh folye?/ Who may been a fool, but if he love?" This is an important section of the passage because it marks unmistakably even for the most literal-minded a substantiated, common-sense, realistic appraisal of Palamon's and Arcite's emotional state and present situation. Hitherto in the poem, if it is literally interpreted, these matters have been presented in the most idealistic, romantic terms, yet as though all this codified behavior were perfectly natural. This, then, is high and sustained incongruity, and Theseus goes on to document his conclusion in detail by pointing out their wounds, depicting them as the wages of the servants of love and hilariously emphasizing the fact of Emelye's ignorance of this "hoote fare." The incongruity lies in the earlier delicacy of treatment of the emotions of these two servants of love contrasted with Theseus' uncompromising earthiness and accuracy. Thus far, the assumption has been implicit that Emelye's lack of knowledge of the whole affair and its consequences in terms of the two lovers' fates is not significant enough to deal with directly from the standpoint of the adherence to courtly ideals. All lovers are fools, then, and Theseus proves it by citing their obedience to the love code supposedly implicit in the poem.

Of great interest here is Chaucer's use of language, which effectively heightens the general incongruity of this section of the passage. He assigns to Theseus, this "noble duc," the most rural and informal vernacular: "She woot namoore of al this hoote fare,/ By God, than woot a cokkow or an hare!" Thus the concepts conveyed, as well as the language by which they are conveyed, complement each other in emphasizing the incongruity of this section of the passage.

Blending a further documentation of his conclusion that the two young men are fools with a delightful revelation of a side of his own character, Theseus goes on to explain that he understands the situation of the two lovers because he himself has, in his time, been stricken even as they are. This is typical of Chaucer's art in portraying his characters believably, precisely, and with consummate naturalness. Without causing him to lose stature as a powerful and dignified ruler, despite the rural language of a few lines before, Chaucer makes Theseus by this refreshing admission a human and understanding man while still maintaining at least the echo of the earlier humor of the passage. Theseus then sweeps to the end of his address with his generous offer of forgiveness on the grounds of his understanding of the young lovers' emotional condition and the request of the queen and Emelye. In the process he poses the condition of friendship and the pledge of the two men that they will never again make war upon Theseus' country or

upon Theseus himself (1815-25). It is in these eleven lines that
Chaucer with great skill and dispatch brings the entire poem to its
turning point. The road is now open for the swift conclusion to
Book II, which decides and outlines the shape of things to come.
It is most significant that these eleven lines of Theseus' address,
while serious enough in themselves, rest upon the established
foundation of the humor of the preceding part of the address.

The effects of the humor in this passage are manifold. In a
particularly precise way it reveals much of Theseus' character in
that he is now shown to be not only the impressive "noble duc"
but also a practical, discerning human being with great insight
into the lives and problems of those around him. Roaming somewhat freely into the realm of speculation, it may be that his
references to the cuckoo and the hare have the sexual implications
now associated with these creatures. If so, Theseus is, within a
few lines, offering the most high-minded, magnanimous (and hard-
headed) forgiveness one might ask for, by way of contrast.

This address goes far toward solving the thorny problem which
the immediate situation has posed for Theseus. He has relieved the
grief of the women, extended mercy to the "woful" young men,
and taken an important step toward removing their political enmity
by making his forgiveness conditional upon their political friendship. All that remains is the love problem, and this passage has
also made its solution a possibility, since Theseus, holding the
upper hand in terms of political and personal domination of those
involved, is now in a position to dictate the rules of the contest
at arms for Emelye's hand.

The significance of the humor, then, is very great. It furnishes
the grounds for Theseus to resolve gracefully and with indisputable
logic a situation which otherwise would have been almost un-
manageable (if one accepts the literal interpretation of everything
leading up to it, including Palamon's characterization of his escape
from jail as a wicked act). The "noble duc" of the earlier part of
the poem, merciful though he might be, could scarcely be expected
to convert his supposedly justifiable rage at two dangerous political
enemies to gentle forgiveness merely because of the grief of his
womenfolk. He also could not appear as a somewhat simple-minded
or even ignoble schemer by directly exchanging his forgiveness for
their friendship. It is his humorous understanding, his ridicule
without malice of love and its effects upon lovers as exemplified by

the woebegone, foolish young pair, which make the resolving of the immediate situation possible as well as believable. Most important of all, the way is solidly prepared thereby for a comprehensive solution to all the problems save one which so far have been posed in the poem.

The significance of the humor here extends, accordingly, into Theseus' final directive concerning the contest at arms. For having swept through his offer of forgiveness, he rides high on the emotional wave resulting from this splendid gesture and lays down the conditions of the contest. The winner will marry Emelye and thus in effect become a member of Theseus' family. The loser's fate is the one remaining problem ("He moot go pipen in an yvy leef"), though Theseus can hardly be unaware of the possibility of death for the loser. Hence the two young men, having been sworn to friendship with Theseus first, will be alienated from each other; one of them is to marry into the family, and there is a good chance that the other will not survive the contest. As political dangers, then, Palamon and Arcite have been disposed of. The women are suitably grateful and Theseus gets a very good press, as it were, for the results of his humorous, carefully thoughtful analysis of the situation. Once more, it is especially significant that some of the most essential material in this entire section of the poem, upon which much of what follows must depend, is thus treated humorously. Hence, humor has the effect of serving an extremely useful series of purposes at this point in the poem, quite apart from its immediate furtherance of the plot.

Professor Peter has quite recently analyzed the Monk's description from the *General Prologue* in terms of its pervasive satire. I know of no authoritative critical disagreement with his conclusions and the grounds upon which he bases them. Some of his remarks are pertinent here in order to illustrate some of the satiric effect of the passage as a whole:

Chaucer uses dialogue only indirectly, keeping for himself the narrator's privilege of suggestive comment. The Monk is an "outrider," one of those who rode out to supervise the properties belonging to the monastery, but the poet's observation that he "loved venery" also contrives to suggest that his excursions were for a very different purpose. Again, by likening the bells on his bridle to the "chapel bell" Chaucer makes a neat ironic comment on one who should only occasionally have been out of earshot

of that bell. Chaucer's attitude is so subtle that sometimes it becomes ambiguous, a fact which in itself adds a provocative interest
to what he is saying . . . and the reader suspects some ambivalence
in the author's attitude toward the Monk. . . . Chaucer's subtlety
is further revealed in his use of literary reference for ironic effect,
as in "But that text held he not worth an oyster" . . . this is
actually a reference to the *Roman de la Rose,* where monks are
said not to prize the *world* at the value of an oyster. Again, the
sly obliquity with which he approaches his characters is also
evident in his use of apparel for satiric purposes, and in the
mounts he bestows on them. As befits one so much preoccupied
with hunting the Monk has a neat, well-groomed palfrey (unlike
the Shipman, who rode a common nag "as he couthe"); the cuffs
of his sleeves are trimmed with grey squirrel, a costly and forbidden fur; and, like the Prioress, he wears an elaborate orna-
mental pin, one end of which is twisted into the quite inappropriate shape of a love-knot. . . . Only occasionally does Chaucer work
in [broad] terms and then, as in the portrait of the Poor Parson, it
is for purposes of commendation, not Satire.[4]

Few would disagree with Peter's textual analysis, but certain
other characteristics of this satiric passage are of at least equal
interest. One discovers, for example, that the outrageous is treated
as though it were perfectly natural, with certain segments of the
passage having structural characteristics that emphasize the
crashing irony:

> The reule of seint Maure or of seint Beneit,
> By cause that it was old and somdel streit
> This ilke Monk leet olde thynges pace,
> And heeld after the newe world the space.   (173-76)

Ostensibly this brief passage accounts for the Monk's concern with
modernity in general and, indeed, with worldly affairs as well. Yet
it actually begs the question; it seems to explain (in the final two
lines with their parallel construction and apparent twin *raisons
d'être* for line 174) why the Monk holds the views and attitudes
he has toward the world. Logically, however, what is conveyed is
that he let old things pass away because they were old—the attitude is implied and unmistakable that he had no use for old
things, including the narrowness or strictness of the founding saints'
rules. The ambiguity of the construction is easily removed by a
careful reading, but it nevertheless serves to emphasize the in-

appropriateness. One expects, then, a clarification to be conventionally presented; instead the inappropriate seems casually but somewhat ambiguously inserted to extend and emphasize rather than
to dissolve or account for the Monk's impropriety.

Later in the description, the same satirical pattern is presented
in a different manner:

> What sholde he studie and make hymselven wood,
> Upon a book in cloystre alwey to poure,
> Or swynken with his handes, and laboure,
> As Austyn bit? How shal the world be served?
> Lat Austyn have his swynk to hym reserved!   (184-88)

Here the inappropriate is so marked that its effect in isolation, as
it appears above, is shocking. Yet it comes at the end of a passage
that has already established the Monk's attitude toward life in relation to his calling, so that the seeming reasonableness of the
rhetorical questions tends somewhat to soften the violence of the
concepts conveyed. This passage is the culminating "explanation"
of the Monk's way of life, with the remarks concerning St. Austin
climaxing the inconsistency of such an existence compared to
what one would normally expect from a religious. The entire description of the Monk is, however, consistent in the unrelieved
inappropriateness, which is successively accented or intensified by
each explanation or reason for or illustration of the Monk's life.
It is both subtle and thorough in detail, as Professor Peter points
out.

In this example of satire one finds no evidence of bitterness or
rancorous cynicism; its bite is very sharp and its effect telling, but
these qualities do not result in the portrait of an evil person.
Perhaps the lack of malice patent throughout the description results in part from the line immediately preceding the above
passage: "And I seyde his opinion was good." This is an obvious
example of what may be called Chaucer's pseudo-naïveté in his
role as the simple observer and narrator. It seems in this case to
evoke the effect of inviting the reader to recognize Chaucer's
transparent pretense of innocent simplicity. It, too, serves to emphasize the irony of the passage.

A passage in *The Knight's Tale* frequently characterized as
humorous is that in which Chaucer, through the medium of the
Knight's narration, comments on the location of souls, presumably

pagan ones, after Arcite's death. Professor Robinson, usually representative of a conservative point of view, comments on the flippancy of the passage.[5] The passage immediately follows Arcite's last words ("Mercy, Emelye!"):

> His spirit chaunged hous and wente ther,
> As I cam nevere, I kan nat tellen wher.
> Therfore I stynte, I nam no divinistre;
> Of soules fynde I nat in this registre,
> Ne me ne list thilke opinions to telle
> Of hem, though that they writen wher they dwelle.
> Arcite is coold, ther Mars his soule gye!   (2809-15)

The principal incongruity here is, of course, in the second line. The expected substance of the line is the naming of the current locale of Arcite's soul; instead the continuity of meaning is delightfully broken, and the reader realizes that he will never know the answer so far as the Knight is concerned.

As in Theseus' address considered earlier, the humor here reveals much of the character of the speaker. Clearly the Knight is uncomfortable on the subject of the future of pagan souls. Deserted by his source of information, which tells him nothing about this important matter, he pleads his case with exaggerated naïveté (". . . ther,/ As I cam nevere, I kan nat tellen wher"). There is a touch of apology, perhaps, in his documentation of why he will discuss it no more—"I nam no divinistre." Again, he has no desire to recount the speculations or opinions of those who have written on the subject. His final statement seems to convey an echo of his ignorance of the finer points of Christian theology—the pagan god is to guide Arcite's soul—but the Knight could also plead the subject matter and setting of the poem as grounds for his unchristian reference. In terms of character revelation, then, this passage reflects the Knight's naïveté and simplicity, which here result in humor of which he is quite unaware. In this respect the humor is more subtle than Theseus' emphatic flippancy.

The significance of the humor again lies in its almost direct resolution of a somewhat delicate situation. Because of the enormously detailed treatment of Arcite's death, his central importance in the poem, and in view of the preoccupation of the thinking medieval person with the future of the soul, the fate of Arcite's soul would naturally be of great interest. The Knight is scarcely the person to explore the appropriate theological doctrine and introduce purely Christian material into a poem already sufficiently mixed in character. The effect of the passage, accordingly, is to account very neatly for the virtual omission of this important matter. Thus a somewhat delicate situation is efficiently resolved by the medium of humor.

The passage also has significance in that it has the effect, from the standpoint of Chaucer's poetic technique, of helping materially to execute an important transition. Just as Theseus' address in Book II, resting upon a foundation of humor, resolved a situation which had been gradually building up since the beginning of the poem and was vital in preparing the way for the future events of the poem, so this short passage performs much the same function in much the same way. By rounding off the long building up of Arcite's death, it humorously resolves its immediate situation, permitting the unfolding of the rest of the plot. Both passages illustrate Chaucer's consummate skill in accomplishing transitions with great economy.

A passage from *The Merchant's Tale*, a single example from a richly abundant series recurring throughout the work, has been treated at some length by Professor Patch, with no authoritative critical disagreement as to the existence of the satire:[6]

> "Rys up, my wyf, my love, my lady free!
> The turtles voys is herd, my dowve sweete;
> The wynter is goon with alle his reynes weete.
> Com forth now, with thyne eyen columbyn!
> How fairer been thy brestes than is wyn!
> The gardyn is enclosed al aboute;
> Com forth, my white spouse! out of doute
> Thou hast me wounded in myn herte, O wyf!
> No spot of thee ne knew I al my lyf.
> Com forth, and lat us taken oure disport;
> I chees thee for my wyf and my confort."   (2138-48)

The irony in *The Merchant's Tale* seems to pervade the entire, story, perhaps because the plot, in the hands of Chaucer, lends itself so completely to his approach to satire and humor. The satire here is less concentrated and less direct than that in the Monk's description. The contexts of the two passages are very different and serve different literary purposes, so that we might expect a different satiric approach. The Monk's description must of necessity be pithier and more immediately striking, as one of many in a series of brief but designedly memorable descriptive portraits. January's address, on the other hand, is part of a generalized, relatively cohesive satiric milieu in its setting of *The Merchant's Tale* and therefore permits a more leisurely, pervasive satiric treatment. Hence the satire here is less tightly knit from the standpoint of a line-by-line consideration.

January's address is, of course, a translation of the Song of Solomon, and is therefore another example of Chaucer's use of literary reference for ironic effect in his satire. I submit that it would be difficult to find a more inappropriate context for a translation of the Song of Solomon than the one in which Chaucer here places it, especially when compared to its original setting.

The most pronounced and emphatic irony is, of course, in the last two lines of the passage. January's inappropriate lecherous preoccupation with young May is stated, echoed, and re-echoed throughout the passage, but the last two lines serve to heighten by restatement the underlying satire of the entire poem: January urges May to come out with him into the garden in which she is eventually to "disport" with Damian in the ultimate act of marital infidelity. Moreover, the garden itself has been designed and constructed on January's instructions in such a manner as to furnish him complete privacy for *his* "disport" with May. Clearly *disport* carries a very effective although unstated complex of meanings that in this specific context goes beyond innocent amusement. And, finally (the culminating irony), January reiterates somewhat unnecessarily in the last line: "I chees thee for my wyf and my confort," subtly but unmistakably emphasizing both the underlying satire of the poem—the utter folly of a lecherous old man in attempting to form a sound, intimate marital relationship with a lovely young girl—and the specific ironic plight of January at this particular point in the poem.

May has already been unfaithful to January in spirit, and it is clear from the straightforward treatment of this aspect of the plot that May and Damian do not experience so much as a single qualm of conscience. At the first opportunity they will inevitably consummate their love. But the importance of their relationship is, in my opinion, the spiritual infidelity it involves, which is treated so matter-of-factly as to seemingly imply that it is a completely natural situation, bound to arise as a result of January's folly—

in turn a specific illustration of an old theme. For the patently lecherous January it is the physical consummation of May and Damian's affair which is so poetic in its fitness. The more important, spiritual infidelity is wasted upon him since, from what one learns of his character in the poem, he would be insensitive to it. Accordingly the youthful lovers are able to deceive him with ease. It is this entire complex of concepts, then, which impregnates this passage—particularly the last two lines—with a significance that embraces the entire poem.

Some of the ironic touches that convey the satiric effect here and that are subtly intertwined with the overall fabric of the poem we would today refer to as "fertility" images. They originate in the Old Testament, of course, and it is Chaucer's delightfully skillful, thoroughly inappropriate treatment of them in *The Merchant's Tale* which leads us inevitably to compare not only the immediate contexts of the two versions of the Song of Solomon but their total contexts as well. The satire, then, becomes delightfully comprehensive. These images include the "turtles voys," "my dowve sweete," the absence of winter, "thyne eyen columbyn," the comparison of May's breasts to wine, and the garden itself. The entirely enclosed garden reminds us of the purpose for its being enclosed and the events which are about to take place in it. To the more imaginative among Chaucer's contemporaries, it also might have been a shocking reminder of the *hortus inclusus* notion. An extreme form of it might lead to the comparison between the lovely enclosed garden and May to Mary's womb (as the enclosing garden for the Christ Child). In any case, as Professor Robertson points out, the implied parallel of such gardens to the paradise of the Old Testament was a recurrent medieval literary figure.[7]

The phrase "my white spouse" is too delightfully ironical to spoil by serious discussion. January's comment that May has wounded his heart is so inappropriate in view of his original intentions and their expression in his subsequent actions that it is scarcely worthwhile to debate the unimportant point as to whether this is self-deception or hypocrisy. That he knows of no stain upon May ("No spot of thee ne knew I al my lyf") may well be a double entendre. That is, it may refer to her character, which would be appropriate in a literal sense in terms of the immediate context of the line, but it may also refer to her body's freedom from physical blemishes. The latter possibility is certainly in keeping with January's own character, and his actions earlier in the poem leave us in no doubt that he is in a position to know such details.

Professor Patch finds the irony here as savage as any in literature. He finds it bitter and cruel, and maintains, in my opinion correctly, that January is "the embodiment of desire in old age" and that he "gathers up all the unsavoury traits of licentious old age in the odor of his own personality."[8] Linking the substance of the tale with the Merchant's own background, he insists that it is sexual frustration which lends bitterness to the story and that therefore the irony in the poem shows "a corrosive, destructive, even a hopeless quality, not unmixed with hatred, and the very opposite of the optimistic instances in the story told by the Franklin." It is difficult to agree that this irony can be so definitely categorized, at least not without an assessment of its total effect. This must be briefly considered because what is being conveyed here is important in determining characteristic properties of Chaucerian satire.

The Merchant does indeed inject his own bitterness and corrosiveness into his satiric narration of the entire tale, but its effectiveness in communicating his state of mind in such a manner that it is shared by Chaucer's audience is at least questionable. Certainly the perceptive reader or listener of today or of Chaucer's time could scarcely fail to be aware of the intensely personal malice the Merchant directs so continually and cuttingly toward May in particular. This becomes the more markedly an individual characteristic of the narrator as one realizes how completely he fails to display genuine concern with any fundamental moral principles. The Merchant clearly attaches more importance to May's physical disloyalty than to the complex of basic violations of morality of which it is symptomatic. One would have, at least partly, to identify himself with the Merchant and his experiences with his young wife in order to share substantially his bias against May. Few would care to do so. The bitterness backfires with ironical moral effect: one at least manages to feel a certain sympathy for May—thoroughly bad lot that she is, for all her charm.

One is left with ambivalent feelings if he accepts Professor Patch's perceptive comments as characterizing the total effect of the satire here. Clearly his characterization of January is substantiated by the tale itself but, granted that the immediate effect of the Merchant's narration is one of bitterness and corrosiveness, such an interpretation cannot be applied to the poem as a whole, and Professor Patch does not attempt so to apply it. He does fail to point out, however, that this immediate effect of the Merchant's bitterness is a kind of means to an end, or a part of a far broader and more important effect in which its function may be described as catalytic. Professor Patch also notes that this bitterness reacts upon the Merchant himself but has little to add to his comment beyond its direct bearing upon the Merchant's character. If one accepts Professor Patch's view uncritically, one is left with a series of impressions which are more misleading than enlightening. The poem is far more than a demonstration of Chaucer's genius in irony boomeranging back upon its teller, or a brilliant exercise of biting satire applied to characters who possess various kinds and degrees of corruptness.

Both January and May are seriously involved in theological-moral violations. January is by far the more guilty: he uses a sacrament of the Church—marriage—in a hypocritical attempt to continue in his old age a life of basest lechery. He knows his desires and life to be wrong in the eyes of the Church. Presumably hoping to achieve salvation by obeying the letter of moral law while continuing to flout it in spirit, he appropriates one of the Church's supreme sacraments to use as a license for lechery. May, fiefed legally to January and implicitly (as would be usual in such cases) without choice, is bound by the marriage sacrament in the eyes of the Church, whatever the personal situation between her and January may be. Like January in one respect at least, she also flouts the spirit of the sacramental-moral law when she first decides to "love" Damian, quite aside from the later physical consummation. In a sense, physical consummation is necessary to carry the point of the tale, because of both January's and the Merchant's insensitivity to spiritual matters—neither of them is capable of discerning the difference between the mere symbol, which they interpret only in terms of the flesh, and the far more important spiritual violations to which the physical act is hardly more than incidental. Thus they must be approached at their own level: through the senses and so thoroughly that January actually observes the act, even if May convinces him that his newly restored eyesight is inaccurate.

Solely in conjecture, if Chaucer had assigned this tale to a churchman, it seems inescapable that its theme of marital infidelity would have to be explored in terms of the Church sacrament and its flagrant violation by May, Damian, and January. But, in fact, while this and other moral and theological violations underlie the whole substance of the tale, the Merchant does not deal with them in any direct way in terms of theological or moral responsibility. The reader is therefore forced to accept the literal substance presented to him; he is also presented with the responsibility of assessing its total effect.

There is indeed more than one kind of irony in *The Merchant's Tale*. That the immediately discernible malice of the Merchant fails to sway the perceptive audience can be easily demonstrated. Does one share the Merchant's view of May (and she is the primary target of his bitterness from the point in the poem where she decides she is going to show Damian a lover's mercy) at the end of the poem? Clearly not, but this fact only gives rise to another problem causally inspired by the inconsistency of the Merchant's irony. His inconsistency is a result of the actual events and characters in the poem, quite apart from his ironic interpretation of them. Thus January's own character and the events of the poem which can be said to have occurred largely as a direct result of it form the powerful motivating forces operating upon May. Accordingly, one must either find inconsistency in the Merchant's irony, as he first directs it at January (thereby constructing the almost overpowering motivation for May's disloyalty) and then concentrates it upon May for falling into the trap thus set for her, or one must share his attitude toward May. The question now arises, if one does not accept the Merchant's assessment of her, just how does one feel toward May? Evidently she suffers no qualms of conscience, and we have no reason to assume that the extent of her infidelities after the end of the poem will be limited by anything but her considerable ingenuity and January's credulity.

I think this problem is most satisfactorily solved by adopting a broader view of the satire in the poem. Besides the Merchant's approach, there is the more far-reaching and malice-free but mocking satire of the literal plot. Thus the events and their timing and execution, culminating in the ending of the poem, are in themselves totally effective satire. It is *this* satire which is effective in the poem and which shines through and displaces the bitterness of the Merchant's, even though the two seem to be intertwined at times. It is this satire which permeates January's address to

May as he urges her to join him in the garden. Despite the savage
and even blasphemous irony of the "Rys up, my wyf" passage,
only through the Merchant's eyes do the events to follow and
hence the poem itself become merely examples of bitterness and
corruption. For the poem is Chaucerian satire at its height, without
malice and unerringly directed toward human folly. Few of us can
sympathize with January as he is portrayed in the poem. There
can be no malice in his receiving retribution of the "poetic justice"
kind.

This satire, therefore, is quite different from the Merchant's nar-
rower, because more personal, bitterness; it is broader of scope
and reveals tellingly and without spite an example of human
folly—another tableau in the Human Comedy. The effect is arrived
at through the failure of the Merchant's irony to achieve the
audience's adoption of his attitude, most specifically toward May.
Stripped of its malice, then, the satire assumes important new
dimensions. Its effects are manifold.

If we assume that the most important satire of the poem is
directed wholly at human foolishness, the moral issues are left to
the Merchant, who constitutes a most uncomfortable and precarious
perch upon which to place them. Fortunately this is actually not
the case, for in its most comprehensive view the range of the
satire's effectiveness is almost startling in its inclusiveness. January's baseness and hypocrisy are satirized to the point where there
is no certain way of telling whether or not he has finally deceived
even himself. His folly lies in giving in to his baseness, in using a
sacrament of the Church both to achieve carnal ends and to escape
the consequences of his past and present carnality by barely adhering to the form—certainly not the spirit—of this sacrament. He
knows better from every standpoint—he is no ignorant churl. His
desires are doubtless natural enough, and we have no right to
blame him for them; his corruptness lies less in his giving in to
them than in the manner in which he satisfies them. His experience, his knowledge of the ancients, the advice he has sought
and received, and his age should all contribute to his knowing
better. With his eyes wide open, he willfully succumbs to his
baseness.

In another sense, an odor of moral offal surrounds January in
the area of social responsibility, not so much from his use of his
position in life to implement his baseness as from his position

itself. Nobility of birth and its consequent social responsibilities are not usually taken lightly in Chaucer's works. By giving in to his lecherousness in taking a young and beautiful wife, he is plainly driving himself into folly, the degree of which is immeasurably increased by the inevitable immorality of his abuse of the sacrament of marriage to gain his way. It is his violation of moral principles which constitutes his greatest folly, and May's disloyalty is his retribution in this life—seemingly an inevitable one.

It might be debated almost indefinitely whether the most severe retribution for January would have been his permanent belief in the sight his eyes beheld, or whether it is more fitting that he should have remained in blissful ignorance. It would seem that the subtler of the two, which Chaucer chose, is by far the more appropriate since the future is left open for the reader's imagination, although any conjectures have been pointed in a very obvious direction by Chaucer.

Seen in terms of this satire, May at first appears merely as a delightful, Alisoun-like instrument of Chaucer's ironic humor. Sadly enough, however, in serving its purpose of exposing and exploring January's folly of allowing his sensuality to become his master, this ironic humor also has the effect of concentrating our attention upon the moral issues at stake far more tellingly than the Merchant's inconsistent polemics. In their social and cultural setting, the events of the poem leave May unquestionably culpable. Despite the motivation she cannot escape responsibility for her actions within the frame of reference of the Church, however repulsive her marriage to January must be. She becomes, therefore, a poignant figure, more sinned against than sinning, and symbolic of the most powerful moral truth conveyed by the poem. The final, the most important result of January's corruptness, then, is that it has resulted in leading another, an innocent, into pathetically unfair and unequal temptation, with a predictable outcome. January's and May's futures can be safely left, as Chaucer has left them, to the theological imaginations of his audience. Whatever Chaucer's intent may have been, therefore, the effects of the most important satire in *The Merchant's Tale* include the important role of subtly but unmistakably focusing attention, however indirectly, upon the human folly in the poem and the grounds for the results of this folly. Its significance lies in the fact that once more Chaucer has employed satire to convey the most vital concepts.

Hence the satire in the tale is not solely a reflection of worldly vice and corruption, presumably perpetual or limited by little more than human whimsy, for at the level of the Merchant's irony Chaucer is not obviously concerned with the violations of religion and morality that underlie the entire poem. The satire here, therefore, is on two levels: the immediately perceivable, bitter irony and sarcasm of the Merchant, which become isolated in him and thus free one's projective processes to embrace the other less direct and richer vein of satire which is central to the poem. Its subtle effect of focusing the attention upon the moral issues at stake by treating the folly of January with its causal roots and its results leads the reader himself to pronounce the moral judgment upon the characters and events of the poem.

A briefer passage from *The Parliament of Fowls* is cited by Raymond Preston[9] as a fine example of Chaucerian humor in comedic proportions, and there has been no significant disagreement with this view. It is in the midst of the discussion of love over which Nature is presiding:

> "Wel bourded," quod the doke, "by myn hat!
> That men shulde loven alwey causeles,
> Who can a resoun fynde or wit in that?
> Daunseth he murye that is myrtheles?
> Who shulde recche of that is recheles?
> Ye quek!" yit seyde the doke, ful wel and fayre,
> "There been mo sterres, God wot, than a payre!"
>
> "Now fy, cherl!" quod the gentil tercelet,
> "Out of the donghil cam that word ful right!
> Thow canst nat seen which thyng is wel beset!
> Thow farst by love as oules don by lyght:
> The day hem blent, ful wel they se by nyght.
> Thy kynde is of so low a wrechednesse
> That what love is, thow canst nat seen ne gesse." (589-602)

One aspect of the humor here, of course, is the underlying incongruity of the animals behaving so utterly humanly in their argument on the nature of love. The duck represents the realist, free of ideals in the sense of courtly love. He commits the widespread human fallacy, clothed in the form of a medieval rhetorical argument, of attempting to reduce emotional matters to his notion of reasonable behavior. The delightful comedy of the last two lines emphasizes the incongruity of this "human" duck's position, in part by drawing attention to the whole allegorical-comical situation and in part by the last line's reference to the stars—no romantic allusion, this! Accordingly, instead of connecting love with the inevitability of the stars or something of this nature, he uses, perhaps a trifle blasphemously, the opposite of the usual, expected relationship. In its lack of harmony as an image and concept designed to be the pithy summing up of his argument, this has the effect of emphasizing the comedy. The penultimate line, with its delightful aural echoes and its praise of what is very likely one of Nature's most ridiculous sounds, is completely comic in its effect.

The most obvious incongruity in the tercelet's reply arises in his very first line and its effect lasts until this bird, too, chooses an even more incongruous image than the duck's, from which he draws an analogy supposed to devastate the duck's views and the duck himself. His whole statement is an ill-tempered blend of false analogy and *argumentum ad hominem* fallacies, couched in the most insulting, ill-bred language. Thus the tercelet betrays himself the moment he opens his beak as anything but an example of gentility, belying the direct description of him in the first line of the stanza. His analogy involving the owl is incongruous in that it does not fit the existing situation. Finally, summing up the spirit of insult implicit in his entire statement, lines 601-2 are ostensibly supposed to dispose totally of the duck's argument by their attack upon his species instead of upon his argument.

The effect of the humor in this passage and its context is carefully analyzed by Preston:

[Chaucer] is giving, with his birds, the comic underside of a human debate which has its relation to that very fine thirteenth-century English poem the *Owl and the Nightingale,* to the procedure of medieval law, and even to the dialectic that taught the schoolmen logical argument. His superior entertainment [in *The Parliament of Fowls*] would be impossible in a culture without the *sic et non* of disputation, without the delimited scepticism which is essential to the thinker. . . . When Dante and Boccaccio are unexpectedly brought together—or a goose, a turtle-dove and a cuckoo become, as we have heard, articulate—we are given the comedy of a poet of a civilization with a philosophy, and not the comedy of the philosophy of a poet. . . . And as we look into the clear mind of the dreamer, at his congress of all too human fowls, we see him more interested in the kind than the genus, and still more interested in the person.[10]

Wilhelm Ewald's contributions to the study of Chaucer's humor have been undoubtedly among the most valuable. The following three briefly treated selections have not aroused scholarly disagreement of any authoritative nature. Ewald's economical treatments of these passages are quoted copiously because they so nearly approach my own interpretations. The first one, followed by Ewald's comment, is from *The Nun's Priest's Tale*:

> So hydous was the noyse, a, *benedicitee*!
> Certes, he Jakke Straw and his meynee
> Ne made nevere shoutes half so shrille
> Whan that they wolden any Flemyng kille,   (3393-96)

". . . auf die zeitgenössische Geschichte findet sich eine humoristische Anspielung. . . . Die entsetzliche Verwirrung, die in der Nonne Preestes T. die Erscheinung des Fuchses auf dem Bauernhofe unter Kühen, Kälben, Schweinen, Enten, Gänsen und Bienen hervorgebricht, wird am Schluss zusammenfassend charakterisiert durch folgenden Vergleich."[11]* Here, again, the underlying incongruity of the animal-human parallels is emphasized and brought to the surface by this direct analogy. The reference, of course, is to the 1381 peasant revolt. The analogy itself is reserved, with Chaucer's uncanny skill in timing, for the last two lines of the passage and thus serves as a dramatic close to the preceding material. Compared to the almost leisurely pace of the first two lines, with the second line casually introducing and thus making possible the analogy, the last two lines move to a close with abrupt and telling swiftness.

The second selection from Ewald is from a part of his work devoted to what he delightfully refers to as Chaucer's "Selbstverspottung."[12] There is no authoritative disagreement with Ewald's comment on the following passage from the Man of Law's Prologue:

*". . . a humorous allusion to contemporary history is found. . . . The frightful confusion which is brought forth in *The Nun's Priest's Tale* by the appearance of the fox in the barnyard among the cows, heifers, pigs, ducks, geese, and bees is in the end collectively characterized by the following parallel. . . ."

> . . . Chaucer, thogh he kan but lewedly
> On metres and on rymyng craftily,   (47-48)

"Als Ch. durch den Man of Laws in dessen Prolog seine Werke auf-
zählen lässt, kann er nicht unterlassen, bei Erwähnung seines
Namens hinzuzufügen."* This is so clearly humor directed by
Chaucer at himself that no useful purpose can be served by further
discussion. Its significance for my investigation lies in its relation
to its context. Through the Man of Law, Chaucer proffers an
extended commentary upon his works, and he is by no means
unduly modest about their range of subject matter and the like.
However, the only reference to the skill and technique of his
writing is, significantly, the humorous passage Ewald has dealt
with. It is nonsensical to maintain that Chaucer considered crafts-
manship of negligible importance in his poetry. Here, therefore,
is another manifestation of the use of humor in the treatment of
concepts Chaucer must have taken very seriously. Again, while
the immediate effect in this and other humorous or satirical passages in Chaucer's works seems merely funny within the lines in
which it appears, its total effect is frequently much more than this.

Another example of humor from Ewald's work pertinent to this
part of my discussion is from the prologue to *The Miller's Tale*.[13]
He considers first, as an introduction to the passage with which he
is mainly concerned, the line and a half which set its context:

> . . . Leve brother Osewold,
> Who hath no wyf, he is no cokewold.   (3151-52)

"Den köstlichen volkstümlichen Gedanken, dass man allerdings
nur Hahnrei werden kann, wenn man verheiratet ist, formuliert
der Müller in seinem Intermezzo mit dem Verwalter in folgender
klassisch knapper form."† Then he proceeds to his main concern:
"Der Müller hat sich aber eine Philosophie zurechtgelegt, die den
Ehemann über alle Eifersuchtssorgen erhebt: Wenn man es sogar
ganz genau weiss, dass die Frau einem betrügt, so soll man es

---

*"As Chaucer appears to enumerate his works through the Man of Law
in the latter's prologue, he cannot resist adding, at the mentioning of his own
name. . . ."

†"The priceless folk saying that in any case one can only be cuckolded
if one is married, the Miller formulates in his Intermezzo with the Reeve
in the following classic, brief fashion. . . ."

doch nicht glauben. Allen Ehemännern gibt er folgende Verhalt-
ungsmassregel": *

> An housbonde shal nat been inquisityf
> Of Goddes pryvetee, nor of his wyf.
> So he may fynde Goddes foyson there,
> Of the remenant nedeth nat enquere.   (3163-66)

Ewald is in my opinion correct in his interpretation of this passage:
"Das heisst also: Man soll sich so wenig um Gottes Heimlichkeit
kümmern wie um die seines Weibes. Dann wird Gott einem mit
Überfluss segnen. Nach dem übrigen—also nach dem, was einem
das Weib dabei bringen wird—muss man eben nicht fragen."†

Considered in their context, these two brief passages cited by
Ewald are part of an identifiable pattern. The first passage cul-
minates the exchange between the Reeve and the Miller and
both confirms and further extends one's information as to the shape
of the tale to come. Having announced his intention to show how
a carpenter was made a fool of by a scholar, with the cooperation
of the carpenter's wife, the Miller replies to the Reeve's protests with an extensive objection in which both of these selections
are included. The heavy sarcasm of "Leve brother Osewold" is
immediately followed by an abrupt and jarring truism which,
however expected it may be, is a shocking contrast to the style
of the immediately preceding *Knight's Tale*, with its genteel echoes
presumably still reverberating in the sensitive breasts of the literal-
minded. This is the principal incongruity of this brief passage.
With its merciless economy it still fulfills many missions: it conveys
something of the Miller and Reeve's relationship from the Miller's
standpoint and confirms and extends one's suspicion of the type
of tale the Miller will tell. It also shows much of the Miller's
lewdness of outlook in both the medieval and modern sense of the
word. Finally, it serves as an appropriate and effective preparation
for the Miller's churlish philosophy of these matters, the core of

---

*"The Miller has laid down as a philosophy that which the married man
holds to be most important of all the anxieties arising from jealousy: even
if one knows for a certainty that his wife has betrayed him, he should
nonetheless not believe it. To all married men he gives the following
instructions. . . ."

†"That is to say: one should concern himself just as little with the secret
affairs of his wife as with those of God. Then God will bless him with
superabundance. Concerning the rest—that is, concerning what one's wife
brings him at the same time—one must not inquire."

which is in the second of the passages. Its incongruity arises in large part from its context, and it is interwoven with the pattern of churlish humor in the Miller's Prologue by its introductory function in relation to the second passage cited by Ewald.

By the time the second passage ("An housbonde shal nat . . .") is reached in the Miller's statement, the tone of his attitude has been set, and the overall incongruity brought out by the contrast between the Miller's Prologue and *The Knight's Tale* assumes a kind of naturalness. By this point in the Miller's prologue, then, one expects the Miller's bawdy attitude and lack of inhibition to be reflected in his every speech. Hence the incongruity of the passage is less dependent upon context, which is already established. Its principal elements of incongruity are, so to speak, self-contained.

Here again certain characteristics stand out as one assesses the effect of the humor in the passage. The analogy equating the divine with the earthy is shockingly incongruous, but, typically, the pithy main point to which the four lines owe their existence is saved for the very last line. It is therefore clear that the effects created by this and the preceding passage cited by Ewald result from a pervasive humorous context which they help create and preserve. Their close complementary relationship of structure, style, and subject matter are so blended with the personality of the Miller that both passages confirm and emphasize what we have learned of him.

An example of Chaucerian satire with which Ewald and others have concerned themselves comes from the *General Prologue*, in which Chaucer devotes some of his most humorous irony to the Friar:

> Ther nas no man nowher so vertuous.
> He was the beste beggere in his hous;   (251-52)

For Ewald, "Von grossartigem Humor zeugt sodann die Begründung, die Ch. gibt, warum der Bettelmönch überall da leicht mit der Absolution bei der Hand ist, wo er eines guten Geschenkes sicher ist."* Further, "Der Bettelmönch versteht überhaupt seinen Handel. Er verkehrt nur mit reichen Leuten, weil—er ist nicht für standesgemäss hält, mit armen Bettlern zu verkehren. Überall aber,

---

*"In this case the superb humor produces the grounds to account for the Friar granting absolution so lightly whenever he is sure to receive a valuable gift."

wo ein Vorteil herausspringen kann, ist er höflich und dienstbeflissen. Ironisch fasst der Dichter seine Kunst zusammen."[14]*

Ewald's comments effectively summarize the preceding material in Chaucer's description of the Friar. Immediately following that of the Monk, it maintains the same rich atmosphere of humorous satire in which the Monk is replaced by the Friar as the central victim. As in the description of the Monk, the Friar's life and the sharp worldliness he practices in the mechanics of his calling are totally inappropriate to anyone who is sworn to devote his life to a begging order or to any other ecclesiastical calling. As one shocker is piled upon another in the descriptions of both the Monk and the Friar, however, Chaucer's technique, which both creates and emphasizes the satiric effect, is clearly apparent. These attitudes and practices are presented as being perfectly natural, and once we accept the first (since all the rest are linked one with another in each of the descriptions), the effect of pseudo-naturalness remains even as the inappropriateness becomes more and more outrageous. Perhaps it is this technique which makes these two descriptions in particular seem so vivid, so true to life. Underlying each one, but especially that of the Friar, is the clear implication that such practices are ostensibly responsible for their success in their calling—at least as measured by some of its standards accepted by the world at large.

The last two lines of the description of the Friar seem to me as obvious as any of Chaucer's satire. The penultimate line is such a shocking allegation that it forces the attention on the ironic aspects of the preceding lines, making it impossible for us to miss any part of the satiric point. Such open emphasis is rare in Chaucer, and is at least indicative of the scope of the satire in this passage. The final line is surely among the most eloquent ironic statements in literature. It complements the heavy, obvious irony of "Ther nas no man nowher so vertuous" with a logic which is perfect in its immediate context but so false in the context of the entire description of the Friar as to emphasize yet again the needle-sharp mockery of the whole passage.

Of the many critical considerations of the humor and satire often

*"The Friar above all else understands the business aspect of his calling. He associates only with wealthy people because—he considers it unfitting for one of his importance to associate with poor beggars. But whenever a profit can be extracted he is always fawning and zealous to serve. Ironically the poet sums up the Friar's professional skill. . . ."

associated with the Wife of Bath, Preston's work on the Wife's philosophy of marriage is among the more detailed comparative treatments.[15] He says, in part: "[T]he ironies of her prologue are more complicated [than the Pardoner's]—the ironies of her prayers for the soul of her last husband, or (at the beginning) the irony of her pretended innocence of the meaning of Christ's words to the woman of Samaria, Christ's words to herself":

> Biside a welle, Jhesus, God and man,
> Spak in repreeve of the Samaritan:
> 'Thou hast yhad fyve housbondes,' quod he,
> 'And that ilke man that now hath thee
> Is noght thyn housbonde,' thou seyde he certeyn.
> What that he mente therby, I kan nat seyn;
> But that I axe, why that the fifthe man
> Was noon housbonde to the Samaritan?
> How manye myghte she have in mariage?
> Yet herde I nevere tellen in myn age
> Upon this nombre diffinicioun.
> Men may devyne and glosen, up and doun,
> But wel I woot, expres, withoute lye,
> God bad us for to wexe and multiplye;
> That gentil text kan I wel understonde.   (15-29)

Preston's comments help establish the context within which these lines appear and contribute toward an understanding of the wife's character and personality. Considered in terms of Chaucer's total treatment of her, one realizes she is not the kind of woman to miss the point of Jesus' rebuke. Preston's opinion is therefore fully justified.

As we have seen in the passages spoken by the Miller considered above, Chaucer's skill in assigning to characters humor which conveys considerable information about them and their personalities is almost uncanny. Here the ironic satire does the same for the Wife. For all its surface obviousness, it is so subtle in its blandness that the Wife builds one inappropriate, unethical—to say the least—edifice upon another with such sweeping, refreshing logic and force of personality that one is compelled, seemingly, to accept her and her earthy marital philosophy on her own terms. This passage obviously reflects her completely self-righteous approach to her astounding marital record, with a hint of future ventures in the field.

From these varied examples of humor and satire and the brief analyses I have made, certain characteristic properties emerge. Concerning Chaucerian humor, it seems to me that eight easily identifiable general properties can be conveniently categorized for my purposes here. Recalling the notion of humor previously cited, we can briefly state that humor is, as I have treated it, incongruity and its perception. The incongruity peculiar to Chaucer's humor is usually identifiable by its sharing of one or more of the following properties:

1. Particularly striking in the shorter passages of Chaucer's humor is the fact that the material immediately surrounding or preceding the humorous passage is so constructed as to emphasize the humor, as in the selection from *The Nun's Priest's Tale* considered here.

2. Similarly, the immediate context in which briefly expressed minor concepts are humorously involved is frequently a logical one. That is, the incongruity of the humorously treated concept is emphasized by its lack of harmony with its immediate context. While this is especially apparent in shorter passages, the same characteristics also apply equally if less obviously to longer, more significant passages. The first two lines of the selection from *The Knight's Tale*, for instance, in which the Knight tells us of the geographical disposition of Arcite's soul, illustrate these two characteristics clearly. Another illustration of the same properties in a quite different kind of Chaucerian humor is the first brief passage cited above from Ewald's work on the prologue to *The Miller's Tale*.

3. Another property often present in Chaucer's humor is some form of equivocation, either on words or entire concepts. Thus in no less than three selections considered, the word "gentil" appears in an equivocal sense, although in the first selection (*The Knight's Tale*, where it is used to describe Arcite and Palamon), it is perhaps somewhat ambiguously used. Certainly the "gentil tercelet" in *The Parliament of Fowls* and the "gentil text" of the Wife of Bath leave no room for doubt that equivocation is involved. On a broader scale, the false analogy in the passage cited from Ewald's study of *The Parliament of Fowls* amounts to an equivocation of concepts.

4. Frequently seemingly inappropriate language, that is language which seems to contradict the knowledge we already have

of the personality of the speaker, is assigned to characters in humorous passages. Perhaps the two most obvious incidences of this in the passages analyzed here are those of Theseus and the "gentil" tercelet.

5. A further property of Chaucerian humor may be described as the presentation of the "realistic" or common-sense view of a situation in humorous terms, while the holders of exaggeratedly idealistic views exhibit shocked amazement and contempt at the realistic offender's expense. This is perhaps best illustrated by the selections examined from *The Parliament of Fowls* and the Miller's Prologue (in the latter's implied contrast between *The Knight's Tale* and *The Miller's Tale*).

6. Often in Chaucer's works an important humorous passage is preceded or surrounded by less sweeping humorous touches. This is evident throughout *The Parliament of Fowls* and, on a less comprehensive scale, in the two passages from the Miller's Prologue considered here.

7. Important humorous passages in Chaucer's poetry often present us with high and sustained incongruity in comparison to their total contexts. If we are to enter into the spirit of the work, we must take a stand. We may have to decide whether the humorous interpretation of important aspects of the work presented to us obtains, or the other seemingly more serious material. Accordingly, if pain, danger to life and limb, and the like accompany the worship of the goddess of supposed courtly love, as in the case of Arcite and Palamon, are courtly lovers fools, as Theseus tells us? In *The Parliament of Fowls*, is the duck or the tercelet "right" on matters of love? In any case, the humor maneuvers the reader into an evaluation of such incompatible views.

8. Finally, when Chaucer feigns innocent naïveté or ignorance in his narrator's role, we frequently find his most delightful humorous effects underneath the innocuousness. Of the passages here cited, Ewald's "Selbstverspottung" analysis of the brief passage from the Man of Law's Prologue amply demonstrates this characteristic.

These eight properties, in one or another combination, seem to me the most important and most clearly identifiable characteristics shared by the extremely varied continuum of Chaucer's humor as it is found in his poetical works. Besides these general properties, it is also characteristic of Chaucerian humor that it is rarely

confined to merely the exhibition of a funny concept. Very often
it serves to resolve a situation which, in its preceding context, is
difficult to manage if the original approach to its various elements
is maintained. The most comprehensive examples of this dealt with
here are Theseus' address and the Knight's account of the whereabouts of Arcite's soul, both from *The Knight's Tale*. The humorous treatment of the situations involved in such passages not only
resolves the immediate awkward state of affairs but also makes it
possible for the rest of the plot to unfold. But perhaps the most
pervading quality of Chaucerian humor is its revelation with economical and telling effect of the more inconsistent, fallacious, or
morally questionable aspects of human behavior and human character. This is directly or indirectly evident in all the examples I
have cited.

From the examples of Chaucerian satire treated so far, it seems
to me five characteristics can be identified. First, one of the most
clearly defined properties found in Chaucer's satirical passages is
the treatment of the inappropriate as appropriate. This is particularly evident in the descriptions of the Monk and the Friar. In
these two passages morally and/or theologically inappropriate
ideals and actions are treated as appropriate. In the passage from
the Wife of Bath's Prologue, the "gentil text," as the Wife interprets
it, at least, is scarcely "gentil" and therefore plainly exhibits this
characteristic.

A second readily apparent characteristic of Chaucer's satire is
the structural emphasis placed on its irony. Just as the essence of
Chaucerian humor lies in incongruity and its perception, his satire
is primarily irony, ridicule, or, sometimes, sarcasm. The analyses of
the Monk's and Friar's descriptions demonstrate the cumulative
effect of irony structurally achieved.

A third property in Chaucer's satire is that often a character's
or observer's reactions to the circumstances of the satire actually
constitute the satire. This is reflected in Chaucer's pose as the
naïve observer in the Monk's description and in the Wife of
Bath's reaction to "that gentil text." Also, the events or circumstances themselves in the immediate or larger contexts may constitute the satire, as in the passage from *The Merchant's Tale*
analyzed here or *The Merchant's Tale* considered as a whole.

A fourth variety of satire in Chaucer often embodies the use of
literary allusion. In the selections considered from the Monk's

description and *The Merchant's Tale,* Chaucer's settings are totally inappropriate to the original contexts of the works to which he alludes. This is especially evident in *The Romaunt of the Rose* allusion in the Monk's description, where, as Professor Peter points out, an apparently deliberate distortion of the original material heightens and emphasizes the inappropriateness. In other instances, as in the Wife of Bath's Prologue and in another portion of the Monk's description, we find theological, textual, or other authority inappropriately interpreted or totally misunderstood by the victims of the satire.

Finally there is a particular approach in Chaucer to our human environment which results in a kind of social satire achieved through his treatment of society on the personal level. The "successful" begging Friar and venery-loving Monk are seen through the eyes of the literal-minded (and hence naïve) poet who, in these passages, typifies the gullible "average" person. In this guise Chaucer brings home to us the utterly fallacious results of human preoccupation with externals or man-made social ideals and the material aspects of culture. For example, the inappropriate ways of life of the Monk and Friar bring them success, according to the false criteria inevitably arising from this almost universal human fallacy. Thus, in exposing social folly, Chaucer's satire assumes its most comprehensive proportions: much of society—that is all its members who confuse the external, man-made aspects of the immediate social order with the timeless, universal ethical needs of humanity—is foolishly mistaken in its sense of values. Clearly Chaucer's satiric concern is not with men but with man.

Chaucer's satire, then, is expository. The most important Chaucerian satire is usually free of cynicism and bitterness; it is instead an exposé of the myriad forms of human folly. In its most significant forms, it is the reader who must supply the moral; that is, in my opinion, its most important effect. Finally, we can identify satire in Chaucer's works by its sharing of one or several of the properties here demonstrated.

Most of the examples of humor and satire cited in this chapter I have considered as either one or the other rather than a combination simply because, for the most part, they were so considered by the critical authorities concerned. It is now apparent, however, that both humor and satire are very much present in several of them. For example, we can readily identify several of the characteristics of humor *and* satire outlined above in the passages cited from the Wife of Bath's Prologue, *The Parliament of Fowls*, the "Selbstverspottung" aspects of the Monk's description, and *The Nun's Priest's Tale*, to specify but four. This significant phenomenon is not only indicative of Chaucer's effective blending of two important aspects of his art, but it should also furnish us considerable insight into his approach to and attitude toward the extremely broad range of subject matter which, as a result of his treatment, is humorous and/or satiric in its effects. Therefore, even if we cannot expect complete consistency in such matters—if, for example, courtly love is treated in such a manner that the effect is humorous and/or satirical in one of Chaucer's works—we should at least not be surprised to find it so treated in some or all of the rest of his works.

It is now possible to return to the two passages from Book II of *The Knight's Tale* (1734-36 and 1748-54), earlier posited as possible instances of both humor and satire. From the standpoint of the various characteristics of Chaucerian humor and satire subsequently derived from authoritatively established examples, it is clear that the first of these two passages shares several of these properties. The context surrounding it is so constructed as to emphasize the incongruity; the immediate context in which "wikkedly" appears is logical (and in which "wikkedly" is incongruous), and there is at least some echo of equivocation. Moreover—and this perhaps tends more to arouse suspicion than serve as evidence—it immediately precedes the important humorous address of Theseus. As shown by the "gentil" tercelet's argument and the two passages from the Miller's Prologue analyzed above, important humorous passages in Chaucer are often preceded or surrounded by less sweeping humorous material. There seem no reasonable grounds to doubt, therefore, that this passage is humorous.

It is equally clear that at least two characteristics of Chaucerian satire, as derived here, are demonstrated by this passage. We find the morally appropriate treated as inappropriate (Palamon's characterization of his prison break as wicked) and Palamon's reaction to his prison break and his present position in themselves constituting, in their irony, the satire. It seems very clear that this passage is both humorous and satirical in its effects.

The second passage concerns the grief of the Queen, Emelye,

and the ladies of the hunting party over the plights of Palamon and Arcite. It, too, reflects the structural emphasis on the incongruity, the presence of the incongruity in a logical context, at least ambiguity in the use of "gentil," and—possibly significantly—is close in locale and subject matter to the important, humorous address of Theseus as well as to the address of Palamon. Accordingly, it is humorous in its effect, beyond reasonable doubt. Considered from the standpoint of possible satire, the passage contains several of the properties derived from established examples of satire: it treats the inappropriate as appropriate, structurally emphasizes the irony (which results in a cumulative ironic effect), betrays in its participants' reactions to the immediate situation the satire itself, and certainly involves in its irony basic social tenets of the characters concerned. Here, too, there can be no reasonable doubt that this passage is both humorous and satirical.

I have outlined the projective nature of the perception, interpretation, and communication of satire and humor in literature, with emphasis upon Chaucer's works. To surmount one of the principal difficulties involved in the interpretation of Chaucerian satire and humor, various characteristic properties common to Chaucerian satire and humor have been derived. If passages in *The Knight's Tale* share these properties—and it is clear that some of them, at least, do—this is demonstrable by the same kind of analysis employed here. It should now be possible, then, to assess in detail the pervasiveness of humor and satire in the whole of *The Knight's Tale*.

III

book one

ROFESSOR MUSCATINE AGREES with Root that Chaucer chose not to be "realistic" in *The Knight's Tale.* Indeed, referring to Professor Baum's suggestions of pervading satire, Professor Muscatine feels that he was "seeking realism of action (or of characterization), for instance, in a poem not written under the assumption of realism of method." It is certainly true that Arcite and Palamon are totally preoccupied with their idealistic love for Emelye. They therefore seem primarily to be mere representatives of this emotional quality and thus abstractions rather than flesh and blood. This in itself makes them vague as characters —they are oversimplified or, to put it more bluntly, exaggerated in their too complete exclusion from their lives of the practical consequences of their love for Emelye. This applies most obviously to the first two books of the poem, but in truth virtually all the events of the poem stem from it.

With this indefatigable idealistic fixation as the motivating force behind its events, the nature of the "method" Chaucer employed in the poem is of central importance. If the "method" were totally unrealistic—perhaps idealistic is a more appropriate term—we would scarcely expect to find evidence of humor or satire involving significant concepts and situations in the poem. It is clear even at this stage in our examination, however, that some significant concepts and situations are treated by Chaucer in such a manner that their effects are both humorous and satirical. If, on the other hand, the "method" were totally realistic, *The Knight's Tale* might well approach the farcical simply because Arcite and Palamon are far too idealistic to be real. They would be entirely incongruous. Professors Muscatine and Root, in common with many adherents to the traditional point of view, would no doubt agree with the implications in Speirs' comment on part of Book I: "How little separates the world of courtly romance from the world of courtly allegory the celebrated garden scene in the first part of the *Knight's Tale* reminds us."[1] Yet some very important aspects of the poem are certainly realistically treated.

Some of this realistic treatment is evident in Book I. For example, we are given a detailed, circumstantial report of Palamon's reaction to his first view of Emelye:

> He cast his eye upon Emelya,
> And therwithal he bleynte and cride, "A!"
> As though he stongen were unto the herte.
> And with that cry Arcite anon up sterte,
> And seyde, "Cosyn myn, what eyleth thee,
> That art so pale and deedly on to see?   (1077-82)

Quite apart from such connotative aspects as the appropriateness of the reaction to the stimulus, as a description these lines permit no doubt to exist on the literal level as to the preciseness of their meaning. Palamon's reaction is documented variously by the Knight's reportorial account of the blenching and the cry, the detail of the simile, and the reaction of Arcite to Palamon's appearance. If the language is figurative, it nevertheless forces us to accept the description at its literal value. Since it is presented to us as a statement of fact, we should presumably evaluate it on this basis.

There are other examples of this realistic treatment in Book I, of which the following are typical and obvious enough to require no comment:

> We stryve as dide the houndes for the boon;
> They foughte al day, and yet hir part was noon.
> Ther cam a kyte, whil that they were so wrothe,
> And baar awey the boon bitwixe hem bothe.   (1177-80)

> This was the forward, pleynly for t'endite,
> Bitwixen Theseus and hym Arcite

> That if so were that Arcite were yfounde
> Evere in his lif, by day or nyght, oo stounde
> In any contree of this Theseus,
> And he were caught, it was acorded thus,
> That with a swerd he sholde lese his heed.
> Ther nas noon oother remedie ne reed;
> But taketh his leve, and homward he him spedde. (1209-17)

Obviously even in varied situations and with both figurative and fairly denotative language, the undecorated facts emerge as the result of this realistic approach.

Still more readily identifiable, as we might expect from the attention given it by the more conservative critics, is the idealistic, highly connotative treatment of situations as concrete as those realistically treated. The garden scene to which Speirs refers is a particularly spectacular example—a portion of it should be sufficient to illustrate this approach:

> Yclothed was she fressh, for to devyse:
> Hir yelow heer was broyded in a tresse
> Bihynde hir bak, a yerde long, I gesse.
> And in the gardyn, at the sonne upriste,
> She walketh up and doun, and as hire liste
> She gadereth floures, party white and rede,
> To make a subtil gerland for hire hede;
> And as an aungel hevenysshly she soong.   (1048-55)

It is evident, then, that both approaches are used in *The Knight's Tale*. Sometimes the realistic or idealistic predominates in one or another passage, but some of each is almost invariably present in every significant portion of the poem. Let us briefly compare Emelye's walk in the garden with its parallel action—Palamon's walk in the dungeon tower—bearing in mind that the passage quoted above was preceded by the highly idealized comparison of Emelye's awakening, her beauty and habits, with the gorgeous garden on this lovely May morning:

> And Palamoun, this woful prisoner,
> As was his wone, by leve of his gayler,
> Was risen and romed in a chambre an heigh,
> In which he al the noble citee seigh,
> And eek the gardyn, ful of braunches grene,
> Ther as this fresshe Emelye the shene

> Was in hire walk, and romed up and doun.
> This sorweful prisoner, this Palamoun,
> Goth in the chambre romynge to and fro,
> And to hymself compleynynge of his wo.
> That he was born, ful ofte he seyde, "allas!"
> And so bifel, by aventure or cas,
> That thurgh a wyndow, thikke of many a barre
> Of iren greet and square as any sparre,
> He cast his eye upon Emelya,   (1063-77)

This, of course, is the material preceding lines 1077-82 earlier considered. The amalgam of the realistic and the idealistic treatments is obvious. Even in the quoted portion of the garden scene there is a touch of homely detail (1050). While my present concern is with Book I, these matters cannot be dealt with in isolation; they recur throughout the poem. With specific reference to Book I, however, the intertwining of the realistic and idealistic is evident in Theseus' meeting with the mourning ladies outside Athens and the conquering of Thebes (892-1000), the account of the discovery and incarceration of Arcite and Palamon (1001-32), and Palamon's and Arcite's reactions to the sight of Emelye and the results in terms of their relationship (1063-1187). The two approaches are more easily separable in the economical account of Arcite's conditional release (1191-1218). Throughout the remaining sections of Book I there are suggestions and touches of realistic treatment, even though most of this material appears to be idealistically approached.

The central consideration always to be borne in mind in any analysis of *The Knight's Tale* is the self-evident one that everything is presented to us by the Knight. He does not "knowingly" in any part of the poem participate in any of its satire or humor. This is accomplished by Chaucer in part by these two approaches to his material. A consistent pattern can be plainly discerned in the narrative technique Chaucer assigns to the Knight, which matches the Knight's own character as it is reflected in his attitude toward the material. It is made up of three stylistic characteristics, fairly broad and occasionally overlapping. None of them is totally free of figurative language, but two consist of a very distinctive kind of figurative language as compared to the third.

The first and simplest device consists of a kind of thoroughly objective reportage. Its similes are homely and uncomplicated, and permit the reader no interpretive leeway. Thus the bars of Palamon's dungeon—at least in that part of the tower where he takes his morning walk—are thick (i.e., present in great quantity) and are of iron as large and square as the structural beam of a house or mast of a ship. If this does not sound probable—and most of us would agree that it is at least unlikely—we still have no choice but to accept the literal substance presented to us, because the exactness of detail allows us no alternative. It is presented as a matter of fact, just as Palamon's reaction to his first sight of Emelye and its documentation by Arcite's comments are presented as matters of fact. The Knight does not interpret or explain in such passages; we are left to do so ourselves.

The second stylistic device, often not entirely separate from the one just described, simply employs a freer use of figurative language still without interpretation or explanation of the passage by the Knight. For instance, Arcite likens his and Palamon's strife over Emelye to two dogs fighting over a bone; are we to take this as read? Or, in Book II, we are left at one important point to decide whether Theseus' colorful depiction of lovers as fools (with Arcite and Palamon as prime examples) is to be believed or not. This device, too, is reportage, but of a more elaborate kind. When either device is used, it is evident that the Knight would be hard put to make literally believable what he is conveying. His problem in the case of the first would evolve from the material itself, while in the case of the second device he would be forced to relate apparently contradictory and inconsistent material to the alleged subject matter of the poem as a whole.

The third device consists of the Knight's *interpretation* of matters of fact; almost invariably subjective, emotional, or idealistic motives are imputed to the action or situation or characters involved when this device is used. This is the idealistic or unrealistic treatment of the material. When figurative language is used in the first two devices, it tends to be homely and specific; often its analogies or similes involve somewhat plebeian or undignified comparisons. The figurative language of the third device, however, results in highly idealized comparisons which in general are subjective or downright emotional in nature.

The interweaving of these devices creates structural contrast and balance. Thus Emelye sings like an angel, while Palamon merely cries "A!" in such a manner and with such an aspect that

Arcite fears for his physical condition. Emelye is the picture of grace during her morning walk; Palamon blenches. The difference in effect between the first two devices and the third is that in the former we are left to evaluate for ourselves material which is presented to us as matter of fact, while in the latter the evaluation is furnished us by the Knight's idealistic interpretations. I think it likely that failure to perceive this pattern in the Knight's narration accounts in part for Professor Baum's pronouncement of the poem as "an imperfect poem, an early work."[2] What seems to be inconsistency in the Knight's treatment of the substance of his narrative disappears when its effects are perceived as part of an identifiable, patterned approach.

The obvious result of the first two devices is to cause us to assess the reasonableness of the matters of fact they assert. From the examples quoted it is clear that our credulity is scarcely equal to the demands of the situation. To accept these circumstantial assertions we must identify ourselves with the Knight who, presumably wishing to convey as convincingly as possible the depth of emotion motivating the events, calls upon his imagination to furnish circumstantial detail. This he expresses as matter-of-fact to substantiate what he imagines to be the true depth of emotion motivating Palamon and Arcite. Since his substantiating material exceeds at times the limits of reasonableness and at other times contradicts concepts established in the total context of the poem, a very confused state of affairs would result if the Knight tried to reconcile them into a believable whole. Chaucer, intentionally or otherwise, has the Knight simply ignore these inescapable implications, thereby requiring us either to identify ourselves with the Knight by also ignoring them or to perceive them for ourselves.

If we question the genuineness of factual matters which supposedly testify to the idealistic emotions motivating the main characters, we naturally question the genuineness or appropriateness of the emotions themselves, which allegedly give rise to these matters. Here, then, Chaucer's artistic ambivalence in *The Knight's Tale* becomes clearly defined. We can identify ourselves with the attitude of the Knight toward his material and, together with Root and the many other adherents to the traditional view, determinedly give ourselves up to the "spirit of romance" and consequently a more or less subjective appreciation. But we can also view the poem from a fresh position free of preconceptions—that of readers unconfined by total acceptance of the Knight's assertions and interpretations. Such a position involves the consideration of the Knight's approaches to his material and the problem of genre, among other things, as aspects of the poem which do not necessarily exclude the possibility of other pertinent qualities. It is from the latter position that the remainder of my examination will proceed.

I agree with many students of *The Knight's Tale* that Theseus is the most vividly and completely drawn character in the poem. I have already cited Professor Muscatine's analysis of Theseus. A very different analysis has been made by Professor Webb, who holds that Theseus is cruel and ignoble and that virtually every reference to him in the poem is therefore ironic. While I agree in part with some aspects of Professor Webb's analysis, I cannot, unfortunately, agree with his principal basis for his findings—that Theseus was being judged by Chaucer in terms of a historical figure, a villain of considerable magnitude. I do not feel we can justifiably consider Theseus outside his appearance in *The Knight's Tale*.[3] Professor Frost, I think, very properly objects to Professor Webb's conclusions on this same basis, but seems to assume that no other basis for these conclusions could exist.[4] I am convinced that Theseus, as Chaucer portrays him for us, is essentially a man of action who, like so many successful incumbents of responsible positions throughout history, seems able to find an ideal or ethical basis for schemes in which he is actually personally interested. This quality, among others, adds to Theseus' personality a dimension of humanness unshared by the other principal characters in the poem.

The Knight is a member of a fading aspect of medieval military society. When he narrates a tale of another military society (suitably far away in space and time) we are scarcely surprised to find its dominant figure a grandly successful military "duc," treated in terms of the Knight's own ideals. But the Knight does not dwell on Theseus' ideals; Chaucer has him extol Theseus only by means of the occasional admiring adjective, and we are ostensibly left to let Theseus' actions convince us, too, of this royal ruler's worth. The Knight does not furnish us explanations of Theseus' possibly complicated states of mind as he does with Palamon and Arcite.

The carefully documented introduction which the Knight vouchsafes for Theseus has many points of interest in its relation to Theseus' treatment in the rest of the poem. From the standpoint of the ambivalence with which I am concerned, Theseus' first appearances in the poem are devoid of any implications beyond the literal meanings of the Knight's language, except when they are considered as part of Theseus' whole treatment. When they are so considered, we can easily perceive a gradual, cumulative inappropriateness developing in the Knight's attitude toward Theseus. That is, they form a criterion, the departures from which are clearly discernible.

The following short passages, with brief comments on their immediate contexts, will demonstrate the establishment of this criterion of treatment:

> Whilom, as olde stories tellen us,
> Ther was a duc that highte Theseus;
> Of Atthenes he was lord and governour,
> And in his tyme swich a conquerour,
> That gretter was ther noon under the sonne.   (859-63)

We may safely assume, in my opinion, that the last two lines are a value judgment. In these lines the immediate situation as the poem opens is most economically conveyed and the Knight's attitude toward Theseus is further advanced. Through this attitude toward Theseus we have a preview of the Knight's attitude toward what he clearly believes Theseus represents. Thus the Knight continues with another value judgment: "Ful many a riche contree hadde he wonne;/ What with his wysdom and his chivalrie" (864-65).

Following the nine lines are three more which are specifically laudatory, if we consider only this immediate context:

> And thus with victorie and with melodye
> Lete I this noble duc to Atthenes ryde,
> And al his hoost in armes hym bisyde.   (872-74)

Making use of the cataloguing rhetorical device of *occupatio*, Chaucer then has the Knight furnish a more detailed account of Theseus' immediate past, in effect actually enlarging upon the situation as the poem opens and establishing the very important matter of Theseus' identity with the qualities of chivalry: "How wonnen was the regne of Femenye/ By Theseus and by his chivalrye" (877-78). In all, only thirty-three lines serve Chaucer to establish the opening situation and the vital matter of the Knight's attitude toward Theseus and, by plain implication, toward chivalry.

But immediately following the introductory passages and in marked contrast to them appears what may be one of the most jarringly inappropriate references to Theseus in the entire poem:

> This duc, of whom I make mencioun,
> Whan he was come almoost unto the toun,
> In al his wele and in his mooste pride,
> He was war, as he caste his eye aside,
> Where that ther kneled in the heighe weye
> A compaignye of ladyes, tweye and tweye,
> Ech after oother, clad in clothes blake;
> But swich a cry and swich a wo they make
> That in this world nys creature lyvynge
> That herde swich another waymentynge;   (893-902)

Considering first lines 893-96, the quality of pride is of primary significance. We can state with fair confidence that the word "pride" occurs in Chaucer's works seventy-four times.[5] A careful examination of each context in which the word appears reveals that in all but six instances its meaning is essentially that listed in the primary position in a typical modern dictionary: An overhigh opinion of oneself; exaggerated self-esteem; conceit. Accordingly, in sixty-eight of its seventy-four occurrences in Chaucer's works, "pride" is used unmistakably to refer directly or indirectly to the first of the seven deadly sins. Five of the remaining six occurrences are in *The Monk's Tale*; each of these is in a context which, to a greater or lesser degree, reflects the above meaning blended with a second one.

The *OED* cites a number of works illustrating the Old English origin of this second meaning, and makes it clear that the following referents apply in some contexts well beyond Chaucer's time: "Pomp, ostentation, display, magnificence, splendor." From what we know of the nonchristian aspects of early Anglo-Saxon culture, I think we may assume that "pride" in this sense was merely another manifestation of the first and most inclusive of the seven deadly sins, according to these five examples from *The Monk's Tale* and—more significantly, perhaps—the *De Superbia* of *The Parson's Tale*. In view of whatever we can gain from Chaucer's works in terms of insight into the man himself and his attitudes toward such

crucial medieval concepts as this, could we reasonably expect any
other treatment of "pride"?

The first of these examples of Chaucer's use of "pride" with this
combination of meanings in *The Monk's Tale* is in the account of
Balthasar:

> For proud he was of herte and of array;
> And eek an ydolastre was he ay.
> His hye estaat assured hym in pryde;   (2186-88)

The remainder of the account graphically describes Balthasar's
catastrophic downfall, leaving us in no doubt that pride is its cause.
Later, in the Monk's account of King Antiochus, there are three
occurrences of "pride" which are especially noteworthy because the
third one clears up any ambiguity in the first two occurrences:

> What nedeth it of kyng Anthiochus
> To telle his hye roial magestee,
> His hye pride, his werkes venymus?   (2575-77)

> Fortune hym hadde enhaunced so in pride
> That verraily he wende he myghte attayne
> Unto the sterres upon every syde,
> And in balance weyen ech montayne,
> And alle the floodes of the see restrayne.
> And Goddes peple hadde he moost in hate;
> Hem wolde he sleen in torment and in payne,
> Wenynge that God ne myghte his pride abate.   (2583-90)

Obviously the "pride" of line 2590 is that of the seven deadly sins,
and there can be no question about equating the other two to it.

The fifth example of this blend of two meanings of "pride" is
in the Monk's account of Croesus, although the total context of
The Monk's Tale by the time this last tragedy is reached leaves
little doubt as to the meaning we are to attribute to the word:

> This riche Cresus, whilom kyng of Lyde,
> Of which Cresus Cirus soore hym dradde,
> Yet was he caught amyddes al his pryde,
> And to be brent men to the fyr hym ladde.   (2727-30)

As in the account of Balthasar, we are left in no doubt that pride,
in the sense of the seven deadly sins, caused Croesus' grisly end
(2740-66).

Chaucer's most complete consideration of pride (and perhaps

the one most nearly reflecting his personal attitude in detail) is in *The Parson's Tale*. These selections amply demonstrate the fusion of these two meanings of "pride" into the one comprehensive, pervasive referent:

And thogh so be that no man kan outrely telle the nombre of the twigges and of the harmes that cometh of Pride, yet wol I shewe a partie of hem, as ye shul understonde.   (389)

Veyneglorie is for to have pompe and delit in his temporeel hynesse, and glorifie hym in this worldly estaat.   (404)

Now been ther two maneres of Pride: that oon of hem is withinne the herte of man, and that oother is withoute./ Of whiche, soothly, thise forseyde thynges, and mo than I have seyd, apertenen to Pride that is in the herte of man; and that othere speces of Pride been withoute./ But natheles that oon of thise speces of Pride is signe of that oother, right as the gaye leefsel atte taverne is signe of the wyn that is in the celer./ And this is in manye thynges: as in speche and contenaunce, and in outrageous array of clothyng.   (408-11)

The only other occurrence of "pride" in Chaucer's works, then, is in line 895 of the principal passage under discussion. In view of the Knight's laudatory references to Theseus in the introductory passages of the poem, we are not prepared to find pride as a sin attributed to the noble duke. Another key word in the line, of course, is "wele," usually interpreted to mean "weal, well-being, happiness, success." But the *OED* maintains that "wele" in one usage refers to "pomp, splendour, rich array"—indeed, it cites this very line as an illustration of this meaning of the word. Thus, if we interpret the line as the Knight ostensibly does, we must assume that "wele" and "pride" are used as "splendour" and "magnificence" —the controlling factor being the assumption that "pride" is used in its Old English sense and hence to be interpreted as a quality worthy of approbation. "Wele" apparently supports this. Yet "wele" supports even more strongly, it seems to me, an interpretation of "pride" as the most formidable of the seven deadly sins, especially in view of the superlative "mooste" intensifying and emphasizing the "pride." In effect, we are told here that no greater pride than that of Theseus is possible, in terms of degree.

From the examples cited earlier it is clear beyond question

that Chaucer's other works reflect no interpretation of "pride" other than as a quality worthy of disapprobation. The similarities of the selections quoted from *The Merchant's Tale* to this particular line and the conclusions we should draw from this seem too obvious to detail. I think we have sound reasons to doubt that this, as the only one of seventy-four instances in Chaucer's usage of "pride" where any slight ambiguity is not immediately and obviously clarified, is an example of praise of Theseus. One tends to suspect strongly these consequently unique referents.

An examination of this line in the context of the remainder of the passage in which it appears is most interesting. As he arrives at the outskirts of the city, Theseus was aware, "as he caste his eye aside," of a company of grieving ladies. Moreover, "swich a cry and swich a wo they make" that no living creature has heard such lamenting. We have here a very subtle incongruity—so subtle that it would be ambiguous were it not for the "wele" and "mooste pride" and the passage containing Theseus' address to the women which follows this selection. The incongruity here lies in the manner in which Theseus perceives the lamenting women: "In al his wele and in his mooste pride,/ He was war, as he caste his eye aside"—yet (and I think the emphasis on the sound is significant) the women were clearly lamenting so loudly ("swich a cry") and in such an excess of woe that never was *heard* such lamenting. But the structure of the passage clearly indicates that Theseus became aware of the women only as he drew abreast of them, by a casual glance to one side. One would expect him to be amply aware of their presence long before he drew up to them because of this woeful din.

Theseus is certainly conscious of the aural aspects of the women's grief, however, as is borne out by the most unchivalric opening questions of his address to them:

> "What folk been ye, that at myn homcomynge
> Perturben so my feste with criynge?"
> Quod Theseus. "Have ye so greet envye
> Of myn honour, that thus compleyne and crye?   (905-8)

This inappropriate demand is followed by material which outlines a situation similar in some ways to that surrounding Theseus' long address in Book II (1782-1825), which was analyzed in some detail in the preceding chapter. In both instances the grounds for these feelings hinge upon the *rank* of the victims, not upon what has happened to them as human beings.

This is clear as the Knight reports Theseus' feelings upon his being told the grounds for the women's lamenting:

> This gentil duc doun from his courser sterte
> With herte pitous, whan he herde hem speke.
> Hym thoughte that his herte wolde breke,
> Whan he saugh hem so pitous and so maat,
> That whilom weren of so greet estaat;   (952-56)

Theseus' "pity" for the women here is not aroused by the terrible tragedy which has befallen them. It is instead an institutionalized emotion—concern that this kind of thing has happened to people of high rank. This is, therefore, not the classical notion of tragedy in the bringing low of the great, since the Aristotelian concept is inseparable from the causes of the fall in all their manifestations.

We derive the effect by the implications of what is left unsaid (that Theseus also feels pity for the specific tragedy of the women's emotional losses), but a close reading demonstrates that what is left unsaid apparently is also unfelt by Theseus. There is both incongruity and inappropriateness in his feeling that his heart would break because of the contrast between the women's former rank and present dejection, but even the Knight would be hard put to wring a stronger or more final pronouncement on Theseus' emotional condition. There is no extension possible. Nothing is left unsaid about Theseus' emotions here, but we cannot help but realize what should have been said—what he should have felt.

Even at this very early stage in Book I, accordingly, it is possible to present definite grounds for considering *The Knight's Tale* from the standpoint of artistic ambivalence. First Theseus is presented as the ideal personification of chivalry and nobility but is immediately afterward depicted as an exceedingly proud man (895). In view of the next 130 lines and of Chaucer's consistent treatment of pride in his other works, it seems extremely unlikely that Theseus' exhibition of pride is anything other than a contradiction of the chivalric, noble attributes earlier ascribed to him. Clearly, this is satire, with structural emphasis placed on the irony and the treatment of the inappropriate as appropriate, alike in principle but far more subtly derived than the examples cited in Chapter II.

The inappropriate moral and theological practices of the Friar and Monk, as Chaucer describes them, are in terms of all too familiar, everyday occurrences observable by almost anyone. But Theseus is in a faraway setting in time and place, a purported example of a kind of life unknown to the Knight's audience in terms of experience. Thus we strive for a meaning of "pride" which exists and, at first glance, seems to fit. In fact, however, it is really too unlikely to stand up in its context of Theseus' treatment in the rest of Book I and throughout the poem, quite aside from its exception to Chaucer's otherwise invariable attitude toward the concept. I have belabored this defenseless line unmercifully because I feel it is of paramount importance in its establishment of Chaucer's ambivalence in the treatment of Theseus practically at the beginning of the poem. In its relation to surrounding passages we find its satire deriving from them as well as heightening some of their own humor and satire.

The incongruity of Theseus' manner of perception of the lamenting women is in part accomplished by the seeming casualness of line 896, giving us almost the impression that it was mere chance that his eye fell upon the women, despite the aural aspects of their grief. In its direct linkage to the preceding line and *its* connotations, any ambiguity in either line tends to become resolved as we see them both as part of a pattern which becomes more distinct as we read on. Line 896, then, is so structurally related to its immediately preceding and later contexts as to emphasize the humorous passage. It also appears in a logical context—Theseus cannot help discovering the presence of the women; only this, the manner of his discovery of their presence, is adroitly and subtly illogical in its effects. Accordingly, it shares the same humorous properties as the examples from *The Nun's Priest's Tale, The Knight's Tale* (2809-14), and the Miller's Prologue which were analyzed in the preceding chapter (classifications 1, 2, 5, and 6).

The third important passage, in which Theseus speaks for the first time, is directly related to the "pride" of line 895. Unlike a shining representative of chivalry or a truly "noble" person, Theseus sounds here extremely worldly and very much aware of his temporal position. His enquiry as to whether the miserable women are envious of his exalted position is both inappropriate and incongruous. It is an unsuitable question in form and content for the supposed chivalric duke to ask a group of grief-stricken women; it is rude—even churlish. Its incongruity arises from the nature of the question itself and the fact that it is addressed to women. In view of the position of women in the social code of literary chivalry, it is virtually inconceivable that envy of Theseus' status would ever occur to them; it would be too far outside their personal frames of reference for the idea to be anything but absurd. Lines 905-8 are accordingly both satiric and humorous in their effects. The satire is in their presentation of the inappropriate as appropriate in both the language used and the concepts conveyed, according to the ostensible chivalric qualities Theseus is supposed to possess.

These same characteristics give rise to some of the humorous effect, too, thus reflecting a direct relation in essential aspects to the analyses in Chapter II of the Monk's and Friar's descriptions in the *General Prologue,* the passage from the Wife of Bath's Prologue, Theseus' address in Book II, and the "gentil" tercelet's remarks in *The Parliament of Fowls* (classifications 3 and 4). The humorous incongruity in turn is derived from appearance of these lines in a supposedly logical context, as in the pertinent passages analyzed in Chapter II (classification 2). Also, like the examples which obtain in Chapter II, both the humor and satire are structurally emphasized in their immediate contexts (classification 1). Accordingly the "pride" of line 895 is linked to Theseus' question in terms of satire, and the incongruities of the manner in which Theseus perceives the women (896-99) are part of the incongruous milieu of the entire context.

In view of Theseus' opening remarks to the grieving women and his "mooste pride," I think the characterization of him in line 952 as "this gentil duc" (the next reference the Knight himself makes to him) should be regarded in the same light as the Wife of Bath's "gentil" text or the "gentil" tercelet or the "worthy" Friar (Chapter II, classification 3). Its relation to the "gentillesse" of the eldest lady's reply to Theseus (920) is obvious; indeed in her assurance that the women are not envious of Theseus' glory and honor (917), the humor and satire pervading this important area in the poem are re-emphasized. Finally, Theseus' preoccupation with the women's fall from "greet estaat" as opposed to the more humanitarian aspects of their tragedy bears a close relationship to his swearing, as a "trewe knyght," to wreak vengeance upon the "tiraunt Creon" (959-61), impliedly on behalf of the women's wrongs. We have here far-reaching social satire: is the true knight imbued with pride and its manifestations, as Chaucer portrays Theseus in this passage, and is the true knight moved to "natural" pity only in terms of external, artifical considerations? If so, the whole concept of chivalry is exposed as something very different in practice from its stated ideals. These lines, then, reflect in every major respect the qualities of the paradigms of social satire analyzed in Chapter II.

Thus far in the poem it is clear that Theseus, usually approached by Chaucer's use of the first and second stylistic devices of the Knight examined earlier, can be consistently and fully interpreted as a character only by viewing him both through eyes other than those of the Knight, as well as the Knight's. We must fully understand the point of view of Chaucer's Knight, but not be bound by it any more than we are bound by the Merchant's point of view in *The Merchant's Tale*. The above analysis plainly demonstrates the subtlety of the effects and their derivation here identifiable. Indeed, with the possible exception of the "mooste pride" of line 895, probably no single one of them would be by itself more than suggestive of satire or humor. Their cumulative effect, however, is so demonstrably strong in terms of characteristic Chaucerian humor and satire that no reasonable grounds exist for questioning the presence of both.

Theseus' importance to the remainder of Book I can be conveniently assessed in terms of his furtherance of the plot and his development as the central character in the poem. Two of the three matters to be considered make up the rest of the section of Book I analyzed so far in terms of Theseus' character. The first of them is simply the conquering of Thebes. This "trewe knyght" keeps his word to the letter and—this I think is particularly significant—"dide with al the contree as hym leste" (1004). Then, in the brief but harrowing glimpse of the aftermath of a chivalric battle, we learn of the discovery by the diligent corpse plunderers of the wounded Palamon and Arcite. Their royal lineage having been established, immediate action is taken:

> Out of the taas the pilours han hem torn,
> And han hem caried softe unto the tente
> Of Theseus; and he ful soone hem sente
> To Atthenes, to dwellen in prisoun

> Perpetuelly,—he nolde no raunsoun.
> And whan this worthy duc hath thus ydon,
> He took his hoost, and hoom he rit anon
> With laurer crowned as a conquerour;
> And ther he lyveth in joye and in honour   (1020-28)

But for the royal young Thebans, life is somewhat different; with this state of affairs firmly established, a single but important transitional line ushers us into the main plot of the poem:

> And in a tour, in angwissh and in wo,
> This Palamon and his felawe Arcite
> For everemoore; ther may no gold hem quite.
>   This passeth yeer by yeer and day by day,
> Til it fil ones, in a morwe of May,   (1030-34)

These two passages, which form the climax of the entire first section of the poem, seem to me among the most skillfully crafted in Chaucer's poetry. They are full of contrasts and in their casual economy convey an enormous variety and range of concepts. The pillagers tear Palamon and Arcite from the heap of bodies, then carry them gently to Theseus' tent. In lines 1022-24 the interrupted regularity in rhythm, achieved by full stops within the lines, is more apparent than actual but is totally effective in forcing extremely heavy emphasis upon the ransomless imprisonment. In lines 1030-32 the concept is emphasized again, this time emotionally. In these fourteen lines, then, we have the sharpest of contrasts superbly drawn between violence and gentleness, military power and military impotence, the fruits of victory and the bitterness of defeat, and joyous, free action and bitter, enforced inactivity. The plot moves forward, the stage is set for the main substance of the narrative, and all the important matters in these lines are clearly and unequivocally subordinated to the one central fact: Arcite and Palamon can never be ransomed and hence must be prisoners "for everemoore."

Obviously the matter of the ransom is of considerable importance; its time-honored place in the chivalric code is quite clear. Much of its significance in *The Knight's Tale* at this point seems to me to derive from Theseus as a personality, whether or not he is a "trewe knyght" with all that implies from the Knight's point of view. G. G. Coulton, in an extended treatment of chivalry, stated: "Being cooptative, therefore it [knighthood] was a free-masonry.

All knights in theory were brothers everywhere." Further, "On its moral side, [knighthood] was based on two eternal principles. The first was that of *noblesse oblige*—privileges implying responsibilities—and the second, that indefinable something connoted by the word 'gentleman' in its best sense; a person not only 'gentle' as we say that a nurse is gentle with a patient, but also in the more literal sense of the word, a person of gens, of race; a pedigree-person, a thoroughbred, so long as his actions do justice to his breeding."

Coulton quoted Malory on the ideal of knighthood obtaining to the Knights of the Round Table: "They were solemnly bound 'never to do outrageousity, nor murder, and always to flee treason. Also by no means to be cruel, but to give mercy unto him that asketh mercy . . . and always to do ladies, damsels, and gentlewomen succour upon pain of death. Also, that no man take no battles in a wrongful quarrel for no law, ne for no world's goods.' " Coulton also cites a passage from *Sir Gawayne and the Green Knight* as evidence of the renowned "noble talk" of knights and considers Chaucer's portrait of the Knight in the *General Prologue* a definition of knighthood. Finally, his ample documentation of the pervasiveness of the ransoming of prisoners as an integral part of chivalric war is decisive, although he emphasizes its financial aspects.[6]

Clearly, if we compare Theseus to the Knight and assess him in light of Coulton's interpretation of reliable sources as well as the sources themselves, Theseus is far from being the "trewe knyght" of the much vaunted chivalric code. Now, Coulton points out that Malory was concerned with contrasting chivalric theory with "the too-frequent practice of his own day," and even if Malory's thoughts were expressed some eighty years after *The Knight's Tale* was written, it seems to me that the poem's effects are related to this purpose of Malory's. Chivalry was fading into the past in Chaucer's day, but certainly the Knight's notion of what it was is a sincere one; it is perfectly clear that his interpretation of these people and events of a bygone era is without guile. It is this fixed idealistic approach to everything in the poem which, in its total consistency, can give rise to confusion if it is not taken into account in every consideration of the characters, plot, language, or setting of the poem. Chaucer employs the first and second devices of the Knight's narration in the description of Theseus and his acts, and the third device in the Knight's interpretive evaluation of Theseus' character or acts.

I see no reasonable explanation that will bring Theseus' failure to grant ransom within the realm of chivalric ideals as Chaucer ostensibly represents them in the Knight's description in the *General Prologue* and through the Knight's narration of his tale. But this state of affairs—one of several comparable ones—does not daunt Chaucer's Knight in his doughty idealism; in his bland naïveté he decisively misinterprets the matter to bring it into line with the supposed ideals motivating Theseus. Hence the "worthy duc" of line 1025 is equivocal beyond reasonable doubt, totally illogical in its context, structurally emphasized in its proximity to the immediately preceding line's contradictory content, and certainly the crowning instance of this kind of humor so far encountered in Book I. Its satiric effect is far-reaching and must be considered in the broader context of Theseus' character in the poem as a whole.

The last direct treatment of Theseus in Book I is in the passage containing the agreement for Arcite's release, cited earlier in this chapter. The matter-of-factness of the first device of the Knight's narrative style here is in direct contrast to the airy idealism conveyed by the third, the interpretive device, in the "worthy duc" of the "raunsoun" context.

Clearly any total view of *The Knight's Tale* must include an analysis of Theseus which takes into account those varied elements of his personality which have direct influence on the principal characters and events of the poem. A great many critics have done this, of course. Professor Webb, for example, finds Theseus in effect gratuitously cruel, while those adhering to the traditional approach to the poem in general hold fairly closely related views of Theseus which tend to resemble the Knight's. But it seems to me that the starting point of any view of Theseus must be that he, unlike any other principal character in the poem, is almost from the very beginning portrayed by Chaucer as an intensely genuine human being, not a collection of institutionalized "natural" reactions to codified ideals. Failure to perceive this in all its implications results in too narrow an interpretation of the work. Much of the effort critics have expended in attempts to assess Theseus' true character seems to have resulted in conclusions of the "black-or-white" variety. Thus Professor Webb is unwilling to credit Theseus with belief in or adherence to any ideals, while those who agree with Professors Muscatine and Frost are apparently unwilling to concede that Theseus' character harbors any notable imperfections.

To consider Theseus ignoble and cruel despite the Book IV funeral oration, to cite but one difficulty, requires a kind of mental elasticity of which I am not capable. On the other hand, certainly his portrayal in Book I is far from reflecting some of the noble ideals that Chaucer implies are inseparable from the chivalric code. One explanation of the principal motivating force behind all of Theseus' major acts and decisions is consistent with every detail of the poem, and I think it is the key to his entire personality. He is first of all a ruler—a wise and responsible ruler whose implied guiding principle is to maintain his realms in peace. In addition to this he is a human being, perhaps made finer by the requirements of military command and political rule as well as by his adherence to some of the qualities of knighthood. But he is also subject to those weaknesses which in a sense define humanity.

I see no need to seek extenuation for Theseus' human frailties or to find them disturbingly inconsistent in an otherwise fine human being. Chaucer, in this respect very much the man of his time, rarely if ever portrayed in his poetry a believable human being who was also free of sin. No doubt he himself had reason to be aware of the human frailty to which royalty is also subject, but it seems to me that through Theseus we are afforded a glimpse of something akin to the concept of kingship evident in so many of Shakespeare's plays. So far as Book I of *The Knight's Tale* is concerned, Theseus, the successful conqueror and ruler, is also equipped with a strong sense of pride and consciousness of his own importance. We should also remember that in wreaking revenge upon Creon as a "trewe knyght" in the service of ladies in distress, Theseus acquires by conquest a presumably wealthy city (he "dide with al the contree as hym leste" after the battle). He thus added greatly to glory, power and, very likely, to treasure already enormous.

The ransom situation is quite different. I think this is not the result of cruelty or satiety in material matters any more than it is the sentence of a "worthy duc" according to chivalric ideals. Is it not instead a situation wherein adherence to the chivalric ideal is incompatible with the possible safety of the realm, or more bluntly, political common sense? Presumably these two young knights, because they are of "the blood roial," are potential dangers far beyond those of ordinary Theban knights. Thus when forced to choose between the chivalric ideal and the practical welfare of his state, Theseus chooses the latter. We may suspect if we please that his concern is more with personal than public welfare, but this amounts to the same thing—throughout the poem Theseus is the personification of the "I-am-the-state" kind of medieval ruler. If Theseus falls under attack, the state falls under attack, just as Thebes fell under attack when Theseus marched against its head. This interpretation of the ransom situation is reinforced by the terms of Arcite's release, by the terms of the tournament for Emelye's hand set up in Book II (which were briefly considered in this light in the last chapter), and by the political reasons for which Theseus (in Book IV) pushes through the marriage—to convert an enemy into a member of the family.

This analysis of Theseus accordingly shows him to be, with all his faults, a man rich in human understanding who is idealistic enough within the chivalric tradition when this does not interfere with what he apparently considers his higher duties as a ruler. He is also a man of decisive and energetic action possessing a most realistic outlook on life coupled with a fine sense of humor. It is true that he shares with others of his "estaat" the "chivalric" notion that tragedy is possible only when those of high rank are involved. But in other matters the warmth and genuine human understanding he alone in the poem seems capable of experiencing, fully demonstrated in Book IV, must be weighed against this.

It is very significant that Theseus' acts and speech, as they appear in Book I, are presented to us in two ways: first, as matters of fact, relatively unadorned—the first and second of the narrative devices of the Knight, without benefit of the Knight's interpretive powers; second, through the interpretive technical device of the Knight's narration, and of this there is only the occasional, adroit touch (the "noble" or "worthy" duke, the "trewe knyght"). But whenever the third device is used, it is invariably to attribute to Theseus praiseworthy motives from the chivalric point of view for acts or feelings which, in their bald and unvarnished matter-of-fact form, clearly cannot reasonably be interpreted in those terms at all. As usual, the effect of these first and second devices is that we furnish our own evaluative interpretation of the material involved.

As a result we find that in major ways Theseus is "unchivalric" by the Knight's own standards, except when it is convenient or when elements of the chivalric code itself have become so far removed from genuine idealism as to be a parody of the humanitarian spirit they purport to exalt. When, however, after each such instance the Knight evaluates by his third device the matter involved as exemplary, unwarranted idealism, we have a series of contradictions that can be resolved only in terms of artistic ambivalence. Moreover we find that these three literary devices are an integral part of Chaucer's narrative style throughout the poem, resulting in similar contradictions for every major character or situation. Because Theseus is central to the poem, the significance of his treatment in Book I lies chiefly in the fact that it is typical of his treatment throughout the remaining three books.

From the swiftly moving aftermath of the battle for Thebes and the ransom context, a single important transitional line thrusts us directly into the main plot: "This passeth yeer by yeer and day by day" (1033). The Knight then waxes eloquent in his description of Emelye; she is fairer than the lily on its stem, fresher than May with its newly blossomed flowers—he is unable to say whether her complexion or a lovely rose is the fairer. He imputes to her a direct message from the season as her motive to rise and pay her respects to May, for "The sesoun priketh every gentil herte." The passage concludes with the similarly idealized account of her walk in the garden, earlier discussed as illustrating the interpretive stylistic device of the Knight's narration.

There is little to comment upon here which has not been amply evaluated by others; Coulton's remark, cited in Chapter I, seems especially appropriate: "her [Emelye's] limits are those of a figure in a stained glass window, compared with a portrait of Titian's." Emelye never descends from her level of abstract idealism, where she is placed by the Knight and maintained by Palamon and Arcite, to that of credible human intercourse. She is never developed any further as a character; the only time she speaks, much later in the poem, she merely documents her incapacity for human emotion. It is noteworthy that here, as in all other situations where she is in any way involved, the Knight's interpretive technique is the means of establishing the ostensible idealistic motivation for her every thought and act.

Palamon's and Arcite's active participation in the poem begins at this point in Book I. It is only after the garden scene that they are identified as personalities. The ransomless imprisonment is the central concept that knits together the preceding parts of the poem and the main plot, partly giving rise to and repeatedly emphasizing the underlying humorous and satiric aspects of the fundamental situation firmly established before Arcite's release. Inevitably it is therefore one of the most important elements in *The Knight's Tale*, and its effects are more comprehensive by far than merely the underlining of their misery, however neatly the "complaint" factor may seem to fit into metrical romance convention and thus tempt us to dismiss it as no more than that.

From the time Emelye appears in the garden up to the release of Arcite (1034-1218) several significant instances of humor and satire are identifiable. After Palamon has explained to Arcite the cause of his cry and his deathly paleness, which Arcite originally attributed to a fresh consciousness of their ransomless, hopeless state of captivity, we are informed by Palamon in detail of the nature of this instantaneous but permanent love wound. No doubt a part of his explanation, which echoes the "figure in a stained glass window" image of Emelye, must have warmed the cockles of the Knight's idealistic heart as he narrated it: " 'I noot wher she be womman or goddesse,/ But Venus is it soothly, as I gesse' " (1101-2). On his knees Palamon beseeches "Venus," if destiny makes it impossible for her to help him escape from prison, to " 'Of oure lynage have som compassioun,/ That is so lowe ybroght by tirannye' " (1110-11). These two lines are the clearest of contradictions to the Knight's characterization of Theseus' actions and motivation concerning the incarceration until death of Palamon and Arcite and the entire matter of the conquest of Thebes.

It is now plain that neither victor nor vanquished finds Theseus' acts toward Theban royalty and hence the city itself falling within the framework of the chivalric code. Theseus quite apparently considered that their political danger outweighed idealistic considerations, and Palamon, who seems imbued with much the same variety of naïve idealism as the Knight, apparently sees the whole matter as a shocking violation of knightly obligation on Theseus' part. The notion that Palamon's "tirannye" charge is merely dramatic—the natural view of any prisoner—is undefendable; Theseus' sentence could not reasonably be otherwise characterized by *chivalric* standards.

We have here, then, striking incongruity and extremely effective —although very subtle—inappropriateness, in that Theseus is in effect accused of acts inimical to the character the Knight has ostensibly established for him and has continually emphasized. By the very absence of enlargement or explanation on the parts of Palamon or Arcite and of interpretive comment by the Knight, the lines are allowed to stand and are tacitly treated as though they were appropriate. Lines 1110-11 are closely related to the descriptions of the Monk and the Friar in the *General Prologue*, cited in Chapter II as examples of satire, in that ideals and acts morally inappropriate to Theseus in his ostensible chivalric role are attributed to him and treated as appropriate. Moreover, in their appearance as the supposed climax of Palamon's appeal to "Venus," these lines are emphasized in their structural and meaning contexts.

In a far more subtle sense Palamon, as the maker of the observation, plainly misjudges Theseus; in his naïveté the larger political issues which are quite clear in Theseus' mind, resulting in the imprisonment without ransom, never occur to Palamon. Even though he assumes that Arcite, after his release, is gathering kindred for a military attack on Theseus, Theseus' sentence remains for him simply "tirannye." Thus Palamon, as the simple-minded commentator here, reflects the third characteristic of Chaucerian satire considered in Chapter II. Just as the satire backfires on Chaucer in his pose as the naïve observer in the Monk's description in the *General Prologue*, the satire here backfires on Palamon.

The incongruity in these two lines is heightened when we realize that there are now three points of view, each unchallenged and therefore presumably equally correct, on the ransomless imprisonment concept: Theseus' implied view that the safety of the state outweighs chivalric custom; the Knight's "act of chivalry" view; and Palamon's "tirannye" view. Part of the incongruity arises from the presence of these two lines in an otherwise logical context and the structural emphasis placed on them. If the Knight's characterization of Theseus' act were correct, we would expect Palamon, a royal knight, to see it in the same light however great the personal sacrifice involved. We are here confronted, after all, with no ordinary run of persons. But instead, in an appeal to "Venus" otherwise consistent with the ostensible spirit of the poem, we find a characterization of Theseus' act in diametric opposition to that previously established. Hence it is illogical both in its immediate context and that of the poem as a whole. Its structural emphasis, resulting from its placement at the end of the appeal, unites with the emphasis derived through the meaning context— it is the climax of the appeal—to heighten the effect of the incongruity.

The rest of the incongruity is more subtle in its effects; we have here what *seems* to be the realistic or common-sense view of a situation, and the terms of its presentation are incongruous. But we do not have the shocked amazement on the part of the Knight or Arcite, or their contempt and "correction" of this view, which we would expect from our knowledge of their known or implied idealistic outlooks. The passage is humorous, then, sharing part or all the properties of the selections analyzed in Chapter II from *The Nun's Priest's Tale, The Knight's Tale* (on the disposition of Arcite's soul), *The Parliament of Fowls,* and the Miller's Prologue (classifications 1, 2, 4, and 5). The humor here is heightened by the presentation of the third of the mutually incompatible views of Theseus' treatment of Theban royalty and hence Thebes itself —the "tyrannye" view. Thus, although the humor and satire in these lines are very closely related, the humor arises from the incongruity of Palamon's characterization of Theseus' sentence itself, while the satire arises from the inappropriateness of attributing to Theseus motives inimical to the Knight's interpretation of his character.

The argument which ensues between the two cousins after Arcite, too, is stricken by the sight of Emelye ("I nam but deed") is among the most delightful sources of humor and satire in *The Knight's Tale*. To savor it fully we must take heed of the constant reminders Chaucer inserts during its progress that in their permanent state of imprisonment, neither Palamon nor Arcite can ever hope so much as to speak to Emelye. This pre-eminent fact at times tends to be subtly camouflaged in the mass of emotional detail, and it seems to me that most if not all critics have failed to perceive its full significance.

Palamon first accuses Arcite of being false and traitorous to his most solemn oath of brotherhood, in which both young men swore, he says,

> That nevere, for to dyen in the peyne,
> Til that the deeth departe shal us tweyne,
> Neither of us in love to hyndre oother,
> Ne in noon oother cas, my leeve brother;

> But that thou sholdest trewely forthren me
> In every cas, as I shal forthren thee,—
> This was thyn ooth, and myn also, certyn;
> I woot right wel, thou darst it nat withseyn.
> Thus artow of my conseil, out of doute,   (1133-41)

Having set up his argument in typical medieval logical form, Palamon sweeps triumphantly to its end by citing Arcite's love for Emelye as decisive evidence of treason to knightly vows in that he is thereby failing to help him.

The argument is riddled with fallacies of contradiction and contains one downright lie, although Palamon is obviously not conscious of it. Since it is presented as a logical argument and as matter of fact, we are certainly justified in examining it in those terms. Accordingly, their oath of brotherhood is a mutual relation—a reciprocal one. Yet Palamon unconsciously assumes that the argument does not apply to himself but only to his "felawe," an assumption which in *its* turn contradicts the oath. Later, of course, Arcite uses exactly the same fallacious argument against Palamon. Hence each interprets this symmetrical relation as asymmetrical with respect to himself. Arcite and Palamon are interpreting a relation symbolically expressed

$$(F_{AP} \equiv F_{PA}) \text{ as if it were}$$
$$(F_{AP} \supset -F_{PA}) \text{ and } (F_{PA} \supset -F_{AP}),$$

respectively, where F represents the relationship of mutual aid. That is, the relation of mutual aid is assumed to be nonmutual, or one-sided, and this contradicts the original oath.[7]

A significant fallacy, too, arises from Palamon's insistence that Arcite has betrayed his vows on the grounds of this fallacious chain of reasoning. Thus Arcite is sworn not to hinder Palamon in love and to help him in all things; because he loves Emelye he has broken his oath. The underlying error, of course, lies in Palamon's equating Arcite's love for Emelye with hindering him in love as well as failing to help him in all things. Obviously, even the most primitive logical argument must be couched in terms which contain exactly the same words or words which have exactly the same linguistically determinable meaning. Palamon's conclusions, therefore, at the very least are not demonstrable within the framework of the argument he presents.

Palamon's patently untrue statement is obviously in lines 1137-38 ("thou sholdest trewely forthren me/ In every cas, as I shal forthren thee"). The "should" and "shall" constructions are important here because the "shal" of line 1138 results in the emergence of a stronger, more positive commitment when we compare it to the subtly milder overtones of the previous line's "sholdest." The fact is, of course, that Palamon will no more help Arcite in the present "cas" than he believes Arcite will help him. Hence in the process of his vain, invalid argument meant to establish Arcite's perfidy, Palamon convicts himself conclusively of the same kind of perfidy —suspecting the presence of a grain of sand in his "felawe's" eye, he fails to see the boulder in his own.

The first part of Arcite's hot rejoinder to this serious accusation maintains a semblance of the logical form set up in Palamon's argument (1153-61). Countering with his own accusation of Palamon's falsity to *his* knightly oath, Arcite contends that the proof of this lies in Palamon's loving Emelye as a goddess. In Palamon's assumption that Emelye is the Venus deity we have an element of the courtly love code most conspicuously emphasized. Yet Arcite immediately scorns such an idea and neither Palamon nor the Knight supplies an objection. Indeed, the notion of any virtually divine attributes of Emelye never arises again in the poem. It may be said, then, that even at this point in Book I, an important characteristic of the courtly love complex is decisively squashed.

For Arcite, Palamon's love is "affeccioun of hoolynesse," while his own love is "as to a creature." To make his reasoning valid a first premise to the effect of "All whose love is 'affeccioun of hoolynesse' are false to their oaths of knightly brotherhood" would be necessary. Clearly such concepts are too extreme to be considered seriously as an effective or rational argument.

At this point Arcite introduces an entirely new spirit into the argument. Veering away from the ideal, he states in effect that all is fair in love and that love is such a powerful phenomenon that it sweeps away all man-made laws (including knightly oaths); man cannot control love (1161-71). Following this implication that their contest of accusations is pointless, in a long burst of realism he makes plain once more their true situation:

> And eek it is nat likly al thy lyf
> To stonden in hir grace; namoore shal I;
> For wel thou woost thyselven, verraily,

That thou and I be dampned to prisoun
Perpetuelly; us gayneth no raunsoun.   (1172-76)

Arcite continues in this vein with the earlier cited analogy of his and Palamon's situation and two dogs quarreling over a bone which is as a result stolen by a bird. Finally, he concludes his outburst with such decisively incongruous reasoning that the whole argument between the two emerges as ridiculous:

And therfore, at the kynges court, my brother,
Ech man for hymself, ther is noon oother.
Love, if thee list, for I love and ay shal;
And soothly, leeve brother, this is al.
Heere in this prisoun moote we endure,
And everich of us take his aventure."   (1181-86)

The beginnings of an acrimonious exchange between Palamon and Arcite set the pattern for the humor which recurs throughout its course. We may well question the substance of the oath itself, but documentary evidence of chivalric vows is extremely sparse and the absence of it in such matters as individual brotherhood oaths forces us to assess this particular one solely in its context. I think we must grant that however suspicious we may find its precise pertinence to the situation here—the condition not to hinder each other in love constituting its single specific article—it must be taken as read. It does have the effect of elevating even the jealousy of these rival lovers almost up to the highly idealistic plane on which their love ostensibly rests.

The fallacies in Palamon's reasoning result in humor derived, in this respect, in the same manner as that in selections from *The Nun's Priest's Tale*, *The Knight's Tale* (on the location of Arcite's soul), and the Miller's Prologue, analyzed in the preceding chapter (classifications 1, 2, 3, 5, and 7). Their context is made logical by the presentation of material in the form of an authentic argument in logic. Also, as a result of its framework of formal logic, the humor is emphasized structurally, sharing this property with the previously analyzed examples cited above. As in the selection from *The Parliament of Fowls* analyzed in Chapter II as an example of false analogy, Palamon's fallacies amount to an equivocation of concepts, and a part of their incongruity arises from this. Thus in his assumption that Arcite's love for Emelye is equivalent to hindering him in love and to failing to aid him in all things, as we have seen, Palamon is assigning a burden of meaning to these words different from that conveyed within the system of formal logic in which Chaucer has him express them.

Palamon's ironic statement wherein he accuses Arcite of failure to help him in accordance with his oath while he, Palamon, will always in *every* case help his brother is, in its falsity, inappropriate. It is plainly treated as appropriate, however, in that Chaucer allows it to stand unchallenged by Arcite and uninterpreted by the Knight. Its satire is therefore derived precisely like that of the descriptions of the Monk and the Friar and the Wife of Bath's "gentil" text, analyzed in Chapter II. Its incongruity arises from its being an integral part of the whole formal argument of Palamon; it is as fallacious as the other components of the argument.

Arcite's counteraccusation derives its humor from the same kind of incongruity as Palamon's fallacious argument since it in fact amounts to a continuation of it. In reminding Palamon of the permanent lack of opportunity for either of them to woo Emelye, Arcite lays the groundwork for his "dog-and-bone" analogy. But there is even a broad hint of the incongruous in his statement that in view of their permanent state of imprisonment it is "nat likly" either one of them will ever stand in Emelye's grace. More significantly, he has idealistically swept aside the whole question of brother-betrayal by his grand statement that love's laws are greater "Than may be yeve to any erthely man" (1166).

Chaucer thus sets up here at least a partial hierarchy of ideals, in which the chivalric one significantly emerges as man-made and thus inferior. The incongruity of Arcite's argument accordingly embraces the entire series of concepts dealt with throughout this section of the poem. It is cumulative in its effects. First the supposedly exalted ideals of knightly brotherhood are totally nullified by the ethereally ordained laws of courtly love, which is completely consistent with the Knight's treatment of Emelye in the garden scene. This lofty explanation of the supreme power of love is expressed in terms of the first and second stylistic devices of the Knight's narration. While in itself the contrast between subject matter and style here is not glaringly incongruous, it tends to emphasize the matter-of-fact attitude of Arcite as opposed to Palamon's insistent impractical idealism.

Chaucer has brought us, however circuitously, to a very neat idealistic impasse at this point. Clearly Arcite's explanation of love demolishes Palamon's argument, which was in any case logically fallacious. But Arcite's argument also destroys itself. Obviously only those possessing the chivalric ideals of a knight are capable of experiencing the kind of love by which Arcite and Palamon are supposed to have been smitten. Yet this emotional state automatically voids the most serious of knightly oaths! In their particular situation, the clash of ideals becomes ridiculously insoluble; one cannot be a "trewe knyght" if he is properly in love, yet he cannot be properly in love if he is not a "trewe knyght." If, therefore, we were to take both their arguments literally, their situation could not possibly exist.

There is a significant if slight degree of resemblance between this idealistic impasse and one which appears in the *General Prologue*. In the description of the Monk and Friar, Chaucer praises them extravagantly for qualities extremely inappropriate to their ecclesiastical callings. But he praises the Parson even more enthusiastically for qualities which are opposite in character and completely appropriate to his position in life. We can easily resolve the obvious inconsistency by assessing all three descriptions in terms of the presence or absence of the humorous and satiric properties discussed in Chapter II. Clearly the Parson's description is to be taken seriously, while those of the Monk and Friar are superbly humorous and satiric. Just as we must decide what is appropriate and inappropriate in the lives of the Monk, Friar, and Parson, so must we decide at this particular point in *The Knight's Tale* whether Arcite's and Palamon's arguments and actions are appropriate to the phenomenon of courtly love.

Such a decision must take into consideration the knightly qualities which, first of all, are a *sine qua non* in order for man to experience this idealistic emotion. Perhaps to make sure that we do just this, Chaucer furnishes us with Palamon's argument. Its content as well as its fallaciousness makes it clear that both young men are living, categorical contradictions of the chivalric qualities they have sworn to exemplify in situations involving courtly love affairs. We are now informed through Arcite's argument that courtly love in effect destroys the foundations upon which its very existence depends. Here, too, Chaucer apparently leaves to us the resolving of a glaring inconsistency, but since both Palamon's and Arcite's arguments are remorselessly self-destructive, we cannot base any conclusions on either one of them. With this the resemblance to the somewhat analogous material in the *General Prologue* ceases—we have no comparable situation to assess in *The Knight's Tale*. We are in fact left to judge for ourselves the whole issue of courtly love as it appears in the poem.

Even though Arcite's grandiloquent characterization of courtly love echoes the idealism of the Knight's description of Emelye, the Knight's device of matter-of-fact reporting makes it clear that he is ostensibly merely quoting Arcite, as he earlier quoted Palamon. But Palamon does not contradict Arcite and, significantly, the Knight's interpretive technique is not employed anywhere in this section of Book I as it is in the description of Emelye. We are justified, then, in evaluating all of Arcite's and Palamon's arguments in this section in terms of the matters of fact they are asserted to be.

Since the two young men's arguments are untenable, it is clear that their own interpretation of what they are experiencing is grossly erroneous. If they are experiencing courtly love, any notion of this ideology as a chivalric, idealistic, and hence highly civilized emotion is obviously fatuous so far as its reflection in their present arguments and actions is concerned. Yet it is perfectly plain that the royal cousins are irrevocably convinced that they have been struck by the idealistic lightning of courtly love. We must accordingly conclude that their error lies in their misunderstanding of what love is. Moreover, virtually every character in the poem, and above all its narrator, shares their conviction that they are indeed smitten with this chivalric love-malady. Also, with the delightful exception of Theseus, Palamon's and Arcite's illusions as to the nature of this bitter-sweet condition are in turn shared by the other characters and, of course, by the Knight.

For the present, it is sufficient simply to note the existence of this idealistic impasse; I shall deal fully with it as its implications and consequences unfold in Book II, together with the whole issue of courtly love in *The Knight's Tale*. Some of its significance in Book I lies in its emergence from the totally fallacious but utterly earnest views of the two young prisoners, as factually reported by the Knight. Its most important effect, however, is that even this early in the poem it makes clear that the motivation for all events to come is an emotion erroneously interpreted by all but one of the leading participants in the poem, not excepting its narrator. This is high and sustained incongruity; lest we lose sight of

it in the actions and pageantry which follow, we have Theseus'
emphatic reminder of it in the passage from Book II already
analyzed (1785 ff.).

The two concluding sections of Arcite's argument emphasize the
humorous and satiric aspects of this idealistic impasse and bring
the entire situation to the edge of ridicule. Arcite, having been as
idealistically wounded as Palamon by the sight of the beauteous
Emelye, now refers to her in quite different terms. His likening
her to a mere bone over which he and his royal cousin quarrel
"as dide the houndes" is indeed the "realistic" or commonsense view
of their situation. It derives much of its humor from its inappropriate language, as compared to the loftiness of the preceding language
in Palamon's and Arcite's arguments and in the garden tableau. In
this respect it is closely allied to the humor in Theseus' long
address in Book II and that of the "gentil" tercelet in *The Parliament of Fowls,* analyzed in Chapter II (classification 4). Here,
again, in the Knight's direct quotation of Arcite's speech, Chaucer
employs the second stylistic device of the Knight's narration. Its
inconsistency remains unexplained and unchallenged either by the
Knight or by Palamon and we are accordingly left to interpret it
for ourselves.

If we take the preceding elements of the young knights' argument seriously, this analogy is clearly highly inappropriate. Since
it remains unchallenged and is not interpreted, it is obviously
treated as though it were appropriate. It is an abrupt stylistic
departure from the intensely serious and highly dignified material
it immediately follows, and it forms the climax of Arcite's reasoning. Hence it is heavily emphasized both structurally and in its
meaning context. It therefore shares the same satiric properties
as the descriptions of the Monk and Friar in the *General Prolgue,*
the Wife of Bath's reaction to "that gentil text," and the extended
passage from *The Merchant's Tale,* analyzed in Chapter II.

No doubt this analogy of Arcite's accounts in part for the
opinion of some critics that he is "realistic" in comparison with
Palamon. At the very least it seems to me his argument here
accurately describes the situation. Yet since it forms the basis for
the crowning absurdity of the entire exchange between the two
young men, Arcite is shown to be (in this section of the poem, at
any rate) perhaps even more unrealistic than Palamon. This short
passage is therefore extremely significant. Whether or not Chaucer

meant it as a wry aside on contemporary life at court, it is a totally unreasonable basis for Arcite's conclusion to his argument, although he specifically grounds his final statements upon it ("And therfore . . . Ech man for hymself, ther is noon oother"). The Knight then makes clear (employing the first stylistic device of his narration) that Palamon and Arcite fall to with a will: "Greet was the strif and long bitwix hem tweye" (1187).

Arcite's realistic appraisal of their situation, then, does not deter for a moment even him from contradicting its unmistakable implications. He is in effect irrefutably demonstrating the uselessness of their quarrelling over a girl neither can possess, then concluding that their proper course of action is to continue the quarrel. Here, too, the ironic inappropriateness and absurd incongruity are unchallenged by Palamon and uninterpreted by the Knight; again we must furnish our own interpretation.

With this passage, the preparation for the remainder of the poem is completed, so far as emotional motivation is concerned. Arcite's release through Perotheus' intervention in no way alters the fundamental states of mind of Palamon and Arcite, although their love for Emelye and jealousy of each other supposedly become much stronger as each envies the other his lot. What remains of Book I is a kind of intensified reiteration of the same symptoms of their love-malady analyzed above. Arcite, like a pendulum, swings from one extreme to another, and again—at least by implication—seems to contradict himself. The Knight reports both his "idealistic" and "realistic" feelings, thoughts, and words, in an amalgam of all three stylistic narrative devices. First, the idealistic:

> How greet a sorwe suffreth now Arcite!
> The deeth he feeleth thurgh his herte smyte;
> He wepeth, wayleth, crieth pitously;
> To sleen hymself he waiteth prively.
> He seyde, "Allas that day that I was born!
> Now is my prisoun worse than biforn;
> Now is me shape eternally to dwelle.
> Noght in purgatorie, but in helle.   (1219-26)

Arcite continues in this vein (and we should bear in mind that he has had but a glimpse or two by way of acquaintance with Emelye), longing for those days of bliss when he was in prison and possibly would have again caught sight of "hire whom that I serve." For this reason he considers Palamon much better off than he:

> O deere cosyn Palamon," quod he,
> "Thyn is the victorie of this aventure.
> Ful blisfully in prison maistow dure,—
> In prison? certes nay, but in paradys!   (1234-37)

Further, as he considers Palamon's happy duress from his own position of miserable freedom, Arcite no longer sees the imprisonment as an insurmountable obstacle in the winning of Emelye's grace by Palamon. This is essentially a contradiction of his earlier view. He says of Palamon,

> For possible is, syn thou hast hire presence,
> And art a knyght, a worthy and an able,
> That by som cas, syn Fortune is chaungeable,
> Thow maist to thy desir somtyme atteyne.   (1240-43)

But as for himself, "Wel oughte I sterve in wanhope and distresse./ Farwel my lif, my lust, and my gladnesse!" (1249-50).

Finally, Arcite soliloquizes at length on divine Providence, Fortune, and man. As in the passages of his argument with Palamon analyzed in detail earlier, there is a juxtaposition in style (from formal to informal and back again) as jarringly obvious as any in the poem:

> Allas, why pleynen folk so in commune
> On purveiaunce of God, or of Fortune,
> That yeveth hem ful ofte in many a gyse
> Wel bettre than they kan hemself devyse?
> Som man desireth for to han richesse,
> That cause is of his mordre or greet siknesse;
> And som man wolde out of his prisoun fayn,
> That in his hous is of his meynee slayn.
> Infinite harmes been in this mateere.
> We witen nat what thing we preyen heere:
> We faren as he that dronke is as a mous.
> A dronke man woot wel he hath an hous,
> But he noot which the righte wey is thider,
> And to a dronke man the wey is slider.
> And certes, in this world so faren we;
> We seken faste after felicitee,
> But we goon wrong ful often, trewely.

> Thus may we seyen alle, and namely I,
> That wende and hadde a greet opinioun
> That if I myghte escapen from prisoun,
> Thanne hadde I been in joye and perfit heele,
> Ther now I am exiled fro my wele.
> Syn that I may nat seen you, Emelye,
> I nam but deed; ther nys no remedye."   (1251-74)

There is little new material in this final speech except for the extensive, detailed treatment of Arcite's love-misery. Also, in some unexplained fashion, he has discovered Emelye's name. But all the important elements of the entire soliloquy are firmly rooted in Arcite's side of his and Palamon's argument considered earlier. His present woeful freedom is thereby directly linked to his earlier lot of ransomless imprisonment, and the paradox is emphasized as he fatuously envies Palamon's "blissful" lot. The stylistic juxtaposition here is also in the same spirit as that of the "dog-and-bone" analogy. Accordingly, these important elements derive their humorous and satiric qualities in large part from their relation to this earlier material.

Palamon's condition at the end of Book I is reported by the Knight:

> Upon that oother syde Palamon,
> Whan that he wiste Arcite was agon,
> Swich sorwe he maketh that the grete tour
> Resouneth of his youlyng and clamour.
> The pure fettres on his shynes grete
> Weren of his bittre, salte teeres wete.   (1275-80)

Chaucer's employment here of the Knight's first and second stylistic narrative devices in this particular manner reminds us of an earlier manifestation of much the same kind of phenomenon. Thus just as Theseus becomes peculiarly "war, as he caste his eye aside" of the loudly complaining women (896), so Palamon's becoming aware of Arcite's absence is similarly—and more than suspiciously—peculiar: "Whan that he wiste Arcite was agon" (1276). The key word, of course, is "wiste" which in this context is relatively unambiguous. As matter-of-fact reportage, then, we have no choice but to assess this line in the sense of "When Palamon *discovered* (or *found out* or *knew*) Arcite was gone."

In isolation, this does not seem especially incongruous or in-

appropriate; in its total context, however, it is emphatically so.
The royal pair, after all, share their "grete tour . . . Which of the
castel was the chief dongeoun" (1056-57), and nowhere in the
poem is there any indication whatever that they were at any time
separated—hence, presumably, the perpetual opportunity for their
constant "strif." There can be no question that Palamon was aware
of every detail of Arcite's release. This is plainly brought out by
the lines which immediately follow the Knight's reportage cited
above and which mark the beginning of Palamon's soliloquy:

> "Allas," quod he, "Arcita, cosyn myn,
> Of al oure strif, God woot, the fruyt is thyn.
> Thow walkest now in Thebes at thy large,
> And of my wo thow yevest litel charge.
> Thou mayst, syn thou hast wisdom and manhede,
> Assemblen alle the folk of oure kynrede,
> And make a werre so sharp on this citee,
> That by som aventure or some tretee
> Thow mayst have hire to lady and to wyf
> For whom that I moste nedes lese my lyf.
> For, as by wey of possibilitee,
> Sith thou art at thy large, of prisoun free,
> And art a lord, greet is thyn avauntage
> Moore than is myn, that sterve here in a cage.
> For I moot wepe and wayle, whil I lyve,
> With al the wo that prison may me yive,
> And eek with peyne that love me yeveth also,
> That doubleth al my torment and my wo."
> Therwith the fyr of jalousie up sterte
> Withinne his brest, and hente him by the herte
> So woodly that he lyk was to biholde
> The boxtree or the asshen dede and colde.   (1281-1302)

It is clear, then, that Palamon is fully cognizant of the essential
circumstances pertaining to Arcite's freedom. Line 1276, therefore,
is incongruous; with line 896 considered earlier in this chapter, it
shares the same properties of humor as the examples from *The
Nun's Priest's Tale, The Knight's Tale* (2809-14), and the Miller's
Prologue, analyzed in Chapter II (classifications 1 and 2).

   This portion of Palamon's soliloquy, like Arcite's, is firmly linked
in all its most important aspects with his side of the argument
which was earlier considered in detail. Accordingly, the emphasis

upon Arcite's political and military opportunities to win Emelye is a perfectly reasonable consequence of Palamon's view of Theseus' "tirannye" and the interpretation of the ransomless imprisonment as political expedience rather than the chivalric practice the Knight obviously believes it to be. Further, there is a subtly implied but very significant intertwining of concepts here which effectively re-emphasizes the idealistic impasse so clearly established in the course of Palamon and Arcite's argument. Since courtly love "is a gretter lawe . . . Than may be yeve to any erthely man," Palamon certainly takes for granted that the grisly conditions of Arcite's release are no deterrent to his cousin's return to Athens as a warrior knight. Should Arcite's forces lose such a war, unless he was fortunate enough to be killed outright in battle, Arcite would be beheaded like a common criminal. Presumably this would be an especially hideous fate for a knight of royal lineage to contemplate.

For Palamon, however, Theseus' decree is a mere man-made obstruction unworthy of serious consideration. The reasoning here is obviously that portion of Arcite's argument quoted above, which also is the foundation upon which the entire idealistic impasse is immovably based. Here, too, the pattern of paradox begun in Arcite's soliloquy is continued. In their quarreling, it was Palamon who immediately took the stand, with conspicuous lack of regard for their ransomless imprisonment, that Emelye was his "lady, whom I love and serve,/ And evere shal til that myn herte sterve." This assumption of possession on the ideal level of someone who cannot be in any way approached on the level of reality seems perfectly natural to Palamon and—since he in no way takes exception to or enlarges upon it—is obviously a part of the Knight's view of the courtly love complex. Arcite attempted to demolish Palamon's stand in part by pointing out the implications of their imprisonment in any attempt to win Emelye. Now, however, Arcite goes even farther than Palamon. If to Palamon, originally, imprisonment had no effect on his love, it seems to Arcite now that imprisonment is an actual advantage to Palamon! Hence, Arcite not only accepts Palamon's earlier premise, but carries it far beyond that young man's unrealistic limits.

Similarly, the two cousins' current views of each other's characters are in sharp contrast to the enthusiastic accusations of moral perfidy they earlier flung at one another. For Arcite, Palamon is now "a knyght, a worthy and an able," while Arcite, in Palamon's present opinion, is now gifted with wisdom and manhood and all the advantages of a great lord. Arcite's freedom, as Palamon contrasts their present situations, at last brings home to this imprisoned idealist the implications of his "fettres" concerning his love for Emelye. Palamon's adoption of Arcite's original view of the prison-love problem is, however, far more subtly effected by Chaucer than Arcite's present fatuity in this matter, as we see from Palamon's assessment of his royal cousin's chances with Emelye as a free and wise man. Thus at first glance Palamon's imprisoned state and his love-sickness appear to be separate causes of his misery (when he first sees Emelye and falls to in the quarrel with Arcite, as well as in lines 1295-98 of his soliloquy). But it is Arcite's freedom (and his qualities as a man which he fears Arcite will employ in his freedom to win Emelye) which really disturb Palamon, who must "sterve here in a cage." It is this which gives rise to the "fyr of jalousie" and its resultant—and (to the Knight) alarming—effects. Clearly, the jealousy is rooted in the love complex.

Palamon's aspect as reported by the Knight in lines 1300-1302 is linked with that which he displayed when he first saw Emelye, when Arcite found him "so pale and deedly on to see." It is as if by this time the Knight had warmed to his theme of love-suffering, for Palamon was originally merely pierced to the heart and moved to shriek while turning deathly pale at the sight of Emelye. Now, however, the "fyr" of jealousy literally grips him by the heart with such maniacal fury that he waxes as red as the box-berry and wanes as gray as dead ashes, by turns.

Palamon, too, pours forth his thoughts on metaphysical matters as he concludes his soliloquy. He touches again upon the ransomless imprisonment (1328-29) and re-emphasizes the unjustness of Thebes' (and, by direct implication, his own) fate (1330-31). Finally, there is an echo of his original view of Emelye when he supposedly mistook her for Venus: "And Venus sleeth me on that oother syde" (1332).

There is, accordingly, a superbly crafted continuity in these two soliloquies, reflected in the variety and degrees of subtlety of their linkage in many significant respects to the poetic material which has preceded them in Book I. Much of their importance as humor and satire, then, is not intrinsic but dependent upon their

relations with this earlier material. Ostensibly they are enlarge-
ments and explanations of matters of central importance to the
entire poem, first identifiable in Palamon and Arcite's argument.
But if we seek a solution to the idealistic impasse or a reasonable
explanation of the two cousins' original reactions to the realistic
aspects of their situations, we seek in vain. And yet, as is perfectly
clear from the analysis above, both of the lovers—even, at last,
Palamon—are thoroughly aware of these realistic aspects and on
occasion approach them in what amounts to a very practical manner. For Arcite, in a burst of homely practicality, clearly likens
their situation to a pair of dogs quarreling over a bone which
neither will, in all probability, ever be able to possess. Far from
acting in terms of this realistic appraisal, he reasons that the quarrel must accordingly continue—obviously with the spirited cooperation of his "felawe."

In his soliloquy, the idealistic Palamon presents what appears
to be a perfectly sound solution to Arcite's situation—gather the
kindred and make war upon Theseus, demanding Emelye as part
of the spoils. But the heroic Arcite is, at least by implication, too
careful of his head to entertain such an idea; in any case it never
occurs to him. Instead, before slinking into Athens disguised as a
"povre laborer," he noisily endures in Thebes "a yeer or two/ This
crueel torment and this peyne and wo" (1381-82). It is obvious,
then, that even the two most idealistic characters in the poem, to
say nothing of Theseus, are shown by Chaucer to be capable of
viewing important aspects of their total situation realistically. This
is of course too slim a foundation upon which to base a claim for
a "realistic" method in the poem, but it certainly precludes the
possibility of even a principally "idealistic" method. Clearly, both
qualities are evident in the most fundamental elements of the
poem.

The paradoxical elements of the two young men's soliloquies,
therefore, remind us anew of their original argument and, inevitably, its fallacious bases. As each now envies the other's lot
and has actually adopted significant portions of his cousin's former
views, the earlier argument becomes even more ridiculous. Accordingly, this last part of Book I presents us with the most
emphatic incongruity we have so far considered, since it removes
the principal cause of the dungeon quarrel. For until Arcite's "dog-
and-bone" analogy and the self-destroying conclusion he drew from

his reasoning, he and Palamon were concerned with the knightly "rights" of each other to love Emelye. Now each concedes the worthiness of the other, in effect, in terms of deserving Emelye's grace. Furthermore, Arcite's present characterization of Palamon's imprisoned state as one of blissful paradise nullifies in its absurdity the one reasonable segment of his original argument: that a man condemned to prison for life stands very little chance to meet and woo anyone. That this fact has now come home to the idealistic Palamon has no effect on *his* earlier argument at all. Book I ends with the solidifying of the essential absurdities of the two young men's argument, leaving the self-contradictory emotional impasse as the unreasonable justification for all the events to come. It is futile to resort to love as a catchall explanation for this state of affairs, since the impasse is genetically presented either as con- clusions arrived at by logical reasoning or as matters of fact which are unelaborated or otherwise explained.

There are, I think, significant relationships between Chaucer's selections from his principal source for *The Knight's Tale* and the humorous and satiric material in Book I so far considered. Many critics have examined in detail the similarities between Boccaccio's *Teseida* and *The Knight's Tale*; a few have discussed and assessed the differences as well. None has considered Chaucer's changes from this principal source, however, in terms of the artistic am- bivalence with which I am concerned in this study. Professor Robinson has carefully summarized and thoroughly catalogued the important contributions made in this area in his second edi- tion.[8] For my present purposes three investigations of Chaucer's uses of the *Teseida* are germane.

Professor R. A. Pratt has most ably collated and extended others' work and presented his results with precision.[9] Perhaps the most significant matter, which in my opinion has not been sufficiently taken into account by any investigator, is Chaucer's omission of all but three *events* of Book I of the *Teseida*. Much has been written of Chaucer's "abridgment" techniques, but it seems to have occurred to no one that an artist whose skill in poetic economy (when he saw fit to exercise it) enabled him to casually sum- marize several hundred lines of an epic in ten lines of his own may have had a discoverable reason besides mere economy. None of the *Teseida*'s other twelve books, except Book VIII, is so ig- nored by Chaucer in *The Knight's Tale* as Book I, and Book

VIII is in any case merely an extension of detail Chaucer amply attends to elsewhere.

Book I of the *Teseida* in fact involves a number of events, the only possible interpretations of which result in serious contradictions of much of what is conveyed to us by Chaucer through the Knight.* The epic paraphernalia in the *Teseida* is perfectly in keeping with the substance of its first book, but Ippolita and Teseo emerge from it as characters entirely different from those we meet in Chaucer's poem. Stripped of its epic framework which, however, is entirely appropriate in the early portions of the poem, Boccaccio's Book I could never be reconciled in terms of characters and events with the Knight's approach to his tale. Boccaccio presents us with matters of dramatic grandeur which he very likely believed would form the proper background of heroic antiquity for an epic in the grand style. Thus we find him recapitulating the classic legend of Ippolita and Teseo, pruned and tailored to suit his artistic purposes.

He begins with the rebellion of all the women of Scythia against male authority. The women in fact slay all the males in the city and elect the mightiest (and, perhaps, the least feminine) of their own sex, Ippolita, as their queen. From then on, any male who comes to Athens and desires to stay is summarily killed. Teseo, the great conqueror, decides to avenge these dreadful deeds perpetrated against his sex and gathers the mightiest armada imaginable to attack the city and annihilate all the women. The women fiercely oppose his landing in a horrible battle which the invading forces barely survive; in the end the women retreat into the city and Teseo besieges it.

Ippolita sends an arrogant message to Teseo, demanding that he state his intentions and threatening to slay all the invaders

---

*The most scholarly edition of the *Teseida* is the exhaustively collated and annotated one of S. Battaglia (*Giovanni Boccaccio: Teseida* [Firenze, 1938]), as Professor Pratt points out. For my purposes, however, the reissue of Ignazio Noutier's edition (*La Teseida di Giovanni Boccaccio* [Milano, 1837]) is more valuable; I am indebted to Professor Pratt's painstaking research for the discovery that this edition was taken from the manuscript section to which Chaucer's manuscript seems to have belonged ("The Knight's Tale," p. 83). All references to the *Teseida* text are based upon the latter edition. I have supplemented pertinent portions of Professor Pratt's English summaries with my own translations and, in Chapters VI and VII, those of Mrs. Paola Boezi Langford. Also, when referring to Boccaccio's characters, I shall use the Italian spellings of their names.

unless they leave. Teseo replies, in effect, that all the women may surrender or die (Canto 111). Mars seems to be favoring the invaders and Ippolita decides to surrender (Cantos 112-14; 117). Teseo enters the city in triumph with all his forces and marries Ippolita. Emilia appears for the first time in Canto 128, as Ippolita's "sorella piccolina"; struck by her beauty, Teseo decides to have her wed to one of his relatives, Acate (Canto 137), and Book I ends at this point. With it, Boccaccio has set the stage for the remainder of his poem, and—up to this point—his epic style is in keeping with the events and people he has presented. Later, when the real subject matter of the poem emerges as revolving around the civilized conventions of an early Renaissance palace love affair and its artificial "romance," one is reminded of an attempt to drive a tack with a sledge hammer. The epic style is simply unwarranted by the substance of the poem.

Chaucer, then, carefully confines himself to mentioning in the briefest possible way only three of the above matters: that Theseus was a great conqueror and the Duke of Athens; that he had conquered Scythia and married Ipolita; and that Emelye was Ipolita's sister. The crucial circumstances surrounding these events are scrupulously ignored. However, we have very good evidence that Chaucer had almost certainly thoroughly assimilated the first book of the *Teseida* and its relationship to the rest of the Boccaccio epic. It seems to me unmistakably clear that *Anelida and Arcite*, the first twenty-one lines of which are almost a direct translation of portions of Boccaccio's invocation in Cantos 1-3, is an artistic blood-relative of the *Teseida*, as far as it goes. Thus *Anelida and Arcite* begins as a full-blown epic and the first hundred lines or so are concerned with appropriately heroic matters, many of which are directly derived from Books I and II of the *Teseida* (lines 1-21, 36-40, 50-66). Then, as in the Boccaccio, the real plot emerges, and although the plots and characters of the two poems differ in detail, they are structurally, stylistically, and in their basic substance nearly identical.

Undoubtedly, whether the bare bones of the subject matter was original with Chaucer or obtained by him from earlier writers, his treatment and development of it are directly founded upon the *Teseida*. When *Anelida and Arcite* undergoes its transformation from an epic to a conventional—almost stereotyped—love complaint, it (like the *Teseida*) fails artistically to survive the inconsistency. Chaucer's attempt to return to his story and, presumably, his use of the epic description of Mars' temple from the *Teseida* (which he used in *The Knight's Tale*) apparently failed to satisfy him. I prefer to imagine that he perceived these flaws very clearly and decided to begin again one day on such a poem, profiting from the *Anelida and Arcite* experience. If this was indeed the case and *The Knight's Tale* the eventual result, we owe much more to *Anelida and Arcite* than is reflected in its poetic qualities. At any rate, we have it as direct evidence that Chaucer was fully aware of the relationship of Book I of the *Teseida* to the rest of the poem.

In the first few lines of *The Knight's Tale*, therefore, there is ample evidence that Chaucer is not only abridging his source but eliminating extremely important elements of it. We need not proceed very far in Book I of the poem to discover some of the reasons for this, and the farther we proceed in even this first book, the more significance this and other changes from its source assume. In the first place, in my opinion, Chaucer conceived Theseus as an able, realistic ruler and a successful human being with qualities communicable within the Knight's frame of reference and not necessarily excluding the artistic ambivalence with which I am chiefly concerned. Can we picture the Knight dealing with Ipolita as the powerful and able slayer of men, ruling a multitude of "unnatural" women who have slain all the males in sight? Possibly, but surely we could not expect him to reconcile in his own mind the wedding by Theseus—whom he persistently regards as the soul of chivalry—of such a creature, to say nothing of conveying it believably to the Canterbury pilgrims.

Directly linked with this complex is Emelye's relation to Ipolita. If she were a royal Amazon, would not Chaucer's problem of having the Knight convert her to a supposedly ideal recipient of courtly love worship be virtually insoluble? I think the epic stylistic approach which prevents artistic harmony within the *Teseida* nevertheless solves problems such as these in that poem. The epic's aura of superhumanity, grandeur of act and character, and consequent sweeping drama permit a certain god-derived mysticism of motivation or inconsistency of psychological reality. But the power of event and character must be maintained throughout such a work, which is not the case with the *Teseida*. The epic, then, can easily surmount some matters of cultural anachronism.

But it would be far too much to expect this particular kind of
thing to be believably resolved by Chaucer's literal-minded Knight,
whose approach to his subject matter is so incorrigibly in terms of
the chivalric code.

We may therefore suspect, even at this point, that Chaucer's
poem is a radically different work from the *Teseida*; it is in fact
so different in every significant respect that I am convinced Professor Robinson is mistaken in characterizing it as a "free adaptation of the Teseida of Boccaccio."[10] When all the evidence has
been accumulated, I think it will be clear that Chaucer's poem
bears essentially no more artistic relationship to its external source
than, analogically, Beethoven's *Diabelli Variations* bear to their
original theme. In keeping with this contention, the significance
of Chaucer's omission of the crucial circumstances of Boccaccio's
Book I and many of the principal events they envelop is primarily that it enabled him to compose a work artistically far removed from its source. It seems to me too little attention has
been paid to the original creative uses he made it serve in its
new contexts and to the entirely different poem in artistic and
psychological character which emerged from these points of departure. The mere arithmetic accounting for specific line similarities cannot be taken very seriously in any assessment of artistic
relationships.

In another detailed study of Chaucer's *Teseida* sources, Professor
Pratt considered many of Chaucer's changes. He is of course correct in stating that Emilia is the most fully characterized figure
in Boccaccio's poem and in maintaining that, in comparison, *The
Knight's Tale* contains "no invocations; classical allusions are reduced to a minimum; the heroine is virtually uncharacterized;
and the amorous psychology is pretty much subdued." Emilia in
the *Teseida* is certainly "a fickle young coquette." Moreover, he
finds "touches of humor, irony and exaggeration" enlivening Chaucer's story; matters of physical description come chiefly from Boccaccio, but not the "tone" and very little of the amorous psychology.
His most important conclusion, despite these findings, is that "the
tone of the *Knight's Tale* is Chaucer's original contribution to his
redaction of Boccaccio's narrative."[11] Professor Pratt's conclusion
is perhaps representative of the most extreme views of those who
tend to look upon *The Knight's Tale* as more or less of an abridged
translation of the *Teseida*. I shall evaluate this school of thought

when enough evidence from all four books of *The Knight's Tale* can be brought to bear on it.

Less recent work which also has important implications for artistic ambivalence and the relationship between *The Knight's Tale* and the *Teseida* is that of Professors Stuart Robertson and Hubertis M. Cummings. Professor Robertson decided that while Chaucer's literal translations from the *Teseida* are primarily more or less set pieces (descriptions, a few speeches, and prayers), the numerous radical changes are almost always on the side of realism.[12] Professor Cummings concluded, in a brief discussion of Chaucer's changes and additions as well as omissions from the *Teseida*, that Chaucer ignored many of the imitation classical elements, employing instead specific material of feudal realism. One of the results of this, he felt, was that Chaucer's poem took on a drastically different "English" atmosphere. He unmistakably implied, however, that *The Knight's Tale* is essentially an abridgment of the Boccaccio source.[13] In this respect his opinion resembles that of Professor Pratt. I agree emphatically with the views expressed here on Chaucer's changes in the direction of realism. Their significance and artistic magnitude, on the other hand, do not seem to me to have been properly assessed either by these able critics or by others.

Concerning Chaucer's significant omission of the key circumstances surrounding the events of Boccaccio's Book I, we find its implications clearly reflected—in a negative sense—in the rest of the poem. His total ignoring of the Amazonian matters, then, makes it artistically possible to place Ipolita as a character in psychological limbo and to reduce Emelye to a psychological nonentity, as opposed to the indomitable, fierce Queen and the unprincipled, flirtatious sophisticate portrayed by Boccaccio. The epic pagan warrior Teseo, moreover, in the *Teseida* is in effect a slaughterer of women (even though they are Amazons). For example, he issues the implacable "surrender or die" edict, after which he baldly takes Ippolita to wife as part of the spoils.

For Chaucer's Knight, however, Theseus is the epitome of chivalric nobility. In the sixth and seventh lines of the poem he is categorically credited with having achieved his greatness with "his wysdom and his chivalrie"! If we bear in mind the humorous and satiric incongruity and inappropriateness arising from the Knight's characterization of Theseus and his acts previously considered here, the implications in terms of artistic ambivalence of Chaucer's vast omissions from and contradictions of his source are obvious. Also, this combination of omission and contradiction serves to emphasize the fact that for Theseus' characterization, as for those of Ipolita and Emelye, Chaucer's source was evidently merely a point of departure, or at most a hazy outline which frequently melts into mirage. With respect to the degree of Chaucer's artistic indebtedness to Boccaccio's *Teseida* in *The Knight's Tale,* then, we may remind ourselves of a later English poet's similar use of Holinshed's chronicles.

The remainder of Chaucer's departures from Boccaccio in Book I of *The Knight's Tale* can be considered more briefly, since they are more specific and hence more obvious. As Boccaccio's Book II opens, two years have passed since Teseo's forces left Athens to attack the Amazon women. Teseo sets sail for Athens with Ippolita and Emilia and enters the city in triumph. At this point (Cantos 25-31), Chaucer joins the Boccaccio for the episode of the grieving women but with far-reaching changes in detail and effect. In the *Teseida* the women await Teseo in the Temple of Clemency; he does not meet them at the side of the road as Chaucer specifically states. Further, Teseo merely asks them who they are (Canto 26); there is no trace of the outburst of Chaucer's version. The women reply in the best epic tradition that each of them was a king's wife, mother, or sister (Canto 28). The implications of these changes in terms of their satiric and humorous effects and, consequently, artistic ambivalence in Book I of *The Knight's Tale* are obvious.

Boccaccio devotes no less than thirty-four cantos to the battle for Thebes, replete with heroic detail. Chaucer covers it, with drastic changes and only three lines of direct quotation, in thirty-seven lines from the time of Theseus' departure from Athens (965-1002)! In the Boccaccio, Teseo issues a formal challenge to Creon, and sees to it that he is given a proper funeral (Cantos 73-76), whereas Chaucer conveys the impression that the whole expedition is one of punishment for Creon's wrongs, the vanquished Thebans and their bodies being treated accordingly. This is, of course, echoed and re-echoed by Chaucer's Palamon later in Book I by his reference to Theseus' "tyrannye." In the *Teseida,* while Teseo gives permission to pillage, it is solely for the purpose of an equal division of the spoils, and the bodies are treated with respect. There is no aura of the grisly aftermath of a medieval battle that Chaucer conveys (1003-10).

While in the *Teseida* Palamone and Arcita are found somewhat as Chaucer writes of their discovery, in the Italian poem the detail of appearance, rank, and so on seems endless. Most importantly, however, while Teseo condemns them to eternal imprisonment, he has them kept in a luxurious apartment in his palace. There they are "served according to their every pleasure, so as to make them comfortable because they were of royal blood" (Canto 99). Book II of the *Teseida* ends at this point.

What emerges from the changes Chaucer made in his creation of Theseus seems obviously significant in relation to Boccaccio's Teseo. When Teseo appears in Book I of the *Teseida* as the implacable, no-holds-barred foe, Chaucer deletes the evidence and has his Knight characterize Theseus as the soul of chivalry. When in the Boccaccio Teseo performs a magnanimous act or extends chivalrously appropriate treatment to the two captive royal knights, Chaucer radically alters the pertinent events either literally or by implication. As a result of the Knight's first and second narrative devices, these events are, in Chaucer's subtly complete reworking of them, reported matter-of-factly enough so that they become not at all the outcome of chivalric courtesy but of hard-headed material or political self-interest. Yet—and this, I think, is most important of all—Chaucer's Knight places the contradictory, idealistic interpretation upon Theseus' every act that his own reportage of the evidence conspicuously fails to warrant.

Chaucer's most pronounced direct deviations from his source in Book I of *The Knight's Tale* are the radical departures from the material in Book III of the *Teseida*. In the *Teseida*, Emilia is very much the flirt and well aware of the presence of Arcita and Palamone. She watches their windows and sings especially sweetly whenever she sees them gazing out at her. Arcita sees her first, and calls Palamone; both of them assume that she is a beautiful, divine goddess (Canto 11). Both weep frequently, sigh endlessly, sleep badly, eat less than formerly, and write many plaintive love songs. Emilia continues to sing all during the summer, but she sings only out of pride in her own beauty, not for love or in praise of love. She is vain, conceited, and selfish (Canto 30). That very fall Arcita is released under the same conditions as in Chaucer's poem, after both young men have found out Emilia's name (Canto 40). There is a long, sad farewell between the two young men (Cantos 75-82), with much weeping and a final embrace. All during their imprisonment together, each has tried to comfort the other. There has been no quarreling at any time and they part on terms of deep affection, commiserating with each other over their hopeless love for Emilia. After a last sight of Emilia on a nearby balcony (Canto 83), Arcita rides sadly off to his banishment (Canto 85), marking the end of Book III.

The garden scene is much the same in the two poems, although Chaucer does not quote Boccaccio directly. The Knight's lyric description is much more ethereal, if shorter, than the corresponding cantos in the Boccaccio. Otherwise, Chaucer's departure from Boccaccio is nearly complete, except for the terms of Arcite's release. He enormously compresses the love-malady aspects of Palamon and Arcite and also makes their symptoms more violent than in the Boccaccio. Their argument is entirely his own creation, together with all the material which evolves from it (the philosophizing, comparison of each other's fate, and the like). In the *Teseida*, one gets the impression of a melancholy withering away of the two young men's spirits, while each wishes the other well and experiences no jealousy. The only hint of a parallel between this part of the *Teseida's* Book III and the end of Chaucer's Book I lies in passages from the latter wherein Palamon finally becomes aware of the implications of his imprisoned state and sadly compares Arcite's freedom to it. In the Boccaccio, during the farewell Arcita says: "You will see her in the spring, but I cannot hope for this" (Canto 77). Palamone replies, in effect, "I shall miss you, but . . . you can travel all the time and thus make your [love] pains less severe" (Cantos 77-78). This is, however, a far cry from Palamon's seizure by the "fyr of jalousie" and Arcite's characterization of Palamon's imprisonment as blissful paradise.

In the Knight's almost allegorically romantic depiction of Emelye in Chaucer's Book I, we have a virtually complete characterization of her for Chaucer's purposes. By roughly approximating *only* this portion of Boccaccio's treatment of her, Chaucer sees to it that she never assumes the proportions of a genuine human being. Yet in the *Teseida* she is by far the most fully developed and extensively treated character and remains throughout a selfish, sophisticated, and superficial girl, wise in the ways of the court. Whatever Chaucer's purposes may have been in creating her as a romantic illusion so different from Boccaccio's Emilia, the sustained humorous incongruity and satiric effects of Palamon's and Arcite's arguments and eventual parade of warring pageantry for the hand of this indifferent, gossamer-like beauty seem to me to be among the most important results.

I am unable to discover any humor in Boccaccio's *Teseida*; certainly in the cantos where the epic style is in harmony with the power of the events and the grandness of the characters, there is none. There is, of course, heavy and sustained irony in the love complex of the poem, but Boccaccio's treatment of the two young men's apparently deep love for a more or less shallow flirt and the lengths it eventually drives them to does not seem to me in any way satiric. It has been posited that much of this aspect of the poem is more or less autobiographical.[14] Accepting this, I confess my impression of the *Teseida* is that it succeeds in communicating not tragedy, but rather a somewhat contrived situation in which the conventions of a period love affair exceed the genuineness of the emotion itself. The poem is not consistent; I do not believe it is by any means a successful epic but rather an attempt at one which does not quite result in the communication of genuine tragedy. In any case the humorous and satiric aspects of *The Knight's Tale* are entirely Chaucer's own, in my opinion; I find no definite trace of either in the *Teseida*.

IV

the love complex

𝒪F ALL THE SCHOLARLY INVESTIGATIONS of the phenomenon of courtly love both as a social code of the Middle Ages and as it appears in literary forms, perhaps the most interesting and detailed is that of C. S. Lewis.[1] In an absorbing consideration of Chaucer's works involving courtly love, Lewis was in part concerned with *The Parliament of Fowls* and warns that "It is here that the exaggerated conception of the 'mocking' Chaucer has produced its most disastrous results." He considers it totally mistaken to believe that Chaucer intended to ridicule "the courtly sentiment of the nobler birds through the criticism of 'the lewednes behinde'" or to believe that Chaucer himself shared the view of the Duck and Goose. Although I agree only in part with these comments, I bring them up here because I wish to make perfectly clear that nothing in this study is intended to convey the view that Chaucer "mocked" or satirized knowingly any genuine human ideal. While Lewis specifically excluded *The Canterbury Tales* from his investigation, it is clear that he considers *The Knight's Tale* an example of Chaucer's courtly love poetry; hence I shall later be concerned with some of his more generalized arguments which are certainly pertinent to *The Knight's Tale*.

Many of the critical sources previously cited make clear that the characterization of Emelye and the garden scene itself are by some considered to reflect important characteristics of the courtly love allegory. Others maintain that *The Knight's Tale* is a metrical romance suffused with courtly or romantic love. My investigation has proceeded, I think, as far as it can profitably go without discussing these questions in some detail. While perhaps most of this material is particularly pertinent to Book II, a good deal of it refers to Book I and indeed is applicable to the entire poem. Thus while many elements of courtly love may seem to be involved in the first two books, it might at first glance seem more appropriate to reserve a discussion of genre until all four books have been examined. Yet courtly love and the metrical romance seem linked together in the minds of many so far as this poem is concerned, and they can conveniently be so examined. In any case, Chaucer's consistency in these areas of this poem, with one exception, makes it possible even at this stage to make generalizations of a relatively broad nature which may be confirmed as the investigation progresses.

In my opinion, the externals of two kinds of treatment of love are readily discernible in *The Knight's Tale*—that of the courtly allegory and that of the metrical romance. Lewis maintained that Chaucer never composed a true love allegory and, indeed, insisted that "in his greatest work, we have the courtly conceptions of love, which Chaucer learned from the French allegory, put into action in poetry which is not allegorical at all." Such a statement reflects my own view of the "combination" seemingly present in *The Knight's Tale*. Emelye, in her two "solo" appearances (the garden scene in Book I and the prayer scene in Book III), has very much the appearance of the love symbol of courtly allegory, the rosebud of *The Romaunt of the Rose*. But as a human being, she is a nonentity. Arcite and Palamon on the other hand, while suffering some of the symptoms of the love-smitten of courtly allegory, ostensibly reflect in their attitudes and actions the characteristics exhibited by heroes of metrical romance. The supposed courtly allegory aspects as we see them through Emelye are accordingly obvious enough. She might well seem to be an echo of the heroines of the love debates alleged to have been held in Eleanor of Aquitaine's court.[2] The supposed aspects of the metrical romance in the love complex are less easy to accept, however, since they unquestionably clash with the concept we are apparently given of the central motivating force of the poem's love complex—Emelye herself—and for other reasons as well.

There is a tendency to refer to a good many medieval poems as metrical romances which probably should either be otherwise categorized or not categorized at all. In fact, it seems to me that in our passion for tracing sources, nailing down facts, and in general searching for similarities, we have been successful to the point that we are at times a little reluctant to credit the medieval literary artists with the original creative abilities many of them possessed. In this case I am glad that Chaucer seems to have done his own categorizing for us, and *The Knight's Tale* can be profitably compared in pertinent aspects to poems with which he was probably familiar and to which he himself referred as romances. Chaucer's own rollicking burlesque of the metrical romance not only reflects his thorough familiarity with the genre's literary characteristics but also contains a list of the most popular ones of his time:

> Men speken of romances of prys,
> Of Horn child and of Ypotys,
> 　　Of Beves and sir Gy,
> Of sir Lybeux and Pleyndamour,—
> But sir Thopas, he bereth the flour
> 　　Of roial chivalry! 　　　(*Sir Thopas*, 897-902)

Still another famous hero of metrical romance is specifically referred to in *Sir Thopas*, just as the Host interrupts the tale:

> Hymself drank water of the well,
> As dide the knyght sire Percyvell
> 　　So worthy under wede,
> Til on a day— 　　　　　　　　　(915-18)

In all, Professor Robinson cites no less than twenty-one romances in which varying degrees of fragmentary and sporadic resemblances to *Sir Thopas* may be found.[3] There is scarcely enough evidence with regard to any individual romance, in my opinion, to justify even speculation about specific sources. Nonetheless, we may safely assume on the basis of this that Chaucer had a thorough literary awareness of at least sizeable portions of these romances.

I resist with difficulty the temptation to which Chaucer's open references to specific romances give rise: that is, to assume that he was certainly familiar with them. If this assumption is unwarranted, the probabilities seem at least great enough to justify

the selection of those we can identify today as the most likely
paradigms of the minstrel romance genre in Chaucer's reading.
They are in any event, I think, sufficiently representative of the
genre as a whole to serve as a basis of comparison between the
metrical romance and *The Knight's Tale* in terms of characterization, certain matters pertaining to knightly quests, love complexes,
and selected elements of literary style. I shall accordingly investi-
gate them briefly from this standpoint.

The Sir Perceval reference is provocative for several reasons.
First, it is from the very early part of the poem and refers to Sir
Perceval the elder (lines 5-8).[4] Second, the love complex of the
poem, in one or two matters atypical of most of the romances,
bears a distinct relationship to that of *The Knight's Tale*. This,
however, obtains with Perceval the younger and is well along in
the poem—Perceval the elder's love material is, in contrast, unlike
that of *The Knight's Tale*. Finally, Manly presented convincing
evidence of Chaucer's intent to satirize the Flemish in *Sir Thopas*,[5]
and Halliwell cited a Flemish translation from the original French
Perceval which was completed in 1350.[6] I therefore think it rather
likely that Chaucer was particularly familiar with *Sir Perceval of
Galles*, but none of these indications is more than suggestive of
this.

Whatever the truth may be so far as characterization is concerned in the love complex pertaining both to Perceval the elder
and younger, we find drastic differences between the women here
and Emelye. There is also, particularly with Perceval the elder,
a great difference in the treatment of the intensity of the hero's
love:

> He[King Arthur] gaffe hym his syster Acheflour,
>> To have and to holde;
> Fro thethyne tille his lyves ende,
> With brode londes to spende,
> For he the knyght wele kende,
>> He bytaughte hir to welde;
> With grete gyftes to fulfille,
> He gaffe his sister hym tille,
> To the knyght at ther bothers wille,
>> With robes in folde.   (23-32)

> To the kirke the knyghte [Sir Perceval the elder] ȝode
> For to wedde that frely fode,

> For the gyftes that ware gude,
>   And for hir ownne sake;
> Sythene, withowttene any bade,
> A grete brydale they made,
> For hir sake that hym hade
>   Chosene to hir make;   (37-44)

Obviously the young couple chose each other as well as having been officially assigned to one another.

It is equally apparent that the elements of Chaucer's mastery of style—the detailed realism, the care in accounting for motivation and, with rare and I suspect purposive exception, the development of characters in terms of their inner emotions as well as their outer acts—are either absent or at best present in crudely rudimentary form in *Sir Perceval of Galles*. The detail in this poem is frequently reserved for the jousts and the battlefield, where both Percevals' deeds assume superhuman proportions, so that realism in the Chaucerian sense is certainly not part of the poet's approach to his material. Aside from Perceval the elder's knightly prowess in combat and the gory details pertaining thereto, he is no more developed as a character than his bride Acheflour. Even so, if we compare her to Emelye, it is significant that, instead of Emelye's exaggerated indifference, she has chosen Perceval the elder "to hir make." Further, she is a happy bride in her husband's wedding-joust triumphs: "And hamewardez thanne rode he,/ And blythe was his bryde" (79-80). It is emphasized by repetition: "And thofe the bryde blythe be/ That Percyvelle hase wone the gree" (81-82).

For Perceval the younger we find ampler consideration of matters of love, although the poet's approach to his material remains the same. The first appearance of the unknown lady reminds us of the tableau of Emelye in the garden, although the setting here is much more in keeping with the courtly allegory than Emelye's, despite its marring by the action:

> Forthirmore ganne he glyde
> Tille a chambir ther besyde,
>   Moo sellys to see;
> Riche clothes fande he sprede,
> A lady slepande on a bedde,
> He said, "Forsothe, a tokyne to wedde
>   Salle thou lefe with mee."

> Ther he kyste that swete thynge,
> Of hir fynger he tuke a rynge,
> His awenne modir takynnynge
>   He lefte with that fre.
> He went forthe to his mere,
> Tuke with hym his schorte spere,
> Lepe one lofte as he was ere,
>   His way rydes he.   (466-80)

This is of course reminiscent of the courtly allegory love symbol. The unknown lady's sleeping state and her unconsciousness of the invasion of her precious emotional sanctity make it possible to compare her to the rosebud in *The Romaunt of the Rose* and this tableau to the dreamer's kiss of the bud after the most elaborate preparations, intercessions, and the like. The rest of the action is hopelessly inconsistent with the scene and its apparent sources, of course, but it does not matter since this poem, like so many metrical romances, is not concerned with consistency.

The other lady, Lufamour, is far removed in her actions from the courtly allegory figure portrayed above. Unwilling to accept marriage from one who has seized her lands and claimed her by right of conquest, she sends to Arthur for aid and Perceval the younger is granted the quest to aid her. He dispatches numberless villains in a day's battle, and Lufamour, inspecting with satisfaction the hideous scene after the battle, invites him to dine. She asks him if he knows who slew these enemies:

> Fulle blythe was that birde brighte,
> Whenne scho sawe hym with syghte,
> For scho trowed that he was wighte,
>   And askede hym in hy;
> At that fre gan scho frayne,
> Thoghe he were lefe for to layne,
> If he wiste who had thame slayne
>   Thase folkes of envy.   (1289-96)

Perceval the younger admits his valor and says he has come to slay her oppressor, whereupon

> And Lufamour, that lele lady,
> Wist fulle wele ther-by
>   The childe was fulle wighte.
> The birde was blythe of that bade,

That scho siche an helpe hade,
Agayne the sowdane was fade
With alle for to fighte.
Faste the lady hym byhelde,
Scho thoght hym worthi to welde,   (1302-10)

Perceval the younger of course finally slays the "sowdan," after King Arthur, Gawain, the Queen, and all the court arrive most opportunely, and Lufamour and her rescuer are married. After a year of bliss, Perceval the younger goes off to seek his mother, and meets on his way a bird of brightest blue fastened to a tree who turns out to be none other than the unknown sleeper. Her troubles arose over the exchange of rings, and the valorous knight realizes he is responsible. There follows a revealing of various magical matters, Perceval the younger slays a giant, and the whole poem ends happily after the hero has made his vow of appropriate sacrificial restitution and done his penance. In its heavy reliance upon the supernatural, of course, *Sir Perceval of Galles* is decidedly unlike the English metrical romances, except for *Sir Thopas*!

The exquisite tableau of the sleeping lady never does become the center around which the poem's love interest revolves, then, and Lufamour actually behaves much like other noble ladies of minstrel romance—that is, she is in fact the aggressor in love. There is a hint that Chaucer knew the sleeping lady scene well and another hint that he was otherwise informed about Perceval the younger. As the youngster leaves the lady's chamber, he (as Sir Thopas does) leaps on his mare—a most unsuitable mount for a knight, but Perceval the younger has not yet been knighted. His dress, for the same reason, is equally bizarre, repeatedly emphasized, and referred to almost invariably as his "wede," the very same word Chaucer uses in the penultimate line of *Sir Thopas* in his reference to Perceval. We are entitled to consider it possible, accordingly, that some of the humor and satire of *Sir Thopas* and possibly the absence of character development of Emelye had its rather misty roots in Chaucer's knowledge of this romance. If this is true, however, the vastly different artistic purposes conceived and carried out with this flimsy material are, I think, typical of Chaucer's genius. There is no question of humor in *Sir Perceval of Galles*. The other details in Emelye's garden scene and their treatment have no objective relationship with the tableau discussed above, but the subjective result is very similar. I submit that

Emelye's characterization (or lack of it) is very little more harmonious with the love complex of *The Knight's Tale* than the sleeping lady tableau would be with the love complex in *Sir Perceval of Galles,* had the poet chosen so to employ it.

The ever present quest concept is, in many metrical romances, somewhat flexible in form. One of its usual characteristics is a time limit within which certain knightly goals must be achieved. It is most often a test of the knight's chivalric worthiness to deserve his lady and the material and social rewards which accompany marriage to a lady of appropriate station in life. Many of the writers of medieval romances were as inconsistent in their treatment of the passage of time and the quest concept as they were in other matters. A case in point is Sir Perceval the younger's exchange of rings with the sleeping girl as a symbol of betrothal and his later betrayal of her by his marriage to Lufamour—surely a *romantic* but not a *courtly* love crime, which is never completely accounted for in the poem. Thus the earlier days of battle, the dinner scene with Lufamour, the court's arrival with the following days of combat, the wedding followed by exactly one year of royal happiness and, finally, the sacrificial seven days of restitutional penance—all are precisely and chronologically treated in *Sir Perceval of Galles.*

But there are obviously several quests, each forming a subordinate part of the principal quest of Perceval the younger making himself worthy of the many and varied rewards revolving around Lufamour. The time limitations of the quests and their separation from each other are, however, for the most part extremely vague or even nonexistent. Nonetheless, the impression conveyed throughout the poem is that Perceval the younger was a man of immediate decision and quick action in every respect, and the quests move rapidly. The longest period of time involved in any single portion of the poem is, in my opinion, the exact year's duration referred to above.

In virtually all of the important metrical romances, the love complex, the quest with its inevitable time element, and stylistic matters are closely interwoven with matters of characterization within the poem. If we compare *Sir Perceval of Galles* to *The Knight's Tale* in these respects, we find Acheflour and Lufamour not only eager to embrace marriage but even openly trying to bring it about, while Emelye prefers spinsterhood and chastity to either hero. Both Percevals are men of quick, decisive, knightly action; the quests are immediately undertaken and their goals are, in general, clearly love's rewards desired or even proposed by the heroine herself.

Chaucer, in his zealous attention to realistic temporal detail, scrupulously accounts for almost every moment of elapsed time in *The Knight's Tale*, and it is *eight years* from the time Palamon and Arcite first see Emelye to the day of their final contest at arms for her hand. To be sure, the quest itself may be said to be only a year. But the preceding seven years are spent, in contrast to the active Percevals, in what amounts to weeping, wailing inactivity so far as any progress is concerned toward what one might assume to be their goal. Chaucer's careful accounting for motivation and his characteristic development of the inner "reality" of his fictive personalities emphasizes, among other things, consistency of motivation and action. Hence our attention is very likely to become engaged by any inconsistency. This is certainly clear from much of the material analyzed so far in this study. His style, which always seems his most polished means of communicating precisely what he wishes to convey, accordingly magnifies any inconsistencies. The inconsistencies in *Sir Perceval of Galles*, however, are in no way inharmonious with the stylistic aspects of the poem. In these fundamental matters *The Knight's Tale* differs conspicuously from *Sir Perceval of Galles*.

Of the six "romances of prys" in the *Sir Thopas* list, *Pleyndamour* is unidentified and, as Robinson points out, *Ypotys* is actually a legend, not a metrical romance.[7] There remain, therefore, four romances to examine: the "Libeux" source, the *Horn Child, Sir Beves of Hamtoun,* and *Sir Guy of Warwick.* The proper name "Libeux" is the Middle English *Libeaus Desconus,* a metrical romance which in one form or another existed in Old French, Italian, and Middle High German. An extremely detailed comparative study of the four versions was undertaken by William H. Schofield.[8]

Interestingly enough, the early part of *Libeaus Desconus* bears a number of resemblances to that portion of *Sir Perceval of Galles* which marks the beginning of Perceval the younger's adventures. Both youngsters arrive at King Arthur's court and ask to be made knights, both set out on quests to succor ladies as yet personally unknown to them, and both lack the knightly appearance and

equipage calculated to impress their peers with their fighting
abilities. In each poem, Sir Gawain is of considerable help in
terms of the donation of arms and equipment. There are other
similarities as well, but none of them is quite as detailed as these.
As is true of many metrical romances whose original sources were
Celtic, magic, sorcery, giants, and the like play important parts
in the *Libeaus*.

In many ways Libeaus Desconus is a romance hero of the
same kind as Sir Perceval the younger. His prowess in knightly
combat is unparalleled, he slays at least one giant (depending
upon the particular version of the poem one is reading), and he
is extremely fortunate in matters of love. Of the several ladies,
one of them (Elena) is the messenger arriving at the court seeking
help, accompanied by a dwarf. She and the dwarf remain with the
hero throughout the poem. For the most part, they either share or
observe his adventures until the lovely lady who is the original
motivation is rescued, falls in love with Libeaus Desconus, and
marries him. Elena, though very beautiful, does not become a part
of the love complex of the poem.

Much of the poet's stylistic approach to his material reminds
one of Chaucer in its emphasis on realistic detail, of which Elena's
characterization is typical. She is described when she arrives at
court as clothed in *tars,* "pelured wiþ blaunner"; she is more
beautiful than a countess or a queen and rides a milk-white horse,
but she is also "all beswette for hete" (p. 7). The dwarf is
described in similar detail, followed by a list of his accomplishments:

> Miche he coupe of game:
> Citole, sautrie in same.
>   Harpe, fiþele and croupe.
> He was a noble disour
> Wiþ ladies in her bour,
>   A mery man of moupe.   (148-53)

While we might expect that such a stylistic approach would tend
to magnify inconsistencies, as I think Chaucer's does in *The
Knight's Tale,* there are so many of them in *Libeaus* which are
simply ignored that one merely accepts inconsistency as a characteristic of the poem.

Libeaus' first adventure occurs shortly after he, Elena, and the dwarf set out from Arthur's court to rescue the imprisoned lady Sinadoun, in whose name Elena has pleaded for a mighty knight "Wiþ herte good and liȝt,/ To winne her wiþ honour" (167-68). Elena and the dwarf are contemptuous of the inexperienced, callow stripling, and Elena emerges from the first part of the poem as a shrew, addressing all manner of disparaging—even insulting—remarks to the young hero. Having beaten a powerful knight in combat and later (as a result of the knight's treachery) several of his cohorts who attacked him in a body, Libeaus wins the apology and regard of Elena. She reverts to the "lovely lady on the snow-white palfrey" characterization and so remains for the rest of the poem, although from time to time she furnishes very practical help to the young hero. In many ways she is the most fully developed character in the poem. Yet one of the inconsistencies in the plot is her frequent disappearance from it, at times when Libeaus is involved in something inimical to his principal quest which she would be unable to condone, and at other times for no apparent reason. During these periods the poet simply ignores her; there is no indication that she has willfully absented herself.

Part of the love complex of the poem takes place as a result of the hero's first encounter with giants. He rescues the lovely maiden Violette, who has been captured by two giants and is being forcibly held by one of them who tries to kiss her. In a fierce battle, Libeaus lops off various limbs and finally presents both giants' severed heads to Violette, who receives them joyfully, while thanking heaven he was made a knight. The hero, Elena, and the dwarf thereupon return the girl to her noble father, who offers his daughter's hand and castles to Libeaus. This the young knight gracefully declines, but only for the present: he says he must first do his duty. The poet leaves out any account of Violette's feelings in this matter, but the adoring hero-worship she hitherto displayed makes it impossible to believe her reaction was like the indifferent one of the exaggeratedly chaste Emelye. This episode marks the first inconsistency in the poet's portrayal of the heroic young knight's relations with the ladies involved in the love complex of the poem. Libeaus Desconus never returns to Violette or thinks of her again.

After other triumphs the young knight and his companions are launched into the famous Île d'Or episode. The gorgeous castle's lady is "roddy as [a] rose" (1322) and beautiful in other ways as well. She is also her father's only heir, and the castle is being besieged by a cruel giant—this one is all black and a thirty-footer. After a really hideously detailed battle, the giant is slain; the lovely lady (la dame d'amour) immediately offers to give the victorious hero her magnificent castle and city and become his wife. The poet in effect says merely that Libeaus Desconus was so fascinated by her that he gave in to her beauty and stayed with her a full year. Nothing further is said about marriage, and we cannot tell whether or not they were actually wed. Elena abruptly reappears in the poem, and she and Libeaus continue on their way. In three days they reach the city of Sinadoun, where once again a knightly battle must be fought before they are admitted to the city. The young hero is of course victorious.

The night of their arrival Libeaus is told of the lady Sinadoun's imprisonment in a castle by two clerks of necromancy, whose talents are such that no one can get to her, although she can be heard crying out from time to time. The lusty hero vows to win her and sets off at once for the bewitched castle, which turns out to be a palace in a city. He rides his horse right into the formal hall, finds a merry party in progress, and finally leads his horse up to the dais at the end of the hall. The knight seats himself on the dais and at once all the minstrels and others disappear, the lights go out, stones drop from the wall, and similar supernatural phenomena occur. Then he is attacked by the two sorcerers, one of whom he kills. The other, to his fearful consternation, escapes. A serpent with a woman's face comes through a window and before he knows it, coils itself around his neck and kisses him. Instantly the serpent turns into the beautiful-beyond-compare and stark naked lady of Sinadoun. She tells him he must be of Gawain's kin because only by kissing Gawain or one of his relatives could she be freed. She at once offers him herself "to wife" and all her fifty-five castles, subject only to Arthur's approval. Libeaus is mightily pleased but, still fearing the possible reappearance of the remaining sorcerer, abruptly rides off and leaves her! Her steward brings her clothing, and she returns to her home castle, where she and her "deliverer" are soon married, to live royally and gloriously "wiþ moche gle and game" (2228) for many years.

Like its counterpart in *Sir Perceval of Galles*, the quest in this poem is somewhat vaguely dealt with in terms of its duration from start to finish. But the two poems are also alike with respect to the passage of time during each individual adventure—a day, three days, the same night, the next morning, a twelvemonth, and the like. The year of loving dalliance before the final quest is also common to them both, and this is by far the longest period of time mentioned in either poem. The impression in *Libeaus Desconus*, too, is one of very rapid action—short periods of travel punctuated by mighty, knightly victories achieved in a matter of hours or a day or two. Other similarities include the extreme youth of the heroes in the two poems, their starting out on quests to succor ladies with whom they are not at the time personally acquainted, and the likelihood of failure in their quests because of their unknightly appearances and lack of chivalric experience. Furthermore, the ladies in each poem who are in any way involved in the love plots are invariably either eagerly acquiescent or, when they are the heroines of the principal quests, aggressors in love.

Clearly, a comparison of *The Knight's Tale* to *Libeaus Desconus* from the standpoint of their love complexes reflects the great differences between Emelye on the one hand and Violette, la dame d'amour, and the lady Sinadoun on the other. They are much like the differences between Emelye and her counterparts in *Sir Perceval of Galles*, except in degree. Obviously in *Libeaus Desconus* the ladies in the love plot are, if anything, in general even more receptively amorous than Acheflour and Lufamour, as opposed to Emelye's ostensible indifferent—even negative—resignation to her fate. The quest complex and its concomitant time elements in *Libeaus Desconus* reflect fundamentally grander events as well as the rapidity of decisive, knightly action which is so characteristic of its hero, in contrast to corresponding matters in *The Knight's Tale*. Although these qualities may be said to be much more emphasized in *Libeaus Desconus* than in *Sir Perceval of Galles*, they are shared by the two poems. Hence Arcite and Palamon, in contrast to Perceval the younger and Libeaus Desconus, are far less heroically decisive in thought and action for seven years; in addition their quest itself does not bear too close an inspection. Palamon and Arcite strive neither to rescue Emelye from mortal or supermortal danger nor to relieve her from distress—it is *they* who are in distress and, not to put too fine a point on it, Chaucer makes it damagingly clear that mere jealousy is in the forefront of their motives.

Stylistically, the most important differences between *The Knight's Tale* and *Libeaus Desconus* from the standpoint of this essay are reflected in the poets' treatment—or the lack of it—of basic inconsistencies in event and character. Despite the realistic detail in *Libeaus Desconus* which at times seems not far removed from Chaucer himself, the almost ever present supernatural complex does much to dissolve the inconsistencies in those areas. Elsewhere they are simply ignored. They are not interpreted by the poet, nor are the internal states of mind of the characters dwelt upon at length, to be followed by logically inconsistent decisions or acts on the parts of the characters concerned.

Chaucer's stylistic technique results in exactly the same kind of thing, as I have shown in the discussion in the preceding chapter of the Knight's interpretation of Theseus, the structure and content of Palamon's and Arcite's arguments and soliloquies, and so on. Moreover, it will appear in other matters of importance to the poem as the remaining books are considered. One effect of this technique is to emphasize and concentrate attention upon the inconsistency, which may be frequently interpreted through our projective processes as humor or satire, confirmable by the approach discussed in Chapter II. One may also maintain that in *The Knight's Tale*, too, such inconsistencies are often ignored—that is, when neither the Knight nor the characters concerned portray, in their absence of explanation or interpretation, any perception of given inconsistencies. But invariably in such instances Chaucer's treatment of the situation is so detailed and the logic points so unmistakably toward a decision or act which would be wholly consistent with the situation that the effect is one of extremely heavy emphasis on the inconsistency itself. This state of affairs does not obtain in either *Libeaus Desconus* or *Sir Perceval of Galles*. I find no trace of humor or satire in either of these poems.

Concerning the poems *King Horn*[9] and *Horn Childe and Maiden Rimnild*,[10] one cannot tell whether Chaucer had one or the other or both in mind from the "Horn Child" reference in line 898 of *Sir Thopas*. The hero is fairly consistently called "childe" in both poems, and neither poem differs significantly in the matters under discussion here. I am considering *King Horn* merely because it was apparently more widely read than *Horn Childe and Maiden Rimnild* in Chaucer's time,[11] and I suspect Chaucer would have been more likely to refer to the more popular of the two.

King Horn is perhaps the earliest of the English metrical romances, dating from approximately 1225. Its love story is concerned exclusively with people of royal rank. Horn, with other youngsters, is set adrift in a boat to save him from being slaughtered by the Saracens who have invaded and mercilessly decimated the population of his father's kingdom. After much traveling over land and sea, he is cordially received into the hospitable realm in which Rymenhild is a beautiful, royal maiden (1-246). Rymenhild falls in love with Horn, whose beauty as a child has gradually changed to the handsomeness of very young manhood as the years have passed. Horn is unaware of Rymenhild's love for him; she becomes a most active aggressor by inviting him to her chamber and declaring her love for him. Horn says he loves her, but (since he does not know his real identity) he cannot grant her request that he marry her because he is of inferior rank. Rymenhild has the king knight Horn and again invites him to her chamber (247-550). Once more she tells Horn that she loves him to distraction and pleads with him to marry her. Horn agrees, but says he must perform deeds of valor and fight well in honor of his lemman with some other knight before they can properly marry (551-60). It is not enough for him to have proudly brought Rymenhild, to her great joy, the gory head of his first Saracen; a quest is in order.

With copious kissing, Rymenhild speeds Horn lovingly on his way (561-85). There is also a public farewell in the great hall of the castle, in which the whole court participates, and Horn is off to kill his first hundred Saracens. He immediately performs this almost superhuman feat and returns briefly to receive the praise due him (586-620). At last, with a final kiss from Rymenhild, he leaves on his seven-year quest, vowing to return at the end of that time and marry his royal lemman (723-41). From line 742 until almost the very end of the poem, Horn carried out a multitude of valiant tasks, helping the weak or vanquished recover their kingdoms or other rightful possessions and finally reconquering what he discovers to be his own kingdom. He has many difficulties and it often looks as though he will be unable to return within his seven years. Eventually, however, he returns in time to his anxious Rymenhild, makes her his queen, and they rule his kingdom in happiness for many years.

Stylistically, the poem's events are treated in briefer, more generalized fashion than those in *The Knight's Tale, Sir Perceval of*

Galles, or *Libeaus Desconus.* The poet exercises the most detail
in his portrait of Rymenhild and the love episode and in the specific
scenes. But such detail as there is is selective. We are not told about
matters of armor or dress, as a rule, but about weapons and the
number Horn kills in given battle episodes. From time to time dialogue slows down the rapid pace. In all, the impression one gets
from *King Horn* is tremendous economy—great events are dramatically described, but series after series of them are compressed
in relatively few stanzas. From the standpoint of style, *King Horn*
and *The Knight's Tale* obviously have not nearly so much in common as, for example, *Libeaus Desconus* and the Chaucer poem.
But here and there Chaucer's Knight seems to echo the *King Horn*
poet's descriptive appellations of the beautiful Horn and Rymenhild the fair in the "noble duc" and Palamon's "Emelye the brighte."
Such appellations are of course typical of many metrical romances.
Chaucer's poetic economies, however, are very different from the
King Horn poet's in that despite their brevity, they convey detailed
realism rather than an air of broad, sparsely supported generality.

In the matters of quest and duration *The Knight's Tale* and
King Horn reflect greater similarities than in matters of style.
Horn must fight with some other knight, he says, in honor of
Rymenhild, and his whole quest is motivated by the desire to
make himself worthy of someone he already loves. This, then, he
shares, with Arcite and Palamon. Also, the duration of seven years
is paralleled in *The Knight's Tale,* up to the point at which Theseus dictates the conditions of the contest at arms to be held at
the end of another year. In these important matters the resemblances are startling, but they are external only. Horn is motivated
in his quest by a lovely lady who is both beautiful and boldly
aggressive in all things pertaining to her own love for him. In this
respect she is strikingly different from Emelye; if Palamon and
Arcite are motivated by a barely animated vision, Horn is motivated by a flesh-and-blood woman who herself takes the initiative
in love. Accordingly, in *The Knight's Tale* the motivation and
potential rewards of the quest are in effect as hollow and artificial
as Emelye herself, since they are all one and the same.

Closely related to this is the matter of duration, for Horn's
seven-year quest is a mighty one, full of grand deeds and dramatic
danger. If Palamon's seven years of amorous complaint and consequent inactivity are enforced, Arcite's certainly are not. It

would seem that love is treated entirely differently in the two poems with relation to quest and duration factors. Moreover, Palamon's and Arcite's quests as such do not really begin until Theseus arranges them, and even so the two young knights are preparing for a single battle only.

Another external resemblance shared by all the poems so far discussed is what might be described as the ultimate royal authority. In *Sir Perceval of Galles* and *Libeaus Desconus* this authority is King Arthur, while in *King Horn* it is the King of Rymenhild's land; in *The Knight's Tale* it is of course Theseus. In the first three instances it is merely incidental to the poems— a convention treated as such. But Theseus is the central figure in *The Knight's Tale,* almost incomparably more fully developed as a character than the supposedly questing heroes. Furthermore, he finds the amorous situation of the two young men both foolish and amusing, rather than the most profoundly appropriate of reason a knight could possibly have to justify his chivalric existence. Thus if for Theseus the love quest seems to be merely a politically useful convention born of human absurdity, for the other royal authorities it is a highly serious undertaking imbued with the ideals and social morality which define and justify the noble life.

The romance *Sir Beves of Hamtoun* is much longer than the three romances discussed above, and more than one and a half times as long as *The Knight's Tale*.[12] Its plot is as swiftly moving in its individual episodes as the others, and its complexity arises from both the sheer quantity of episodes and their variety. Like *Sir Perceval of Galles* and *Libeaus Desconus*, it is a redaction of an originally Celtic romance, and has an even heavier reliance upon the supernatural than we find in these two romances. At the same time, while all the poems under consideration in this chapter are at least tacitly Christian, Christianity is given an entirely different dimension in *Sir Beves of Hamtoun*. For Sir Beves is as much a champion of the Church as of anything else, and if sometimes his faith seems almost to bring him the troubles of a martyr, from time to time he is saved from hideous death or catastrophic misfortune by prayers or miracles. Furthermore, the essentially Christian emphasis upon virginity and its defense at all costs is startlingly direct and graphically detailed throughout the poem.

In *Sir Beves of Hamtoun* women involved in the love complex are much more important to the plot than their counterparts in the three romances so far discussed. This is largely a result of the degree and kind of emphasis placed upon both romance-approved and church-approved methods for the surrender of virginity. I think it likely that the poet responsible for the English redaction was at least sporadically concerned with making the poem a Christian polemic and may well have at times so tailored his sources.* If this was the case, his success was meager, for while the Christian characters are on the whole within the fold of the godly and the pagans usually more or less "naturally" wicked, there are notable exceptions in each category. Possibly the authority of the various sources was in the long run too hard to resist, hence the inconsistency in the polemic element. At any rate, the various competing kinds of supernaturalism, Christian and pagan or simply unspecified, result in a poem of very mixed character with a multiplicity of inconsistencies even within its Christian elements.

Of the two women chiefly concerned in the love complex of the poem (one can scarcely refer to them as "ladies" of the order of Acheflour, Lufamour, la dame d'amour, Violette, Sinadoun, or the improbable Emelye) the most fully developed as a character is Sir Beves' bride Josian. The other, Sir Beves' mother, appears only in the first part of the poem and is never referred to by her proper name. It is her truly shocking acts arising from frustrated love which brutally force her stripling son out into a cruel world. The poem starts out not unlike *Sir Perceval of Galles* in that we are first told of the marriage of the hero's father, the father's death, and the mother's relationship with her son. Like Sir Perceval the younger and Libeaus Desconus, Sir Beves, at the beginning of the poem, is looked upon by the other characters as quite incapable in every way of performing the tasks he undertakes. But while many aspects of the quest and duration complex, the love complex, and the supernatural elements are similar in all three poems, all these elements are carried to much greater extremes in *Sir Beves of Hamtoun.* Thus Sir Beves' father, Sir Guy of Hamtoun, decides

*Kölbing decided a complete compilation of all the various versions of the poem known in his own time was a task "too extensive for a single writer" (p. xxxv). Accordingly, such an opinion on the possible polemic intentions of the English redactor as I have here expressed is necessarily speculative and not readily confirmable.

in his old age to marry and is granted by the King of Scotland the hand of his daughter. She prefers a younger man, but to no avail:

> Þis maide ichaue of y-told,
> Faire maide ȝhe was & bold
>   And fre y-boren;
> Of Almayne þat emperur
> Hire hadde loued paramur
>   Wel þar be-foren.
>
> Ofte to hire fader a sente
> And he him selue þeder wente
>   For hire sake;
> Ofte gernede hire to wiue:
> Þe king for no þing aliue
>   Nolde hire him take.
>
> Siþe a ȝaf hire to sire Gii,
> A stalword erl and hardi
>   Of Souþhamtoun.
> Man, whan he falleþ in to elde,
> Feble a wexeþ and vnbelde
>   Þourȝ riȝt resoun.
>
> So longe þai ȝede to gedres te bedde,
> A knaue child be-twene hem þai hedde,
>   Beues a het.
> Faire child he was & bolde,
> He nas boute seue winter olde,
>   Whan his fader was ded.   (31-54)

This mismatching forms the background to the countless wicked conspiracies and acts against Sir Beves which are to follow.

After the boy's birth, his mother longs anew for a younger lover, unscarred by the battles of war. She insists that such a man, instead of preferring to be in church to making love to her, would love her by day and night, "Cleppen and kissen wiþ al is mizt/ And make me blis" (65-66). She sends a messenger to her former lover, to state that she will send her husband to a certain forest on the first day of May. Devoun, the lover, is to kill Sir Guy, after which she will give Devoun her "all" in love. Sir Guy is foully killed, and Beves' mother is as good as her word, having received from her lover Sir Guy's bleeding, severed head. She joyously marries Devoun the very next day.

Young Beves knows what his mother has done and bravely calls her a whore and murderer. She beats him and has him removed by the good Saber, whom she charges to murder the boy. Sprinkling pigs' blood on Beves' clothes, Saber tries to convince the boy's mother he has duly performed the murder. Instead he has disguised young Beves as a shepherd boy. The seven-year-old cannot bear the sounds of riotous merrymaking from his father's palace after the wedding; killing the porter with his staff, he enters the great hall and tries to kill Devoun when the latter refuses to give him back his property. His mother finally sells the handsome lad as a slave to heathen merchants, who in turn take him to Armenia and give him to King Ermin, father of the beauteous Josian.

Despite his refusal to become a heathen, Beves at fifteen is appointed the king's chamberlain. Ermin also promises to knight him, having seen him kill and behead a fierce wild boar and watched him slay no less than thirteen mounted attackers although he had only a broken lance with which to defend himself. Josian, like Rymenhild, has her father knight Beves for these feats. The accolade comes in time for Sir Beves to repel the invading hordes from Damascus, whose king has demanded Josian as his price for refraining from the utter destruction of Armenia. Ermin, delighted with Sir Beves' victory, allows Josian to go to the young knight's chamber and help him remove his armor. She tells Sir Beves then that she loves him so deeply that she will die if he does not become her lover. Sir Beves refuses, saying he is of too low rank. This self-denigration angers Josian, and in turn Sir Beves leaves her in a huff, but Josian returns another time to his chamber and wins his love by promising to become a Christian. They kiss each other happily, and Sir Beves seems at last to have his future appropriately settled, what with a lovely, royal lemman, a magic horse (Arondel), and the mighty sword Morgelai.

I have dealt with this first quarter of the poem in some detail so that the obvious relationships between the women of the love complex in this romance and those of the others considered may be more easily assessed. So far, with the exception of the perfidy of Sir Beves' mother who is motivated by her earlier love for young Devoun, we find the aggressiveness in love of the women in this romance typical of that of the ladies in *Sir Perceval of Galles*, *Libeaus Desconus*, and *King Horn*. They are correspondingly atypical of Emelye in this respect. As the poem progresses from Sir Beves and Josian's first kiss, far from being a recitation of rewards falling to the deserving young Christian lovers, it becomes a veritable catalogue of martyr-like trials. The trials hinge upon treachery, deceit, supernatural evil, and endless assaults upon Josian's militantly preserved virginity. Her defense against these would-be possessors of her virtue is as ruthless as the reacquisition by Sir Beves' mother of her original lover.

The young lovers' vicissitudes begin when King Ermin is wrongly informed that Sir Beves has deflowered Josian. The king treacherously arranges to have the young knight incarcerated in the deepest and darkest of dungeons, informing Josian meanwhile that her lover has returned to England and married the king's daughter there. As the hero combats poisonous flying adders and the like in his dungeon, Josian's father marries her to King Yvor of Mombraunt. Josian suspects Sir Beves is actually being kept from her and so preserves her virginity by a charm (although in at least one version of the poem she employs the more prosaic means of a chastity belt). The charm apparently works, for Yvor is thrown by Sir Beves' horse Arondel, and suffers a broken crown. With the help of prayer, Sir Beves at last manages to kill his guards and escape from his dungeon. With God's help, he overcomes all manner of physical, human, and superhuman obstacles en route to Jerusalem. Here he is confessed by the Patriarch, who enjoins him never to marry anyone who is not a virgin.

Sir Beves then disguises himself, eventually reaches Josian, and agrees to take her home to England with him, but only on condition that she is still a virgin—a rather blunt answer to her protestations of love and loyalty. She somehow convinces him that she is a virgin, and they arrive in Cologne after all kinds of dangerous encounters with dark magic, to which Josian is fortunately immune since she is not only a king's daughter, but also a queen (presumably because she is still married to Yvor, who was not killed by his fall from Arondel), and because she is a virgin. The bishop baptizes Josian, while Sir Beves continues his adventures. He is saved from death in a battle with a fearful dragon by diving into a well which had been purified because it had been the bathing place of a local virgin. This the dragon cannot enter, of course; Sir Beves, refreshed by the holy water, slays the monster.

Leaving Josian behind, Sir Beves goes to England to recover his estates from Devoun and his mother. Josian is persecuted by an earl named Miles who, since she has told him she will not surrender her virginity outside of marriage, marries her against her will. On their wedding night, at the crucial moment, she manages to strangle the earl with a girdle. Rescued by Sir Beves from being burned alive by the authorities, Josian is brought to England by him, and he wins the battle with his stepfather. He then appropriately disposes of Devoun in a cauldron of molten lead, while his mother falls to her death from the top of the castle as she watches the spectacle. At last Sir Beves and Josian are married, and Josian has twins during the first year of their marriage.

Sir Beves next gets into trouble with the King of England and is forced to leave the country. Politics now enter, and after many more colorful adventures the poem ends with one of Sir Beves' sons becoming betrothed to the heiress of the English throne, while the fatally ill Josian dies happily in her husband's arms even as he expires from grief over his impending loss.

Apart from the greatly increased importance of Christianity in the poem and the related constant emphasis on virginity which results in the women playing more decisively active roles in its plot, the rudiments of the poem's love complex are clearly present in one or another of the three romances discussed above. In terms of characterization, the women here amount to extreme but more or less logical extensions of Acheflour, Lufamour, la dame d'amour, Violette, and Sinadoun, with the possible exception of Sir Beves' mother. What the poem conveys in her character and actions as well as those of Josian is that as a result of their greater significance in the plot, the women's share in its progress is much like that of the male characters in other romances. Only the motivating factors are different. Hence Sir Beves' mother's violation of practically every moral law to enjoy a youthful lover results in her playing the role usually taken by the "bad" knights of the other romances, whereas Josian's defense of her virginity and her love for Sir Beves result in her playing the same kind of part as a "good" knight in the other romances. It is evident that, when threatened, the virginity of Lufamour, Sinadoun, and Josian evokes a basically similar response in each of them which contrasts sharply with Emelye's response to the same threat in her prayer to the chaste Diana. Indeed, the differences in degree if not in kind between the women in *Sir Beves of Hamtoun* and those of the other romances merely emphasize the more fundamental differences between Emelye and her counterparts in these other poems.

There are at least two points of similarity between the love complex of *The Knight's Tale* and that of *Sir Beves of Hamtoun*. The external one involves the durational aspects of the quest as well as the love complex. Sir Beves' quest is, in effect, a long series of "intermediate" quests linked on the one hand to his eventual marriage to Josian and on the other to the simultaneous recovery of his estates in England. He is constantly being subjected to all manner of trials and tribulations, arising from both human and supernatural villainy, while in the process of attaining these twin goals.

As in *Sir Perceval of Galles*, *Libeaus Desconus*, and *King Horn*, we are carefully informed of the duration of the subordinate or "local" quests, but the time elapsing between them and the total time lapse between Sir Beves' father's murder and the end of the poem is, I think, impossible to discover. I should hazard a minimum of thirty-five years, but this does not take into account any possible supernatural precocity in battle of Sir Beves' twin sons, which could telescope the duration considerably. At any rate, Sir Beves endures seven years imprisonment in the frightful dungeon of the King of Damascus, during which period his love for Josian remains as constant—but subject to her continuing virgin state, of course—as Palamon's and Arcite's love for Emelye. Thus, if the external resemblance here seems significant, we must remember that Sir Beves' hideous torments during his imprisonment were such that his life was in constant danger quite aside from any love pangs he may have experienced. These the poet does not in any way dwell upon. Hence if there is superficial resemblance between the enforced inactivity in love and quest matters of Sir Beves and Palamon, the magnitude of the trials of the two knights is of a very different order. Similarly Sir Beves' heroic response to the seven-year trial and the valorous acts by which he gained his freedom are in sharpest contrast to Palamon's reaction to his plight and the manner of his escape from it. Finally, if we contrast Arcite's use of disguise at Theseus' court with that of Sir Beves at King Yvor's court, we find Arcite merely fulfilling his lovesick desire to be near Emelye, whereas Sir Beves' subterfuge is a planned preliminary to carrying off the willing Josian.

More fundamental, perhaps, is the similarity between *The Knight's Tale* and *Sir Beves of Hamtoun* in the matter of the heroes' very personal devotion to the heroines and the large degree of direct action in the poems which stems from this. Neither Sir Perceval the younger nor Libeaus Desconus has any personal acquaintance at all with Lufamour or Sinadoun. Instead they have commitments transmitted by third persons that the beleaguered ladies will marry them when the knights relieve them of existing perils. Nonetheless, when the couples meet at the point of successful conclusion of the quests, they obligingly fall deeply in love. But King Horn and Sir Beves have personal commitments from their lemmans at the outset of those quests which in all ways involve the love complexes. Also, while Rymenhild is not directly involved in the major events of Horn's quest, Josian is very much an active participant in Sir Beves' principal quests from the moment she appears in the poem. We are therefore constantly reminded of the essentially personal nature of Sir Beves' love for Josian, despite the superimposed condition of virginity as a *sine qua non* for its eventual fruition through marriage. The nature of Sir Beves' devotion to Josian is, of course, dramatically confirmed at the end of the romance—he is unable to live without her. It is this kind of male devotion which is ostensibly expressed in *The Knight's Tale* by the avowals and acts of Palamon and Arcite; but the parallels, when seen in terms of the *whole* love complex of *The Knight's Tale*, practically disappear.

Fundamental as the similarities between the two poems may seem in these respects, the basic *emotional* difference in the relationship between Emelye and her would-be paramours and Josian and Sir Beves' relationship reveals that the resemblance is apparent rather than real. For if Palamon and Arcite are prepared to risk their lives over their devotion to Emelye (albeit always within the too elaborately defined conditions dictated by the conventions of their social environment), the goal of this extravagant emotional display is psychologically nonexistent. She is not attainable emotionally, whereas Josian as a goal of a quest is not only clearly eager to consummate her love for Sir Beves but is also emotionally already attained as a goal. Hence Sir Beves' romantic quest and his eventual *Liebestod* are completely sound psychologically (granted, of course, the conventions of romantic love), while Emelye's emotional sterility renders Arcite's and Palamon's love stories psychologically unsound and correspondingly unconvincing within the same convention.

It is primarily Emelye's emotional sterility which serves as a measure of the differences in elements of style between *The Knight's Tale* and *Sir Beves of Hamtoun*. If we fail to discover in *Sir Beves of Hamtoun* the superbly crafted realism so characteristic of Chaucer's poetic style, we nevertheless find blunt realism which, from time to time, seems to serve the poet chiefly as a means of conveying motivation in an extremely economical manner. The passages quoted are typical of this stylistic characteristic. The poet's stylistic approach to Sir Beves' mother and Josian is as bluntly realistic as his portrayal of Sir Beves in battle. We seek in vain for the clearly conveyed nuance or sensitivity to feminine psychology which is so much a part of Chaucer's artistry. The result, naturally enough, is that the women in the love complex of *Sir Beves of Hamtoun* are portrayed not only as originators and aggressors in love matters but also as performers of decisive physical acts that are usually left to the male heroes or malefactors in the romances hitherto considered. In these conclusive respects they are indeed very different from Emelye.

Josian at least differs from Emelye in another respect, for in one of the poem's minor inconsistencies she takes part in a delightfully unique episode—one which has no counterpart in any of the romances Chaucer alludes to in *Sir Thopas*. This is the quarrel between herself and Sir Beves when she first tells him of her great love and then calls him a churl for refusing to marry her merely because of his protestations of low rank (1089-1124). Sir Beves replies to the effect that he really comes from the best of blood lines and furiously rides off, vowing he will never see her again (1125-34). Josian soon seizes an opportunity to apologize, and the two confess their mutual, undying love (1179-1200). This thoroughly human lovers' quarrel is atypical of the poet's approach to both Josian and Sir Beves in general and stands out the more as a result. It is obviously totally uncharacteristic of any element of the love complex in *The Knight's Tale*.

While there is much stark, realistic brevity of style in *Sir Beves of Hamtoun*, there is also a good deal of vagueness in the poet's treatment of a number of important concepts, and this gives rise to inconsistencies similar to those of the other romances under discussion. Typical of these is Josian's virginal state after seven years of marriage to King Yvor; the poet concentrates so heavily on this highly desirable condition throughout the poem that we are amazed to find it airily dismissed with merely the statement—in all but one version—that she preserved it by some undisclosed charm. At first, when Yvor is thrown by Arondel, it is implied that his injuries are fatal. But he lives to fight Sir Beves years later, and in any case Josian is clearly still married to Yvor when Sir Beves carries her off. This kind of inconsistency, of course, is nowhere found in Chaucer's careful, realistic approach to his material in *The Knight's Tale*.

The last metrical romance from the list in Chaucer's *Sir Thopas* which remains to be discussed is *Guy of Warwick*. Of the five mentioned this is the longest by some seven thousand lines.[13] While we have met with most of its fundamental material in the same or different forms in one or another of the four romances so far considered, three important matters are distinctly different. First, from the very beginning it is clear that Guy's origin is not noble; he is the son of the Earl of Rohaud's steward. This state of affairs is directly related to the treatment afforded Guy by the heroine early in the poem, and as a result we see her embodying very different and more carefully delineated personality traits at the beginning of the quest than our other heroines. Later in the poem she becomes a more conventional participant in the love complex. Finally, this romance is even more pronouncedly Christian than *Sir Beves of Hamtoun*. In fact, after all the magnificently surmounted trials of his impressive seven-year quest, Sir Guy spends only a matter of days in wedded bliss with Felice la Belle before departing upon a lifetime pilgrimage.

Felice, the lovely daughter of the Earl of Rohaud, is portrayed in great detail as the most intellectually accomplished lady in the land. She has spurned all suitors, for she finds none worthy of her. When young Guy, handsome, accomplished, and beloved cupbearer to his lord, is called upon to serve the haughty beauty in her chambers, he falls hopelessly in love. For some days he suffers the pangs of his malady, much as Arcite and Palamon suffer in *The Knight's Tale*. While the poems differ in this matter perhaps chiefly in that Guy's torments are motivated by a heroine whose personality and accomplishments are fully treated, another striking

contrast is the decisive action Guy takes to help himself. Moreover, his is a private sorrow—it is not bruited about. For many
years no one but Felice is aware of it. Fearing his hopes will be
dashed, he nevertheless confesses his love to Felice, who unhesitat-
ingly threatens him with drawing and quartering for presuming
to seek her love—his rank is too shockingly low.

After a few more days of agony, Guy returns in desperation to
plead his suit again. This time Felice points out that he is ignoring
her command to cease annoying her, thereby making a fool of
himself; by way of acknowledgment of his attentions, she will take
pleasure in having her father hang him for her. When Guy insists
he would welcome such an end to his present condition of unrequited love, she softens enough to tell him she could never
love one of his rank. He should therefore try to get himself
knighted and become famous for deeds of valor; then she will
grant him her love. This Guy does, vanquishing many mighty
knights, kings, and emperors of France, and receiving offers of
love and marriage from lovely ladies.

But when Guy returns to Felice, she informs him that her
unequivocal condition for marriage (although by now Guy is
somewhat dear to her) is that Guy must become the most renowned,
noble, and valorous knight in the entire world. Guy then departs
upon the familiar seven-year quest, performing deeds throughout
the medieval world which make his name and noble valor the
glory of the godly and the terror of the heathen and other wicked
wights everywhere. His strongest temptation in love lasts an entire
year, just before his triumphant return to England, when he nearly
allows himself to love and marry a beautiful, wealthy, and grateful
princess who is deeply enamoured of him. He finally tears himself
away and returns home to Felice. They are married in a grand
ceremony, and the wedding celebration lasts a fortnight.

These events comprise approximately the first two-thirds of the
poem. Sir Guy's pilgrimage—which frequently takes on all the
important aspects of another greatly lengthened quest—and his
and Felice's deaths take up the remaining four thousand lines.
Guy of Warwick does not differ fundamentally from the other
four romances in terms of its quest and duration complex, but it
deals with these matters much more elaborately. Although Sir
Guy overcomes giants, dragons, monsters, and all manner of human malefactors, much as Sir Perceval the younger, Libeaus Des-

conus, King Horn, or Sir Beves do, he is often accompanied by loyal and redoubtable brother knights. Accordingly, the descriptions of combat often involve considerable attention to the knightly prowess of all the "good" knights. Moreover, Sir Guy takes the oath of brotherhood with the valiant but usually unlucky Sir Tirri, and often is called upon to alleviate his sworn brother's misfortunes. At times, too, some minor attention is given to political and even individual psychological motivation behind the royal or imperial warring in which Sir Guy takes part. These are the principal factors which account for the relatively greater length of *Guy of Warwick*.

It is true that the quest and duration complex has external similarities to that of *The Knight's Tale*, but like those of the romances discussed earlier, Sir Guy's seven-year trial is far more heroic in its nature and outcome than Palamon's and Arcite's. The Christian elements in the poem are much like those in *Sir Beves of Hamtoun*, except that there is no obvious intent on the poet's part to make the poem a religious polemic. In the latter third of the poem, in fact, the Christian aspects of Sir Guy's pilgrimage approach superficiality. He is constantly doffing his humble pilgrim's garb and mien to battle for Tirri, for a former friend, or for an unfortunate knight or king. The distinction between the earlier quest and the actual pilgrimage, for all practical purposes, is that in the former he sought the human prize of Felice, while in the latter he undertook to do good deeds in the name of God.

Felice's character and personality differentiate her clearly from Rymenhild, Lufamour, Sinadoun, or Josian, so far as the early part of the poem's love complex is concerned. If her attitude to Guy's original protestations of love is both frigidly and angrily hostile by turns, she gradually allows herself to encourage him as her demands are met. By the end of his quest, she confesses she has turned down many a royal suitor in his favor and is deeply, irrevocably in love with him. From this point onward in the poem she becomes the ideal heroine of romance. Felice and Guy are so happy to be wed at last, the poet tells us, that she conceives a son on their wedding night. As a personality she is the most fully treated of all the heroines here discussed, but the detail applies almost entirely to the account of her education, a few comments on her beauty, and her two long dialogues with Guy—all of which take place within the first few hundred lines of the poem. She is completely different from Emelye in terms of her personality and consequent reactions to the prospect of marriage as well as in the fullness of treatment accorded her by the poet. Upon Sir Guy's departure on his pilgrimage for the rest of his life, which takes place fifteen days after the wedding, Felice devotes herself entirely to charitable works. She sees Sir Guy again only as he dies in her arms and in a fortnight joins him in death. The poem's ending is accordingly reminiscent of that of *Sir Beves of Hamtoun* —an almost perfect example of romantic idealism.

Stylistically, there are traces here of the careful psychological detail so typical of Chaucer's poetry. As is true of the other four romances, however, when the poet waxes realistic, it is with a bluntness that frequently strips the events and characters concerned of psychological believability. Thus we are told of Felice's unique education and learning and what amounts to her nobility of soul, only to find this inconsistent with the manner of her early refusal of Guy:

> 'Guye,' quoth Felice, 'thou doost folie:
> Woll thou for my loue dye?
> After my fader y woll sende,
> And telle him euery worde to the ende,
> That thou him doost grete disworship
> Whan thou desirest my shenship;
> In this Courte he shall dampne the
> Highe to hange, to please me.   (629-36)

I submit that this kind of inconsistency might be found in Chaucer's poetry only when he had a specific purpose in mind, such as the "gentil" tercelet's comments analyzed in Chapter II. I find no trace of humor or satire in the substance of either *Sir Beves of Hamtoun* or *Guy of Warwick*, and whatever inconsistencies are not absorbed by the reliance upon supernatural phenomena are simply ignored. In any case, there is no fundamental resemblance in style between *The Knight's Tale* and *Guy of Warwick*.

Finally, much might be said against comparing *The Knight's Tale* with the minstrel romances which Chaucer satirized in *Sir Thopas*. Yet if we turn to the classical romance or to the medieval romances of significant literary stature, the very different evidence leads us to essentially the same conclusions. Thus Statius' *Thebaid*, Boccaccio's *La Teseida*, and Chaucer's *The Knight's Tale* are almost literally worlds apart. The Statius is a classical epic, the Boccaccio is in one dimension an Italian Renaissance *court* love affair in which the slightness of subject matter and Emilia's character do not warrant Boccaccio's imitations of epic stylistic paraphernalia, and Chaucer's poem is a medieval work of artistic and philosophic character entirely different from either of the others. The Orpheus of classical antiquity is no more the medieval character in *Sir Orfeo* than Chaucer's Theseus is the mystic superhuman of classical legend and poetry. The transfer of classical iconography to medieval Christian associative doctrine—whether the parallels were real or only imputed—had become a tradition by Chaucer's time, as Professor D. W. Robertson has recently pointed out. The Old French *Eneas* reflects the same phenomenon.

Chaucer was not unique, of course, in his treatment of serious subject matter in the metrical romance genre with lightness, humor, or satire. Chrétien's *Cligés*[14] or Jean de Meun's cynical antifeminist satire in the *Roman de la Rose* are cases in point. But no medieval poem which even approaches the importance of *The Knight's Tale* reflects such effective satirization of the literary forms in which the chivalric material had appeared for so long. Finally, such matters as the treatment of the quest concept and the characterization of the heroines in such works, as compared to their counterparts in *The Knight's Tale*, enable us to form the same conclusions as obtain with the minstrel romances I have considered in detail here. Thus Soredamors in *Cligés*, Guinevere in Chrétien's *Chevalier de la charette*—indeed, as she appears in virtually all versions of the Arthurian romances—and Morgan la Fey in *Sir Gawain and the Green Knight* are developed far more fully as medieval love objects of various kinds. Time sequences and the nature of the quests themselves in these works are almost without exception conspicuous examples of the traditions of literary chivalry. The characterizations and performances of their heroes may be similarly contrasted with the extravagant deficiencies of Palamon and Arcite.

Turning briefly to courtly love or, more properly, certain of its literary aspects which impinge upon my investigation of *The Knight's Tale*, one finds a more clear-cut situation than obtains with the metrical romance. Although we may be in doubt as to the extent of Chaucer's work with that most popular of all the courtly allegories, the *Roman de la Rose*, we have his own word for it

that he was one of its translators. The goddess of Love rebukes
the unhappy Chaucer in *The Legend of Good Women*:

> Thow art my mortal fo and me werreyest,
> And of myne olde servauntes thow mysseyest,
> And hynderest hem with thy translacyoun,
> And lettest folk to han devocyoun
> To serven me, and holdest it folye
> To truste on me. Thow mayst it nat denye,
> For in pleyn text, it nedeth nat to glose,
> Thow hast translated the Romauns of the Rose,
> That is an heresye ageyns my lawe,
> And makest wise folk fro me withdrawe;
> And thynkest in thy wit, that is ful col,
> That he nys but a verray propre fol
> That loveth paramours, to harde and hote. (G text, 248-60)

I think there can be no reasonable doubt that Chaucer was
referring here to that portion of Jean de Meun's 18,000-line extension of Guillaume de Lorris' original fragment wherein woman
is mercilessly satirized as an object unworthy of courtly love or
of any other idealistic consideration. As Professor Robinson points
out, even though there is strong doubt as to whether Chaucer ever
actually translated this portion of the poem, the *Roman de la
Rose* was for Chaucer and his contemporaries "a book of heresy
against the God of Love."[15] Clearly, then, Chaucer here identifies
himself as a transgressor against idealistic love.

Professor D. W. Robertson, Jr.'s recent critical analysis of courtly
love raises rather than settles certain problems which must be
considered;[16] a detailed solution of them must be reserved for a
future study because limitations of space and scope here do not
permit the full exploration they deserve. Surely Professor Robertson's painstaking investigation of Andreas and related sources is
invaluable, but some of his most sweeping conclusions seem to me
untenable. One of his primary assumptions is reflected in virtually
all modern scholarship in this area: that the existence of a "code"
of courtly love must involve flesh-and-blood human beings successfully adhering to its provisons, which in turn must specifically
involve documented criteria. Hence, one must suppose, we find
the widespread concern with the virtually unique *De Amore* and
the literal interpretation of literary models. Indeed, as Professor
Robertson points out, one authority has gone so far as to account

for courtly love at least partly on the basis of an alleged shortage of eligible young ladies. In any case, Professor Robertson's treatment of the works of Andreas, Chrétien, Jean de Meun, Chaucer, and others results in his concluding that, in the first place, "courtly love" is a term coined centuries after the phenomenon it purports to refer to, and that in effect exhaustive research demonstrates very different dimensions of the phenomenon from those often attributed to it. For him it is merely that love which is "for delight," is passionate, and involves a "corruption of the reason . . . thought to be a manifestation of original sin"—especially as it is treated by Andreas.[17] In sum, the peculiar attributes many critics have found characteristic of aristocratic courtly love (courtesy, *morum probitas*, service, professions of adoration, and so on) are mere selfish techniques motivated by guilty passion with the constant object of either simple fornication or some other direct violation of scriptural law.

Furthermore, since the *De Amore* seeks to help the young lover achieve his goal and at the same time "encourage him to be sensible about his problem," it must follow that at least sometimes conscious hypocrisy with relation to Christian theology is involved. (We may assume, then, that the notions of secrecy are manifestations of guilt.) Marriage, for the best of reasons, lends itself to the only love man may properly submit himself to—that ordained in the sacraments, with the act of love completely free of sin only when performed for the purpose of begetting children. For this reason—that is, not because of the binding responsibilities of marriage, but because of the veniality of "love for delight"—"courtly" love and the sacrament of marriage are wholly incompatible.

That this interpretation is substantiated by many medieval moral philosophers Professor Robertson documents superbly; that it is a complete one or the only possible one it is difficult to agree. For it leads, most reasonably, to such conclusions as this: "Although Arcite actually falls into the lover's malady, whereas Absalon only pretends to do so, there is no real difference between the love expressed by Palamon and Arcite on the one hand and that expressed by Nicolas and Absalon on the other. It is, in all of these instances, love 'for delight.' Chaucer has, as it were, played the same 'melodie' in two different keys in the two opening tales of his collection."[18] I trust few of us would wish to equate the conscious desire of Absalon and Nicolas for fornication for its own

sake with the bedsome Alisoun, and the emotions Palamon and
Arcite believe themselves to be experiencing over Emelye. "Love
for delight" in that its object is not divine—yes; but there *are*
"real" differences, surely, in its forms.

I find it impossible to believe that lovers behaved in literal
accordance with so-called courtly love as it has been codified by
such critics as Lewis and Dodd from the many literary models.
No one ever died from the pangs of such an emotion, the direness
of its catalogued symptoms notwithstanding. To cite purported
evidence of its literal existence is to insist that human beings in
fact lived its provisions which, as Professor Robertson points out,
would be a practical impossibility. But to deny its existence as an
ideal on the grounds that documents and some literary manifestations concerning it demonstrate it to be theologically wrong is
going too far. Whether we agree with their conclusions or not,
Dodd and Lewis, among others, have established that at least
some medieval lovers were portrayed in literature as though they
believed themselves to be adhering to an ideal of love sufficiently
codified to be consistently identifiable. If only literary lovers approach the ideal rather than historical ones, this is not to say the
ideal didn't exist. One might as well insist Christianity was nonexistent in Chaucer's time because its adherents in the Christian
world failed to reflect Church doctrine in their actions. But surely
many of them believed in the ideal and, as many do today, tried
to live up to their Christian obligations, often conceiving themselves to be exemplifying the ideal even in the very process of
violating its doctrinal forms.

Let us not eschew the testimony of personal experience in such
matters; many a man must remember a time—alas, long ago in experience if not in years—when the loved object assumed the hues
of what to him now may seem absurd perfection. But it was not
absurd at the time. It is unnecessary to cite instances of what
men and women have performed under the influence of such an
emotion; although it may glorify the self, it often takes the form of
extreme self-sacrifice, and its effects are ennobling in more than a
few of its manifestations. If, as twentieth-century psychologists
maintain, it is merely a response to the reproductive drive, then
one can but say that many of the smitten are unaware of the fact.
I prefer to think that such ignorance on their part need not be
categorized as mere "subconscious" carnality, if indeed our social

scientists are right. We can at least agree that throughout the history of Western civilization man's needs have remained constant, while his means of satisfying them have changed as his culture has changed. We may conclude that for at least some in the medieval era, what we now call courtly love was celebrated as a response in part to the "perfection" attributed to the love object, with the inevitable concomitant assumptions of infinite superiority and virtual unattainability. Thus human beings acting on a basis that the humanly impossible is the only important human reality should be expected to respond with similar contradictions to much that goes on around them.

It will not do to oversimplify the whole matter, as some modern critics do, by maintaining that there were many kinds of "courtly" love, some of which involved marriage, public avowal of the love relationship, and other immoderate extensions of the provisions of the ideal. We are to conclude, according to such a view, that the English poets so interpreted courtly love. We need only consult the literary models which are in fact the source of the ideal to determine that many of the continental poets were as prone to confuse "courtly" and "romantic" love as their English contemporaries. Of the romances considered here, *Sir Perceval of Galles* illustrates the point sufficiently. On the other hand, *Troilus and Criseyde* is one of the most eloquent literary illustrations of the provisions of courtly love. Obviously, within their limits there are variations, but the provisions themselves may be clearly enough defined so that they must be respected if we are to attempt any classification of courtly love at all as a distinct variety of aristocratic emotional experience in medieval literature.

These are some of the problems the solutions of which remain to be substantiated in a forthcoming study. The concept of courtly love embodied here is that of the ideal expressed in terms of the quasi-codification exhaustively developed and carefully demonstrated by Lewis and Dodd particularly. I do not believe that literal adherence to these codified provisions existed outside the literary models. But no doubt in Chaucer's time, as in ours, lovers conceived themselves to be responding to idealistic love in literal accordance with the poetic ideal—mistaking its imaginary provisions for reality and its currency in the minds of their contemporaries for proof of its truth. One cannot doubt that courtly love existed as an ideal, but living in terms of man's codification of it was demonstrably impossible, however hard one may have tried and however successfully one may have deluded himself into believing his actions were in total harmony with it. It seems to me that *The Knight's Tale* demonstrates all these matters very well, for Arcite and Palamon believe themselves to be adhering to the *provisions* of an ideal which cannot be literally adhered to by human beings. Were they appropriate courtly lovers, the "realism" Chaucer has employed in their development would have to be exchanged for another kind of make-believe—the allegory.

In any event, it is scarcely necessary to catalogue the satiric or merely facetious treatment Chaucer so frequently accorded courtly lovers; among the more striking examples are, perhaps, Damian and May's affair in *The Merchant's Tale* and Absalon's priceless performance in *The Miller's Tale*. Lewis' exhaustive researches led him to the conclusion that courtly love involved four major concepts—humility, courtesy, adultery, and the religion of love—together with a host of other necessary conditions of which utter secrecy was paramount.[19] Moreover, since marriage was considered totally incompatible with love, the courtly lover was predestined to woo and win ladies already married. The achieving of his lady's grace, which is to say having a completely and intensely consummated erotic love affair with the lady's joyfully dedicated cooperation, was the conventional reward of the lover who faithfully obeyed the courtly love code. No more convincing evidence of Chaucer's learned familiarity with these matters need be sought than that so obviously presented to us throughout *Troilus and Criseyde*. Even in the early *Anelida and Arcite* fragment the courtly love code is fully treated.

In view of these considerations, it is clear that Emelye is portrayed by Chaucer in *The Knight's Tale* only partially in terms of the courtly love code. Her first appearance in the garden, as I have pointed out, seems more or less to echo the tableau elements of the courtly allegory. In addition, Arcite, Palamon, Theseus, and the Knight himself share the assumption that the "hoote fare" here is courtly love. But this assumption is as much an illusion as Emelye herself, for whatever the oddities of plot we may take for granted in the courtly allegory, the principles of its love complex are as fixed as the quasi-dogma outlined above.

In *The Knight's Tale* the all-important rule of secrecy is not only broken but becomes a travesty in Palamon's inexcusable—from the courtly love standpoint—public outburst. Palamon's and Arcite's object is *marriage*, arranged for them by none other than Theseus, himself a former servant of the god of love! Indeed, far from granting grace to either contender, which is the lady's inviolable prerogative within the courtly love code, Emelye (if we take her characterization literally) regards the whole affair as a prospective, unwelcome assault upon her virginity, and she is not even placed in a position by Chaucer to specify the terms of service of her unwanted "servants." Her response to this, in contrast to the cruel disdain of the ladies who adhere to the courtly love code, is one of graceless surrender to the inevitable. It cannot be maintained that she is merely holding out for a long time in keeping with the noble lady convention. Chaucer, as we shall see, does characterize her to the extent that her reluctance to embrace *any* emotional experience greatly exceeds the aristocratic dissembling to be expected in the earlier stages of a courtly love affair. Indeed, always, if we interpret her literally, her harried suitors could serve her best by doing nothing. Finally, while Palamon and Arcite suffer so insistently that they, too, transcend even the rigorous requirements of courtly lovers in this respect, the code-authorized reward of their lady's grace is never to be theirs. This is, of course, because it must be freely bestowed by the lady, flowing forth from her own freely professed and—eventually—erotically shared love.

There is no room in the complex of courtly love for such heretical violations of its code as these. All motivation for performing knightly prodigies in the fulfillment of courtly love thus disappears. We must therefore conclude that its external elements in *The Knight's Tale* are spun from the gossamer of illusion, since the poem violates essentially all of the most important requisites of courtly love convention.

It is evident, then, that courtly love is not involved in fact in the love complex of *The Knight's Tale*, even though some of its external characteristics are apparent therein. We find also the same situation obtaining with romantic love as it is treated in the representative romances discussed here. Thus in terms of characterization we find the counterparts of Palamon and Arcite in these romances men of decisive action, motivated by the certain goals of requited love, the righting of injustice, and material gain.

Emelye's and Theseus' counterparts are even more decisively in psychological contrast with one another. If Sir Guy's Felice seems

atypical of heroines of metrical romances at first and correspondingly closer to Emelye, she eventually falls in love with Sir Guy
and in every other respect fills in the mold of the ideal romantic
love goal. Felice's inconsistency lies in her original crude resemblance to the lady of courtly love evolving into the conventional
heroine of metrical romance—a mixture which does not become
an artistic amalgam. Emelye is neither the heroine of courtly
love allegory nor the loving affianced of romance. In the romances
the ultimate royal authorities, while hazy in outline in *Sir Beves
of Hamtoun* and *Guy of Warwick*, take the love complexes with
uncompromising seriousness in contrast to Theseus' public levity.
In terms of the quest and duration complex, external resemblances
between the romances and *The Knight's Tale* are insignificant
when we examine the nature of the quests themselves and the
manner of their fulfillment, to say nothing of the goals. Only in
The Knight's Tale is the love goal the *sole* purpose of the quest,
and if this reminds us of courtly love rather than romantic love,
we must bear in mind the marriage factor and Emelye's reactions
to the quest's outcome.

Turning to stylistic considerations, while we take for granted
the inconsistencies which seem characteristic of the romance genre,
the elements of realism and psychological believability in *The
Knight's Tale*—which are direct results of Chaucer's poetic style—
so emphasize its inconsistencies as to preclude our taking them for
granted in that poem. Moreover, the kinds of inconsistencies
involved in *The Knight's Tale* are different from those indigenous
to the romance genre, as I have pointed out earlier in this chapter.
Our conclusion is accordingly unavoidable: *The Knight's Tale* is in
no fundamental way related closely to either the poetry of
courtly love or that of medieval romance, and the love complex
of Chaucer's poem is in reality not that of the courtly allegory nor
the romantic love of the metrical romance.

We have now arrived at the heart of the matter of Chaucer's
ambivalence in *The Knight's Tale*, the central purpose of my
examination of the poem. So far as the traditional point of view is
concerned, we may agree with comments such as those of Professor
Root and give ourselves up to the "spirit of romance," accepting
literally and uncritically the external characteristics of courtly love
and the medieval romance as our criteria of such an appreciation.
But it is now clear that these external characteristics are in fact

fundamental contradictions of the substance of the poem, which accordingly will not bear examination in terms of paradigms of the genres whose qualities it is assumed to reflect. When we couple with this the pervasive humor and satire of Book I, we have convincing evidence even at this relatively early stage that *The Knight's Tale* may also be interpreted as a delightful satire, not only of the characters and social environment portrayed in it but also of the literary genres it ostensibly resembles. Further, the effect of the significant differences between *The Knight's Tale* and its *Teseida* source, some of which were analyzed in the preceding chapter, supports such an interpretation. The remainder of my essay will consist of the consideration of Books II, III, and IV to the end of confirming these findings.

V

book two

Book II of *The Knight's Tale* begins with an account of Arcite's lovesickness which would be positively harrowing were it not for the conclusion of the passage and if his sufferings were not causally rooted in the highly artificial situation obtaining during the last three hundred lines of Book I. We learn that when he arrived home in Thebes from his imprisonment he swooned many times a day because, as the Knight tells us (no doubt with a perfectly straight face), "For seen his lady shal he nevere mo" (1357). Then, in a comparatively subtle use of the *occupatio* rhetorical device which results in the conveyance of both humor and satire, Chaucer has the Knight begin the catalogued account of Arcite's alarming condition, and we are confronted with a host of frightful symptoms. No one recognizes his voice, and his appearance and behavior are those not alone of a sufferer of love's malady but also of a madman. Furthermore, this goes on for "a yeer or two," until Arcite "upon a nyght in sleep as he hym leyde" has a dream in which Mercury appears before him. Arcite, acting on Mercury's advice, immediately leaves for Athens, having looked in a mirror and decided he was so totally changed in appearance he would be unrecognized. Posing as a common worker, he fetches and carries so diligently that he becomes a house servant in Emelye's residence. He has risen to this station in the ranks of the employed because, the Knight says,

Wel koude he hewen wode, and water bere,
For he was yong and *myghty for the nones,*
And therto he was long and big of bones
To doon that any wight kan hym devyse.

(1422-25; italics mine)

These first seventy-five lines of Book II are very closely related in their humor and satire to the long quarrel between Palamon and Arcite as well as to the final events in Book I. In the two young men's argument, something very similar to the *occupatio* device employed here was involved. That is, a potentially endless catalogue of points and counterpoints was brought to an abrupt halt by Arcite's "dog-and-bone" analogy. Here the catalogue of Arcite's woes comes to an equally abrupt halt with the account of Mercury's appearance before him in his sleep. The immediate reactions of the individuals involved in these two situations are much the same in that they are direct departures from what we might expect in view of what has led up to them. Thus Arcite's analogy, far from being acted upon by both young men in terms of its perfectly sound reasoning, results in their actually intensifying their quarrel by absurdly misinterpreting its unmistakable implications. Similarly, we would hardly expect Arcite's lurid deterioration, presented to us as a matter of fact by the Knight, to cease immediately after he hastily proceeds to Athens. Even if we were to take all this literally, it is impossible to escape the fact that Arcite's situation with regard to winning Emelye is not one whit changed, nor does he intend to try to change it. The humorous effects of the "dog-and-bone" section of Book I are similar to those resulting from the ending of the *occupatio* section of Book II under discussion here, except that we now have no less than two direct contradictions.

Chaucer, through the Knight's shockingly detailed first and second narrative devices, informs us that Arcite simply cannot sleep at all. We may well decide, in assessing this and other similar statements which are presented as matters of fact, that this is hardly likely to be the case for the duration of "a yeer or two." Nevertheless, we are scarcely prepared for a direct contradiction within twenty-three lines! Moreover the contradiction is emphasized so strongly and in such a manner that it is hard to believe it is not purposive on Chaucer's part. Perhaps lest we err in assuming that Arcite's dream of Mercury came to him in a swoon or possibly even a lover's daydream, it is spelled out for us with unmistakable precision that it occurred when Arcite was *asleep*! Even the word "dream" seems to be carefully avoided:

> Upon a nyght in sleep as he hym leyde,
> Hym thoughte how that the wynged god Mercurie
> Biforn hym stood and bad hym to be murie.   (1384-86)

Upon awakening Arcite clearly takes all of Mercury's advice, ostensibly even the "be murie" portion of it. If we care to consider this matter from a logical standpoint (and by his insistent collection of evidence pertaining to Arcite's condition, the Knight reminds us of Palamon's reasoning in the argument of Book I), we are confronted with the obvious fallacy of contradictory assumptions. That is, Arcite cannot be "biraft" of sleep and see Mercury in his sleep. From the standpoint of the properties of Chaucer's humor and satire analyzed in Chapter II, it is clear that the material immediately surrounding the passage cited above is such that the incongruity is heavily emphasized; its context is a logical one. In these respects, therefore, its humor is like that of the selections from *The Nun's Priest's Tale* and *The Knight's Tale* (wherein the Knight comments on the disposition of Arcite's soul), considered in Chapter II (classifications 1 and 2). The humor also resolves a situation which would perhaps be difficult to manage if the same approach to it were maintained as that in its preceding context; hence this passage is in this respect, too, like the Knight's account of the whereabouts of Arcite's soul and Theseus' extended address examined in Chapter II.

While I have described the context surrounding this contradiction as a logical one, I mean this in a relative sense only—all of the material embraced by the *occupatio* device consistently conveys the severity of Arcite's sufferings. If, however, we compare it with corresponding situations in romance or courtly allegory, we find that it amounts to a gross exaggeration of the love complaint convention. Even in *Troilus and Criseyde*, while Troilus endures the conventionalized agony of the courtly lover, the goal of these sufferings is the winning of Criseyde, who cooperates properly in accordance with the courtly love code. She is throughout the "wooing" portion of the poem a paradigm of motivation for the courtly lover. Emelye obviously is not, by any stretch of the imagination, the courtly allegorical heroine to furnish the necessary erotic motivation or soul-fulfilling reward for either Arcite's or Palamon's love torture.

By way of contrast, the inconsolable knight in *The Book of the Duchess* has the irrevocable loss of his lady as the firm courtly love foundation for his grief. Chaucer's use of the courtly allegory for such a purpose in this early work is certainly a bold departure from medieval poetic precedents, but it is very much in harmony with the fundamental conventions of the genre.

A more tangible measure of the unwarranted exaggeration of Arcite's pains—and, of course, those of Palamon as well—is the time element. Troilus, for example, does not suffer nearly as long during his wooing of Criseyde, if only as a result of Pandarus' sometimes hilarious activities as a one-man ways and means committee. In *The Merchant's Tale*, Damian's comparable condition also is soon alleviated. Yet Arcite's most extreme symptoms continue for "a yeer or two" (actually two years), while Palamon's acute phase of the same illness continues for all of seven years! Moreover, neither young knight has the faintest intention of making any specific effort to woo Emelye. Of the romances here considered only *Guy of Warwick* is in any way comparable; young Guy survives two attacks of similar lovesickness, but each lasts only for a matter of days. Furthermore, he presses his suit and almost immediately is able to achieve Felice's firm agreement on the conditions of wooing and winning her. His seven years are therefore largely a recital of heroic steps toward his specified goal, while his year of indecision in matters of love hinges only upon the quandary of which willing lady he will choose. It is clear, then, that Arcite's sufferings, no less than those of Palamon, are grossly and unwarrantably exaggerated within the literary conventions that traditional critics maintain are implicit in the poem.

The second contradiction is contained in lines 1422-25, which I have quoted above. Serving at the palace gate as a common carrier, Arcite immediately achieves his conspicuously unheroic goal:

> And shortly of this matere for to seyn,
> He fil in office with a chamberleyn
> The which that dwellynge was with Emelye;   (1417-19)

Two lines after this comes the passage quoted earlier, in which I have italicized the contradiction.

The contradiction here is even more strongly emphasized contextually than the one involving Arcite's sleepless state. In the Knight's detailed list of Arcite's symptoms at the beginning of this section of Book II, the appearance of his visage and the thinness of his body are linked together, along with his many other ills (1361-82). Hence when Arcite takes up his mirror and we are again vouchsafed an account of his facial appearance, his total bodily condition in effect is likewise being re-emphasized— we have no reason at all to believe they are no longer linked with each other. He is so changed in appearance, then, that he succeeds in remaining unknown in Athens for years. We are therefore justifiably startled to find that almost immediately upon his arrival "the nexte way" in Athens he is an exemplary physical specimen, "yong and myghty for the nones," although apparently his face remains marked by the effects of his love-malady.

So far as structural and contextual matters are concerned, then, this contradiction shares the same humorous and satiric properties as the selection from *The Nun's Priest's Tale* and the Knight's account of the disposition of Arcite's soul, analyzed in Chapter II (classifications 1 and 2). But unlike the contradiction involving Arcite's sleepless state, the resolving of a situation otherwise difficult to manage does not seem to be involved here. It is, indeed, a gratuitous inappropriateness ignored by the Knight. The inappropriate is treated as appropriate, and this glaring inconsistency as well as that involving Arcite's sleepless state share the same fundamental satiric properties as the descriptions of the Monk and Friar in the *General Prologue*, analyzed in Chapter II.

In one respect, both Arcite's and Palamon's lives from the time Arcite is released from prison until Theseus arranges for the grand lists are similar. Despite the marked external differences in their plights, at the end of the seven years neither one is nearer than the other to winning Emelye. Both suffer mightily, and if Palamon is unable to woo his lady from his dungeon, it never occurs to Arcite that he himself is one whit better off. Arcite, then, spends his first two years of freedom in violent lovesickness, the next two years as a humble page in the same household in which Emelye lives, and the final three years as Theseus' squire. As the Knight tells us, he does his very best to make a good impression on all the court and is well thought of by Theseus; each year he receives his income from Thebes, which he is careful to spend unostentatiously. During the five years he is in Athens, Arcite as a matter of course retains his disguise.

As Professor Robinson points out, Arcite's pseudonym—Philostrate—Chaucer took from Boccaccio's *Filostrato*. Its proper meaning derived from the original Greek is "army lover," but Boccaccio evidently understood it to mean "vanquished by love" as a result of connecting the second element with the Latin "stratus."[1] It never occurs to Arcite during this entire period to attempt to woo Emelye in any way—his ambitions rise no higher than being able to look at her from time to time. All things considered, by no stretch of the imagination can Arcite be described as a courtly, heroic, or valorous lover in terms of the courtly allegory or medieval romance genres. Leaving Arcite "in this blisse"—yet another contradiction which becomes clear only after Arcite's song —the Knight returns to Palamon.

Palamon, of course, is no more heroic during these seven years than Arcite, although Palamon's tribulations are admittedly much more severe:

> In derknesse and horrible and strong prisoun
> Thise seven yeer hath seten Palamoun
> Forpyned, what for wo and for distresse.
> Who feeleth double soor and hevynesse
> But Palamon, that love destreyneth so
> That wood out of his wit he goth for wo?
> And eek therto he is a prisoner
> Perpetuelly, noght oonly for a yer. (1451-58)

This passage—particularly the redundancy of the last line—reminds us once again of the delightful, literal-minded naïveté of the narrator from whose selective view this tale is presented to us. The Knight goes on to state that he is not the man who is able to "ryme in Englyssh proprely" Palamon's martyrdom (1459-60)! I am reminded by a colleague that the notion of Palamon as a martyr, stoically welcoming the divinely ordained rigors of authentic persecution, is so delightfully and obviously incongruous as to need no discussion. Chaucer then briefly launches into a superbly crafted change of style, in effect creating a relief from the Knight's first and second narrative devices almost exclusively employed up to this point in Book II. The change is prepared for by the Knight's rhetorical question in line 1456, which is a mild depar-

ture from the matter-of-factness of its preceding context. Within
a half-dozen lines the Knight's third narrative device appears, as
he interprets the nature of destiny for us:

> It fel that in the seventhe yer, of May
> The thridde nyght, (as olde bookes seyn,
> That al this storie tellen moore pleyn)
> Were it by aventure or destynee—
> As, whan a thyng is shapen, it shal be—
> That soone after the mydnyght Palamoun,
> By helpyng of a freend, brak his prisoun
> And fleeth the citee faste as he may go.   (1462-69)

It is barely possible that the reference to authority here is not as
conventional as it seems at first glance; the Knight's protests are
perhaps suspiciously in accord with the truth. *The Knight's Tale*
is a very different poem indeed than its legendary and literary
sources might be expected by the literal-minded to inspire. In any
case, there is a suggestion of yet another contradiction in this
passage: "aventure" can scarcely account for Palamon's obviously
carefully planned and aided escape, and if "destynee" is responsible, it is certainly operating in a peculiarly human way!

Palamon hides timidly in a nearby grove ("With dredeful foot
thanne stalketh Palamon"), and thus ends his seven years of
imprisonment during which his overwhelming concern (re-emphasized in line 1455) has been a hopeless love for someone he
has seen only occasionally at a distance and who is totally unaware
of him. Comparing his trials and his response to them and the
manner of his escape from prison to the corresponding seven-
year experience undergone by Sir Beves, for example, we find no
grounds for ascribing any form of knightly fortitude or heroism to
Palamon.

On a less sweeping scale it is also significant from the standpoints of satire and humor that now Palamon himself plans to make
his way by night to Thebes, gather an army, and make war upon
Theseus in an effort to win Emelye or die in the attempt. Inevitably we are reminded of the paradoxical situation at the end
of Book I as Palamon and Arcite envy each other's lot. Obviously
what Palamon now plans to do and assumed Arcite would do
some seven years before contrasts sharply with Arcite's unheroic
activities—he has been in fact as inactive as the imprisoned Pala-

mon. Thus the paradox is now complete and shares the humorous
and satiric qualities I have ascribed to its original appearance at
the end of Book I.

The Knight's description of the dawn and early morning seems
to be an echo of that other May morning, long ago in Book I,
when Emelye was so idealistically blended with the idyllic beauty
of the flower garden. Here Chaucer's Knight blends Arcite with
the lovely English May as Arcite arises, and to pay his respects to
this lovers' season, "Remembrynge on the poynt of his desir," leaps
on a fiery courser and rides off in the fields to "pleye" (1488-
1503). Never one to bask in his own emotions in silence if he
can help it, Arcite turns his literal mind to the task of composing
a song expressive of his reaction to the beauty of nature surrounding him ("And loude he song ayeyn the sonne shene") after
arriving at the crucial grove. The lovely gaiety of the preceding
poetry is then shattered by this raucous bit of doggerel straight
from Arcite's creative soul:

> "May, with alle thy floures and thy grene,
> Welcome be thou, faire, fresshe May,
> In hope that I som grene gete may."   (1510-12)

Obviously the humor here is heavily emphasized in that it is
decidedly incongruous with its stylistic context and is structurally
stressed. Of the several selections analyzed in Chapter II whose
humorous properties this brief passage shares, the most obvious
one is that from the prologue to *The Miller's Tale*, originally cited
by Ewald (classification 2). Even more striking, of course, is the
relatively rare *rime riche*, here employed by Chaucer in such a
manner as to convey the effect of humorous word-play in an
Elizabethan sense, for "May" is certainly a pun, the effect of which
is magnified by the *rime riche* technique. The word-play involving
"grene" is particularly effective humor partly because Arcite is so
patently unaware of it.° Hence this passage also shares those

---

°The word-play throughout the passage is particularly significant in that
so far as I know it is the earliest literary instance of the use of "grene" in this
sense. Yet in this context it is unmistakable. Thus the initial "May" is, of
course, a double entendre for "Maid" or "Maiden" and the multiple play
on "grene" embraces the season's color and freshness, the youthful freshness
of a young girl, and, finally, the incongruously vulgar reference to the
physical aftermath of a virgin maiden's first sexual experience. Even though
the *OED* places the earliest literary allusions to this folk belief much later

properties of equivocation common to the "gentil" tercelet selection from *The Parliament of Fowls* and related examples, analyzed in Chapter II (classification 3).

The fearful Palamon, watching from his hiding place, fails to recognize Arcite, whereupon:

> Whan that Arcite hadde romed al his fille,
> And songen al the roundel lustily,
> Into a studie he fil sodeynly,
> As doon thise loveres in hir queynte geres,
> Now in the crope, now doun in the breres,
> Now up, now doun, as boket in a welle.
> Right as the Friday, soothly for to telle,
> Now it shyneth, now it reyneth faste,
> Right so kan geery Venus overcaste
> The hertes of hir folk; right as hir day
> Is gereful, right so chaungeth she array.
> Selde is the Friday al the wowke ylike.   (1528-39)

Since the Knight's usual formality of style is employed by Chaucer throughout this section of the poem up to Arcite's outburst quoted above, this passage is obviously another example of stylistic juxtaposition. Its humorous and satiric effects are therefore derived in the same manner as those of the stylistic juxtaposition in Arcite's soliloquy at the end of Book I, discussed in Chapter III.

The first part of Arcite's complaint is part and parcel of the satiric substance of *The Knight's Tale*—a theme which has had many variations thus far in the poem. Arcite at last sees himself for a moment or two as a man rather than an unrequited lover:

---

than Chaucer, the Middle English "grenehede" is used by Chaucer elsewhere as "wantonness" in the modern sense of the word (see Walter W. Skeat, *The Student's Chaucer,* Glossarial Index, p. 50). Further, green was the color of inconstancy. Chaucer's puns are few and far between, although perhaps there are more than many of us suspect. Here their effects complement the stylistic juxtaposition by an extended and decisively abrupt change in approach to Arcite's much vaunted "idealistic" love for Emelye. The shift from the noble images of the charging courser and wooded grove in all its May beauty to those of the lowest peasant vulgarities is swift and devastating in its clarity. Yet unmistakable as the word-play seems, when the passage is closely examined, it is very subtly executed—so subtly that the literal-minded simply fail to perceive it. This is highly sophisticated poetic technique. As a link in the evidence of Chaucer's artistic ambivalence in *The Knight's Tale,* it seems irrefutable.

> Of his [Cadmus'] lynage am I and his ofspryng
> By verray ligne, as of the stok roial,
> And now I am so caytyf and so thral,
> That he that is my mortal enemy,
> I serve hym as his squier povrely.   (1550-54)

Thus although he blames Juno and Mars for the fall of Thebes and his family in a general sense, it is clear that even in his own eyes Arcite's behavior through these years is scarcely that of a valorous royal knight.

The last part of the complaint is another installment of Arcite's love misery, replete with such alarming symptoms that he expects death momentarily, and he concludes (somewhat absurdly, in view of the preceding part of his complaint):

> Of al the remenant of myn oother care
> Ne sette I nat the montance of a tare,
> So that I koude doon aught to youre [Emelye's]
>   plesaunce."   (1569-71)

The entire song is a contradiction of line 1449, wherein the Knight has said, "And in this blisse lete I now Arcite." Obviously Arcite's life during his years in Athens is by no means blissful—he is always falling into these states "as doon thise loveres in hir queynte geres." As a contradiction, its humor and satire are derived in the same manner as those of the two direct contradictions considered earlier in this chapter. But there is another dimension to the humor of this implied contradiction; it also is an equivocation of concepts, sharing in this respect the same properties as the false analogy in the selection from *The Parliament of Fowls* originally studied by Ewald, analyzed in Chapter II (classification 3).

There is yet another contradiction at this point, for no sooner has Arcite uttered the last word of his song when, "And with that word he fil doun in a traunce/ A longe tyme, and after he up sterte" (1572-73). But at the same time, Palamon, when he had heard Arcite's tale, "As he were wood, with face deed and pale,/ He stirte hym up out of the buskes thikke" (1578-79). Since he immediately begins his verbal castigation of his "felawe," it is clear that no "long tyme" has elapsed for Arcite's trance or swoon to pass. This, too, shares the same humorous and satiric properties as the more obvious contradictions considered earlier in this chapter.

As we know, after Arcite's release from prison, Palamon was able to discern knightly qualities in his cousin (1285-93). Now, however, he reverts to his earlier opinion of Arcite's character:

> . . . "Arcite, false traytour wikke,
> Now artow hent, that lovest my lady so,
> For whom that I have al this peyne and wo,
> And art my blood, and to my conseil sworn,
> As I ful ofte have told thee heerbiforn,
> And hast byjaped heere duc Theseus,
> And falsly chaunged hast thy name thus!   (1580-86)

Thus Palamon is still interpreting the symmetrical relationship established by his and Arcite's oath of brotherhood as an asymmetrical relationship, giving rise to the same humorous and satiric effects as in its original appearance in Book I, analyzed in Chapter III. This time, too, Palamon is guilty of the very matter of which he accuses Arcite, since he himself has "byjaped" Theseus by escaping from his prison.

Characteristically, Palamon castigates the only aspect of Arcite's behavior as a royal Theban that we would expect another royal Theban to find thoroughly praiseworthy. Anti-Theseus activity would appear to be a duty rather than a misdemeanor. Palamon overlooks the real issue in Arcite's situation—that he has failed to wage war on Theseus and fulfill the proper knightly role of military royalty. Arcite's disguise is of course unheroic but surely not immoral with respect to Theseus. Yet Palamon persists in this naïvely mistaken view which amounts to a feeling of obligation to Theseus, whose "tyrannye" both have to thank for their original ransomless imprisonment. Palamon carries it to the most illogical extreme possible when he later reveals Arcite's identity to Theseus and characterizes his own escape from prison as an act worthy of severe disapprobation. Certainly no provisions of chivalric or courtly love could be interpreted in such a way that either Palamon's or Arcite's acts at this point in the poem could be described as immoral with reference to any knightly obligation to Theseus.

Palamon next manages to entangle himself in what can perhaps best be described as a triply fallacious logical quagmire. Having vehemently asserted that Arcite is not to love Emelye and that he himself has no weapon, he neatly combines the *argumentum ad baculum* and confident-manner fallacies in no more than three lines:

I drede noght that outher thow shalt dye,
Or thow ne shalt nat loven Emelye.
Chees which thou wolt, for thou shalt nat asterte!" (1593-95)

Hence Palamon has appealed to force rather than reason to per-
suade Arcite that he should cease loving the beauteous Emelye,
but in fact he lacks the force to fulfill his threat. Moreover, in
spite of all this he is still confident he will slay Arcite. Such
confidence in the face of a furious Arcite who himself is armed
with a sword is patently absurd, the more so since Palamon is
aware of at least one of the pertinent factors which nullify both
his threat and any reasonable chance of his carrying it out.

Arcite, having made it clear that he refrains from killing Palamon
then and there only because Palamon is mad with love as well as
weaponless, openly disavows their oath of brotherhood—for "love
is free." He offers to

... bryngen harneys right ynough for thee;
And ches the beste, and leef the worste for me.
And mete and drynke this nyght wol I brynge
Ynough for thee, and clothes for thy beddynge.
And if so be that thou my lady wynne,
And sle me in this wode ther I am inne,
Thow mayst wel have thy lady as for me."
This Palamon answerde, "I graunte it thee." (1613-20)

Thus Palamon, whose life is evidently at Arcite's mercy, graciously
grants Arcite the favor of accepting the necessary arms and ameni-
ties from Arcite which will put Arcite's life in jeopardy! Here we
have what amounts to an asymmetrical relationship (Arcite's proposal) being interpreted as a symmetrical relationship by Palamon,
who in reality has no choice. Arcite is dictating terms, not requesting a favor. Since neither contestant perceives the fatuously
unreasonable aspects of his situation and the Knight fails to interpret these matters for us, we must assess these passages ourselves. We find the same properties of humor and satire here as in
the original argument between Palamon and Arcite in Book I,
where Palamon failed to perceive the conclusions his own reasoning clearly indicated, and both young men failed to perceive the
equally inevitable conclusions implicit in Arcite's "dog-and-bone"
analogy.

Another aspect of Arcite's reasoning in this prison argument

leads directly to the idealistic impasse which itself is fallacious
since it is based on the contradictory assumptions within his
argument. Arcite's statement that his "love is free" in line 1606
echoes his fallacious reasoning in the Book I argument. It is clear,
therefore, that not only the central motivation of the entire plot
complex of *The Knight's Tale* is firmly rooted in fallacy, but also
that there is a continuous chain of fallacious reasoning extending
throughout the poem. Obviously this would be necessary in order
to maintain any psychological consistency of character and action
at all, once the fallacious basis of the central motivation was
established.

There is, of course, a parallel to this particular situation in *The
Knight's Tale* to be found in *Sir Thopas*. Sir Thopas "priketh over
stile and stoon" seeking the elf-queen he intends to woo,

> Til that ther cam a greet geaunt,
> His name was sire Olifaunt,
>   A perilous man of dede.
> He seyde, "Child, by Termagaunt!
> But if thou prike out of myn haunt,
>   Anon I sle thy steede
>   With mace.   (807-13)

Undaunted, Sir Thopas replies, just as Palamon replies to Arcite,
as though he were not at all at the giant's mercy:

> The childe seyde, "Also moote I thee,
> Tomorwe wol I meete with thee,
>   Whan I have myn armoure;
> And yet I hope, *par ma fay,*
> That thou shalt with this launcegay
>   Abyen it ful sowre.
>   Thy mawe
> Shal I percen, if I may,
> Er it be fully pryme of day,
>   For heere thow shalt be slawe."   (817-26)

Whereas Palamon presumably relies upon the trusty chivalric code
to deter Arcite from slaying him on the spot, the heroic Sir
Thopas "drow abak ful faste," as the unchivalric giant cast stones
at his fleeing prey. But I submit that the marked similarities to
Arcite and Palamon's situation are not coincidental.

As Palamon and Arcite meet the next morning, the Knight

treats us to yet another contradiction and also reminds us of the shattered oath of brotherhood in his unconscious irony:

> Ther nas no good day, ne no saluyng,
> But streight, withouten word or rehersyng,
> Everich of hem heelp for to armen oother
> As freendly as he were his owene brother;
> And after that, with sharpe speres stronge
> They foynen ech at oother wonder longe.   (1649-54)

The satiric and humorous implications in the two young knight's speechless greetings and the characterization of their helping each other with their armor as "freendly," together with the "owene brother" allusion, are plain enough to require no further comment. We cannot here assess the Knight's gory account of their battle on the basis of its matter-of-fact presentation, since his later "thou mightest wene" subtly removes the responsibility for these exaggerations from himself to his audience.

The Knight's lengthy detail in his discussion of providence and destiny supposedly accounts for the coincidence of the arrival of Theseus and his hunting party in the grove. Palamon answers Theseus' demand for an explanation of their solitary battle in the passage analyzed in detail in Chapter II. The remainder of Book II is also considered in detail in Chapter II from the standpoint of satire and humor.

Books IV and V of Boccaccio's *Teseida* are Chaucer's immediate source for Book II of *The Knight's Tale*. Unlike the Knight's account of Arcite's two years of violent lamenting, in the Boccaccio version Arcita changes his name almost immediately after his release from prison and dejectedly travels to Boetia with his entire retinue. Although Boccaccio devoted several cantos early in Book IV to Arcita's love plight (Cantos 4-10), his plaints are eloquently melancholic as opposed to the lurid violence of the dangerous state depicted for us by Chaucer's Knight as matters of fact. In the *Teseida*, Arcita does not arrive in Thebes for some time (Canto 12), and he remains there only very briefly. He is deeply saddened by its state of destruction and travels on to Corinth and finally to Messina (Cantos 13-18). There he takes service with Menelao—presumably as an unknown knight, since his sufferings have greatly changed his features. After a year with Menelao he goes on to Aegina where he spends his time as a menial servant of Pelleo, often grieving over his unattainable love; he becomes still more drastically changed in appearance and even his voice changes (Cantos 19-30). Finally he seems resigned to death: "Finche al veduto termine pervenne,/ Dove si ruppe'l fil che'n vita il tenne" (Canto 31, lines 7-8). Having learned that Acate (to whom Emilia had been promised by Theseus) has died, Arcita determines to return to Athens and takes passage on a small Athenian ship (Cantos 32-37).

Several fundamental differences between the *Teseida* and *The Knight's Tale* are evident here, besides the significant contrast in the nature of Arcite's love-malady in the two poems. Boccaccio treats Arcita's dolorous condition with the suave elegance of genteel convention, while Chaucer's unsophisticated Knight distorts convention with the exaggerated extremity of his graphic catalogue of symptoms—especially in view of the closely related matter of Emelye's characterization. Also significant, of course, is the matter of Arcite's alias—in the Boccaccio Arcita changes his name to Penteo immediately upon his release from prison, and remains incognito throughout his various travels, long before he makes his way back to Athens. Chaucer's choice of the Philostrate alias obviously is an important change which, for the purpose of my investigation, seems among the most delightfully subtle examples of humorous and satiric effects we derive from his use of literary allusion. In the *Teseida*, of course, Arcita actually marries Emilia but he is indeed "vanquished by love" since Venus causes him to be crushed by his horse (Book IX, Cantos 83 and 4-8); but in *The Knight's Tale* Arcite is vanquished not by Venus, but by Saturn. The whole affair is merely an accident so far as the characters in Chaucer's poem are concerned. In any case, Chaucer has Arcite call himself Philostrate only while he is in Athens and, according to the Knight's contradictory characterization, "in this blisse," while obeying Mercury's admonition to "be murie." Since Arcite is clearly achieving all he seeks to achieve at this point with respect to his love affair, he is scarcely "vanquished by love."

Acate is simply left out of *The Knight's Tale*, even by inference, although who can say Chaucer did not have his role in the *Teseida* in mind as Arcite outlines his own and Palamon's situation in the "dog-and-bone" analogy of Book I? At any rate, Chaucer's invention of Arcite's dream of Mercury is an interesting contrast to Boccaccio's less dramatic means of motivating his Arcita's return to

Athens. Thus, in the Chaucer, so grave is Arcite's malady, it seems, that nothing less than a god's pronouncement can spur him into action. In fact, we find his apparent recovery only partial at best, and he is far from being "murie" or the heroic lover of allegory or romance during his period of disguised servitude.

To a degree, the same applies to Boccaccio's Arcita, but the *Teseida* is, in my opinion, devoid of humorous and satiric effects, and Arcita somewhat mundanely decides to return to Athens principally because his only effective rival for Emilia's love is dead. Since he has so far appeared in the *Teseida* as a melancholy young man sadly enduring his lot until death will release him from a love-cross he bears in social anonymity, we hardly expect him to suddenly turn heroic. Boccaccio even refers to him as Penteo from the moment he changes his name. In *The Knight's Tale* Arcite does not endure his grief in anonymity—he brandishes it publically for two years in his royal Theban setting. While we may expect little of the dejected Penteo in the way of heroic acts, it is clear that he is measurably more heroic than Chaucer's supposedly love-maddened Arcite and a more believable figure within the conventions of the courtly allegory and metrical romance genres. Thus Chaucer's Arcite merely seeks proximity to Emelye, while Boccaccio's obviously intends to woo her.

In the *Teseida* Penteo decides his appearance is so altered that he can serve Teseo without being recognized. He accordingly returns to Athens and at once prays in the temple of Apollo that he will not be recognized in his guise of a humble servant (Cantos 38-47). He manages to be taken into service in Teseo's retinue, and his physical health soon improves (Cantos 48-50). At "una mirabil festa" he sees his beloved once again—she is by far the most beautiful lady there; he is overjoyed (Cantos 51-53). Emilia recognizes Penteo as Arcita, but no one else does. She wonders why he has returned—or pretends to—and, significantly, does not identify him to anyone. She also pretends she has never seen him before (Cantos 56-58).

Penteo soon becomes beloved by Teseo over any other servant and manages to keep his love hidden from everyone but Emilia, whom he tries to woo at least with his eyes. Emilia is fully aware of his love, but she feigns ignorance of his very existence, since she herself is not in love. It is very clear, however, that she is not at all displeased with the situation (Cantos 59-61). In order to keep his desires hidden from others ("Ed e' non gliele ardiva a discoprire"), Penteo is wont to sleep alone in a grove outside the city, where he can sing his love-complaints in privacy (Cantos 63-73). In the morning he sings prayers to Phoebus and Venus, to the end that Emilia might return his love. One morning he reviews his sad lot in song—his imprisonment by Teseo, the love in his heart, his unwanted release from prison, his disguise as Penteo during his subsequent unhappy travels, and his foolhardy action in returning to Athens since Emilia's beauty has abolished his fear of Teseo (Cantos 75-89). This particular morning it happens that one of Palamone's servants chances to be passing by and, overhearing Penteo's lament, rushes off to the palace and reports it to Palamone (Cantos 79-90). Book IV of the *Teseida* ends as Penteo, unaware that he has been overheard, joyously returns to Athens.

Chaucer, of course, omits entirely the prayer to Apollo and its surrounding material. In *The Knight's Tale* it is unmistakable that Arcite's sole purpose in returning to Athens as Philostrate is to be near Emelye—he clearly has no intention of wooing her, and she has no idea at all of his "hoote fare." It is equally unmistakable in the *Teseida* that Arcita disguises himself as Penteo not only to be near Emilia but to woo her and win her love as well. Accordingly his prayer to Apollo that he remain unrecognized is in complete harmony with the fulfillment of this conventional desire. There is no humor or satire involved here. The prayer would be merely superfluous in *The Knight's Tale*. Obviously, in *The Knight's Tale* Arcite's unheroic role also appears more pronounced by Chaucer's omissions—Emilia's flirtatious attitude and the fact that she recognizes the disguised Arcita—which emphasize anew the differences in her characterization between the two poems; we may well conclude that Chaucer's Arcite is indeed the fool Theseus says he is later in Book II.

Penteo is measurably less foolish. This is because he is much more like a conventional courtly lover, while—at least from the standpoint with which I am chiefly concerned—Chaucer's Arcite is a delightfully exaggerated misrepresentation of this literary phenomenon. Thus Chaucer has him conscientiously work his way up to Theseus' favor, while Boccaccio simply places him in Theseus' court immediately upon his arrival in Athens, as befits the conventionally vague treatment of such matters in the world of epic or romance. Hence in *The Knight's Tale* Arcite's motivations and acts throughout this section of the poem do not bear the perceptive scrutiny Chaucer's realistic treatment invites; in short, Arcite simply doesn't succeed as a valorous knightly lover.

The improvement in Penteo's condition in the Boccaccio occurs quite apparently as a result of his not unfounded hopes of attracting Emilia and possibly winning her love. After all, she recognizes him and even flirts with him but does not give him away, and his physical health and joyous spirits at the end of Book IV do not surprise us. The condition of Chaucer's Arcite, on the other hand, is a series of contradictions to the Knight's characterization of his "blisse" and Mercury's admonition to him to "be murie." This is brought out in the song of complaint, which is very much milder in the *Teseida* than in *The Knight's Tale*. Moreover, this section of the *Teseida* is not only a complaint but also Penteo's conventional lover's prayer that Emilia be inspired to reciprocate his passion (a prayer Arcite would obviously consider unforgivably presumptuous).

But the most significant difference between the two poems here is the disguised lovers' relations with Theseus. Boccaccio's Penteo is free of fear of Teseo, and no political implications are involved —at least not directly. In the *Teseida*, Thebes is utterly destroyed, and in any case neither Palamone nor Arcita ever brings up the question of waging war upon Teseo. Moreover, Boccaccio's epic Teseo is sufficiently ruthless to make the ransomless imprisonment unobtrusive. But as a result of Chaucer's changes in the complaint in *The Knight's Tale*, wherein Arcite refers to Theseus as his mortal enemy and himself as "so caytyf and so thral" for serving the great duke, his present unheroic life takes on unpatriotic tinges as well.

Book V of the *Teseida* opens with a treatment of Palamone's fears that Arcita might have been released from imprisonment through Emilia's intercession with Teseo. When the servant reports what he has overheard in the grove, Palamone decides he must escape and "possa conquistare/ per arme Emilia"—by fighting Arcita, of course, not Teseo (Cantos 1-14). There follows a relatively complicated escape plan proposed by the loyal servant and successfully carried out with the aid of another Theban (Cantos 15-26). Palamone spends the night comfortably in a nearby inn and the next morning arms himself carefully before proceeding to the grove where Arcita is sleeping (Cantos 27-35). Their meeting and battle are very different from those in *The Knight's Tale* and must therefore be dealt with in some detail. They recognize each other almost at once, Palamone addresses Arcita affectionately ("dolce amico caro"), and it is clear that even on his way to challenge Arcita his friendly regard for him remained undiminished ("O bell'amico molto da lodare"). Palamone reiterates his love for Emilia and says he realizes that Arcita loves her, too. Pointing out that they cannot both have her, he asks Arcita to grant her to him. Arcita counters with the request that instead Palamone concede her to him, Palamone's dear kinsman. Palamone regretfully concludes they must settle the problem with their swords, although Arcita tries to suggest other solutions.

Finally Palamone insists, requesting Arcita to prepare himself for the worst since he believes he, Palamone, will surely win. Arcita, tragically conscious of the destruction of their family when Thebes fell, reluctantly prepares for the battle, horrified that the last of the royal Thebans are fated to kill each other. Arcita strikes Palamone mightily, and Palamone appears to be dead. Arcita bathes his face and weeps over the loss of his brave companion, but Palamone recovers from the blow at that moment and vows he will give no quarter despite Arcita's pity. They pray to Mars, Venus, and Emilia, and fight fiercely and long but are too evenly matched for the battle to be decisive. There is much more detail than I have given here, of course, but this redaction, embracing Cantos 36-76, adequately illustrates the significant differences between the Boccaccio and Chaucer versions in this vital matter up to this point.

The battle continues as Teseo and Emilia enter the grove some distance away with a hunting party. Emilia comes upon the battle alone, and Palamone and Arcita intensify their efforts as they recognize her. She calls Teseo, who arrives and watches the fighting with great interest. Finally Teseo rides up to them and asks them why they are fighting and who they are, to which Arcita replies merely that they are knights who are testing their valor for love. Teseo again asks their identity, but Arcita refuses to tell him unless Teseo promises the two combatants "la pace vostra." Teseo immediately grants this, and each young knight identifies himself by name in turn, without derogatory comment about each other. Teseo asks for the details of their love affair and who the lady is, whereupon Palamone courteously relates the whole affair. Throughout his brief recital, he makes no hostile comment whatever about Arcita.

Teseo, deeply moved by Palamone's story, replies that he himself has often committed folly because of love ("E per amor sovente folleggiai"); he will therefore pardon them but only on condition that they abide by what he is about to ask of them. This Palamone and Arcita gladly promise. Teseo says that he could ask for no finer man to bestow Emilia upon than either of them, but since both cannot have her the matter must be settled by arms. In a year each must return with one hundred companions to take part in a contest in Teseo's battle-theater. Whoever drives out the other party shall wed Emilia; the loser—and this seems to me especially significant—shall obey her judgment. Book IV ends as Teseo takes them all back to the palace as his honored guests; the entire scene is completed by Boccaccio in only twenty-eight cantos (77-105) from the time that Teseo and Emilia first enter the grove.

The differences between the *Teseida* and *The Knight's Tale* in these vital details are very important from the standpoint of Chaucer's artistic ambivalence. The oath of knightly brotherhood between the two cousins is entirely original with Chaucer. Throughout *The Knight's Tale* it is a central factor in the love complex, in the entire motivation which gives rise to the action of the poem, in the matters of quest and duration, and, most obviously, in the attitudes of the two young men toward each other and toward their competition in love. I have dealt in some detail with the humorous and satiric effects we may derive from this in Books I and II of the poem. Certainly Chaucer's establishment of this relationship of knightly brotherhood between the two cousins in *The Knight's Tale* is not in itself an especially significant departure from the Boccaccio. But his artistic use of it to permeate every major element of the poem in skillful combination with other more significant changes from the Boccaccio source furnishes us some of our most convincing evidence that *The Knight's Tale* is a very different work from the *Teseida*. At this point the results of the evidence so far accumulated may be said to demonstrate that in the Chaucer poem different emotions and a misunderstanding of them react upon different people in entirely different ways with very different artistic effects than in the *Teseida*.

If we were to interpret literally Palamon's denunciation of Arcite to Theseus in *The Knight's Tale,* we would be face to face with one of the naïve Knight's most fundamental contradictions. These "gentil" paradigms of royal chivalry could scarcely treat the knightly oath of brotherhood so treasonably. It cannot be maintained that the oath is dissolved by Arcite's renunciation of it (1604-5) since, as I have demonstrated earlier, the oath establishes a symmetrical relationship, and its renunciation by one member would invalidate it if and only if it were an asymmetrical relationship. Apart from this, for all of his alleged bitter hatred of his "felawe," Palamon has not attempted to renounce the oath at any time. The humorous and satiric effects of this are derived in the same way as in the other contradictions discussed above; thus both young men misinterpret the provisions of their oath of brotherhood and its connections with their love problems. Hence they misinterpret their entire relationship.

It is hard to find the acts of the foolish wicked, and when they painstakingly infer absurd conclusions from the plainest evidence they themselves present, we are likely to find their acts ridiculous. I submit that Palamon's series of misunderstandings of idealistic matters in his address to Theseus in Book II may be so interpreted. In the *Teseida,* this situation never arises, of course, or any situation which resembles it. It is clear throughout Boccaccio's poem that relations between Palamone and Arcita are always affectionate and the necessity of bearing arms against each other both consider tragically regrettable. Literary convention dictates the characterization, action, setting, and style in the *Teseida,* and while more than one literary genre is involved, in my opinion, any given section of the poem is in all important matters consistent with the genre concerned. Neither humor nor satire seem to me anywhere discernible.

Palamone's comfortable night at the inn and his preparatory arming of himself in the *Teseida* are in delightful contrast to Chaucer's treatment of these matters. Emilia is the only lady directly referred to in Teseo's hunting party in the *Teseida,* and far from being disturbed at the plight of the two contestants, if anything she enjoys it because of its reflection upon her own desirability. This is in harmony with her pleased awareness of the disguised Arcita's love of long standing. Paradoxically, Teseo is presented by Boccaccio as much more of a "noble duc" than by Chaucer when he first discovers the identities of the two combatants. He instantly pardons them and, although he acknowledges that their follies are the result of love, he takes the situation very seriously, believing Palamone's and Arcita's actions to be wholly admirable. Thus in *The Knight's Tale* Theseus' first reaction to the situation—death for Arcite and Palamon—and the consequent grief of the women with all its satiric and humorous effects are entirely original with Chaucer.

Similarly, the very different characterization of Chaucer's Theseus as compared to Boccaccio's Teseo is reflected by the total absence in the *Teseida* of any possible political considerations or the necessity to pacify mere women in Teseo's arrangement for the great contest at arms. Finally, if perhaps autobiographical experiences are involved in Emilia's flirtatiousness and general lack of seriousness in the first several books of the *Teseida*, she is in other respects the conventional love object of courtly and medieval romance. Chaucer omits any reference to her authority over the loser of the contest at arms, in keeping with his entirely different characterization of her.

The significance of these fundamental differences in terms of humorous and satiric effects and hence artistic ambivalence in *The Knight's Tale* are now, I think, plain enough to make further discussion of them redundant. We may summarize the findings of Chapters III, IV, and V from the standpoints of principal source changes and Chaucerian humor and satire as confirming the hypotheses and method of investigation outlined in the Introduction and Chapter I. In our perception of satire and humor in *The Knight's Tale* through the operation of our projective processes, we find that the passages with which we have been concerned share the same satiric and humorous properties as one or more of the passages cited in Chapter II which have long been considered representative Chaucerian humor and satire. Further, at least through Book V, the *Teseida* source of *The Knight's Tale* is clearly devoid of both humor and satire; its form is mixed, but it is a work of unrelieved seriousness and even sadness which frequently is not in keeping with its epic style. The humor and satire in *The Knight's Tale*, therefore, are solely the effects of Chaucer's artistry —indeed, many of the changes from his source so far considered are significantly involved in the derivation of much of the humor and satire of the poem.

VI

BOOK THREE

ook III of *The Knight's Tale* shares important qualities with the *Teseida* to a greater degree than any of the other books, while Book IV owes much of its literal content to the *Teseida*. Accordingly a somewhat more detailed comparison of corresponding areas of the two poems is particularly meaningful here.

In Chapter I comments of various critics on the *Teseida* were cited which are indicative of a widespread opinion that the subject matter of the poem does not warrant the epic style. Up until the point at which Palamone and Arcita fall in love with Emilia, it seems to me that the *Teseida* is a successful epic, as I have stated in Chapter III. Emilia, flirtatious and shallow as she is, is the most fully developed character in Boccaccio's poem; whether or not she is the Fiammetta to whom the poem is dedicated, she certainly is not a convincing epic heroine.

Except for her frivolity, however, she is a successful blend of the heroine of courtly allegory and the heroine of medieval romance. Still we cannot picture battling over such a frivolous prize on the scale depicted in the *Teseida*, and even Boccaccio seems to have arrived at more or less the same conclusion, since in Book VII of the poem he has Teseo state to the great crowd before the beginning of the lists:

172

Ma esser ciò com'un palestral giuoco.
E non credetti che tutta Lernea
Sotto gli regi Achivi si movesse
Per sì poca di cosa;

(Canto 4, line 8;
Canto 5, lines 1-3)*

Thus Teseo, considering the whole affair to be of interest only to those immediately involved, is astonished to see the entire country turn out for "sì poca di cosa." Palamone's and Arcita's genteel love for Emilia and their equally genteel regret at the necessity for recourse to arms is scarcely the substance from which an epic poem may be expected to emerge.

The Knight's Tale diverges even farther from the epic genre than the *Teseida*, according to the differences between the two poems discussed in Chapters III and V. Moreover, in his first two books Chaucer provides all the events, motivation, and characterizations which make up the total foundation upon which Books III and IV of *The Knight's Tale* depend. For the more literal-minded, then, Chaucer's poem reflects the characteristics of courtly love and metrical romance. For those who may also interpret *The Knight's Tale* in terms of its artistic ambivalence, its pervasive satire and humor are among its most salient characteristics. From both standpoints, however, it is clear that Chaucer's approach to his material is certainly not epic. Hence we find that Book III of *The Knight's Tale*, wherein Chaucer derives more than half of his material from the *Teseida*, is even more inconsistent with the rest of *The Knight's Tale* than Boccaccio's Books VI and VII are with much of the *Teseida*. It is here that, for the first time in our comparison of the two poems, there is a close literal resemblance between them in areas of substance and genre: the substance of both poems fails to warrant the extravagant epic paraphernalia both poets make such liberal use of at this point in their respective plots.

The other quality shared by the two poems in the portions under discussion is, to a large degree, their literal content. It is interesting that in all the studies of the relation of *The Knight's Tale* to its principal source, the unique aspects of the dependence of Chaucer's Book III on the *Teseida* have not been found especially sig-

*. . . . but that this be like a tournament.
I didn't believe that all Learnea
Under the Greek kings would bestir itself
For such a small thing. . . .

nificant. Yet even the arithmetical basis of comparison, which seems so popular as a means of assessing Chaucer's artistic debts, indicates a radical difference in Chaucer's use of the *Teseida* in Book III.

Of the 2,250 lines of *The Knight's Tale*, only 744 correspond even approximately to the *Teseida*. If these 744 lines were relatively evenly distributed throughout *The Knight's Tale*, one might be mildly justified in forming the easily tested hypothesis that Chaucer's poem is a consistently structured redaction of the Boccaccio. But approximately two-fifths of these lines are in Book III alone. Slightly over three-fifths—61 per cent or 460—are accordingly distributed throughout Books I, II, and IV of *The Knight's Tale*. Book I contains 118 lines which merely approximate lines in the Boccaccio; none of them corresponds to the Boccaccio closely enough to amount to direct translation. Book II contains only 81 lines which may be traced to the *Teseida*, none of which is a direct translation. Book IV contains a total of 264 lines derived from the *Teseida*, 51 of which are essentially direct translations.

Expressed in terms of percentages, 23 per cent of Book I and 15 per cent of Book II loosely resemble portions of the *Teseida*, while 42 per cent of Book IV resembles the Boccaccio source—about 7 per cent amounting to translation. But some *47 per cent* of Book III is derived from the *Teseida*, although only about 8 per cent is direct translation! Thus Book III not only accounts for nearly two-fifths of Chaucer's *total* debt to the *Teseida*, but also fragments of about one-half (284) of its 601 lines may be found in Boccaccio. We might therefore suspect merely on these simple arithmetical grounds that Book III would differ in other ways as well from the rest of *The Knight's Tale*—especially from the first two books. I hasten to add that in my opinion far too many specific conclusions concerning Chaucer's literary relations to Boccaccio and others have been advanced by critics on the dubious evidence of such numerical analyses as this. The phenomenon is sufficiently widespread that I solicit the reader's indulgence for belaboring what is surely obvious—the statistical evidence cited here is at most provocative, an obvious "lead" indicating a possibly fruitful line of investigation. It of course cannot demonstrate or imply that *The Knight's Tale* is imbued with tragedy, humor, or satire, or any other literary characteristic.

The significant differences between the *Teseida* and *The Knight's*

Tale so far considered certainly demonstrate that Chaucer's poem is in every major respect distinctly unlike the Boccaccio. As it happens, this is reflected in the number of lines in Books I and II of *The Knight's Tale* which loosely correspond to various lines in the *Teseida*. Of the 1,021 lines in Chaucer's first two books, only 196 may be traced to the *Teseida*—more than four-fifths of Chaucer's material in these decisive books is in no direct way derived from Boccaccio. Moreover, the material Chaucer made use of from the *Teseida* here, as is obvious from the discussions in Chapters III and V, is confined to such superficial matters as names of characters and mechanical details of setting and plot. Yet even in these matters, we have found that Chaucer sometimes made drastic changes which were consistent with his own very different artistic treatment of the legendary setting, events, and characters of the Italian poem. These factors are important as a background to any consideration of Book III, together with the actual state of affairs in *The Knight's Tale* at the end of Book II. All the circumstantial details of pomp and circumstance pertaining to the preparation for the grand lists do not alter the fact that the prize at stake is the hand of a woman who is apparently completely uninterested in both contestants; indeed, she insists she prefers a life of chastity to the "hoote fare" of love or marriage.

Book VI and approximately two-thirds of Book VII of the *Teseida* roughly correspond to Chaucer's Book III. Boccaccio's Book VI begins with a detailed account of the luxurious life enjoyed by Arcita and Palamone during the year preceding the great battle. They remain in Athens as Teseo's guests and do everything they can think of to impress Emilia. Boccaccio dwells upon the unforeseeable mutations of Fortune which will determine the fates of the two young lovers (Cantos 1-5). They remain the closest of friends and entertain day and night; they have goshawks, falcons, and hounds—throughout the year both spend enormous sums of money on these activities (Cantos 6-8). Palamone and Arcita are very generous with their wealth and hold many jousts; each tries hard to win favor in Emilia's eyes by his acts of valor and largess (Canto 9). But despite their affection for each other and the delightful life they are now leading, each of the royal Thebans is determined to win Emilia through victory in the lists or die in the attempt (Canto 10). During the year each invites many friends—some of whom are renowned in battle—to take part in the great contest, and other important preparations are also made (Cantos 11-12).

Chaucer, of course, omits completely any mention of the activities of Palamon and Arcite during the year of preparation. Certainly their relations with one another could not have been friendly, in view of their attitudes and activities in both Books I and II. In any case, Chaucer disposes of them by packing them off to Thebes, and we hear no more of them until they return the following year prepared for battle. This gives Chaucer's Knight the opportunity to expand upon what is obviously closest to his heart—the complex grandeur of a proper chivalric theater in which to decide an issue of love:

> I trowe men wolde deme it necligence
> If I foryete to tellen the dispence
> Of Theseus, that gooth so bisily
> To maken up the lystes roially,
> That swich a noble theatre as it was,
> I dar wel seyen in this world ther nas.
> The circuit a myle was aboute,
> Walled of stoon, and dyched al withoute.
> Round was the shap, in manere of compas,
> Ful of degrees, the heighte of sixty pas,
> That whan a man was set on o degree,
> He letted nat his felawe for to see.
>   Estward ther stood a gate of marbul whit,
> Westward right swich another in the opposit.
> And shortly to concluden, swich a place
> Was noon in erthe, as in so litel space;
> For in the lond ther was no crafty man
> That geometrie or ars-metrike kan,
> Ne portreyour, ne kervere of ymages,
> That Theseus ne yaf him mete and wages,
> The theatre for to maken and devyse.   (1881-1901)

The very first line has shades of humor and satire which set the tone for much of what is to follow in the entire book. The literal acceptance of the character of the Knight as he appears through his narrative—and hence the literal acceptance of his interpretation of the poem—seems to me the principal reason for the traditional point of view documented in Chapter I. Nothing in Chaucer's poem reveals so clearly, in my opinion, the Knight's exaggerated preoccupation with anything which can be construed as chivalric as this passage. Consequently, assuming others to share his preoccupation, he believes he would be considered negligent if he does not launch into his almost interminable digression! Despite the hint that he himself would prefer to get on with his story rather than dwell on details so minor he might easily forget to mention them, we realize from what we have so far learned of him how thoroughly the Knight relishes his idealized, exaggerated descriptions of the theater and its temples.

The first and second narrative techniques—the "reportage" devices—which Chaucer has the Knight employ here result in every detail of the description appearing as a matter of fact. These devices also clarify one of the most significant matters in Book III, which is also one of Chaucer's sharpest departures from Boccaccio. While Chaucer follows Boccaccio's description of the theater and the temples faithfully in every important detail, he puts Boccaccio to shame in epic matters. My guess is that with modern engineering methods it would take an army of laborers and at least hundreds of sculptors, artists, architects, several million tons of materials, and so on to erect the tournament theater—not to mention years upon years of time. Boccaccio, much more believably, has it already erected and the temples part of the city's religious facilities, while Chaucer has everything custom-built for this specific contest.*

The effect of this fundamental departure from the Boccaccio is also very important because the epic characteristics in their milder form in the *Teseida* are already far in excess of what the subject matter can bear. Even Boccaccio seems to have been aware of the *Teseida*'s inconsistency in this respect, as is reflected in Teseo's address to the assembled populace quoted above. But by having the grand theater constructed especially for Arcite's and Palamon's group contest and including in it the three temples, Chaucer's Knight is at the very least enormously enlarging the original excessive proportions of the comparable material in the Boccaccio. If we bear in mind the implausible motives and fallacious reasoning which supposedly account for all the events

*Unless I have failed to find it, we have as yet no linear English translation of the *Teseida*, nor even a summary sufficiently detailed to make such matters clear. I must accordingly beg the reader's indulgence—here and elsewhere—for my own lengthy treatment of portions of the *Teseida* which comprise the only easily available substantiation for my conclusions.

and relationships in which Arcite and Palamon involve themselves, together with Emelye's characterization and consequent attitudes, I think we must recognize that Book III can be interpreted from one point of view as high and sustained satire throughout. Accordingly, the twenty lines here quoted are merely the introduction to a catalogue of pageantry which has the effect of illustrating the lengths man will go to in order to reap the harvest of his folly. The way in which this effect is derived becomes clearer as we perceive the full significance of Chaucer's manipulation of his source material.

Having begun his Book VI with an account of the extravagantly luxurious lives of the two royal Thebans as they await the appointed time for the lists, Boccaccio continues with a long series of epic descriptions of the famous knights who are to take part in the battle. As the great day approaches, Palamone and Arcita ask their men to come (Canto 13). Ligurgo, a brave and mighty king, is the first of Arcita's men to arrive (Canto 14). Next comes Pelleo, another great king who is also a famous conqueror (Canto 15). His appearance is impressive, for he is dressed all in cloth of gold covered with precious jewels. Even his saddle is made of gold, and he brings a number of his nobles with him who are also richly clad and who hope to win honor and glory in the lists. The populace of Athens is full of admiration for Pelleo's grand procession (Cantos 16-19).

Then Niso arrives, followed by Agamennone, who rides on a vehicle drawn by four huge bulls. Agamennone is very large and strong; he has a large, black beard and his dress is unusual, not for its ornamentation but for its fierceness—it is the pelt of a bear (Cantos 20-22). After Agamennone come Menelao, Castore, Polluce, and Cromi, who is wearing a lion's pelt (Cantos 23-27). Then, one after another, Ippodomo, Nestore, Evandro, Peritoo, the Duke of Naricia, Diomede, Pigmaleone, Sicheo, Radamante, Sarpedone, Auchelado, Ameto, and a great many others arrive—all accompanied by squires, servants, and other subordinates (Cantos 29-55). Nestore is conspicuous for his rich armor, Evandro for his bear's pelt whose nails are covered with glistening gold. Evandro's elaborately ornamented shield contrasts with Peritoo's crown of laurel. Many have come from distant lands; all desire to seek fame and honor by their performances in the lists (Cantos 58-64).

The last seven cantos of Book VI of the *Teseida* are devoted to the appropriate reception of the dukes, kings, princes, and knights, and to Teseo's royal entertainments given in their honor. They do not believe that Palamone and Arcita are foolish to go to such lengths for such a great and worthy love:

> Nè furon folli Arcita e Palamone
>   Tenuti da chi seppe i fatti loro,
>   Se l'un s'era fuggito di prigione,
>   E l'altro, oltre al mandato, a far dimore
>   Nella vietata bella regïone,
>   Per acquistar così fatto tesoro:
>   Nè s'ammiraron se non voller loco
>   Dar l'uno all'altro all'amoroso foco.   (Canto 67)*

Never have such a great number of noble persons been gathered together in the city before, and there is a great deal of feasting and celebration (Cantos 70-71) with which Boccaccio ends Book VI.

Book VII of the *Teseida* opens with the approach of the day of the lists. The people of the city are in the theater; Teseo leads in all the nobles and addresses the crowd (Cantos 1-3). In addition to the significant remarks quoted earlier in this chapter, Teseo also informs the people that they are all aware of the issue at stake and of his arrangements for its settlement. He insists that the battle should savor of love, not of hatred: "Dunque amorosa dee questa battaglia/ Esser, se ben discerno, e non odiosa" (Cantos 3-8). He explains further that Palamone and Arcita are to choose one hundred men each; the winner will be granted Emilia and will have all the glory (Cantos 11-12). Palamone and Arcita then choose the best of all their noble guests to make up the total of two hundred fighting men, and Teseo leads them back through the city to the palace (Cantos 15-20).

On the day before the great battle, Palamone and Arcita make their prayers to the gods (Canto 22). Arcita makes his prayer to Mars, praising the god for his great power and acknowledging his

---

*Neither were Arcite and Palamon
  Held as fools by those who knew about their affairs,
If the one escaped from jail
And the other, against orders, had lingered
In the beautiful, forbidden region,
So as to acquire such a treasure as this:
Nor is it surprising if they did not want to give away
One to the other in the flame of love.

own puniness without the aid of the mighty god of war. Arcita promises Mars to adorn his temples and credit him with all the glory if Mars gives victory and its delights to his humble petitioner (Cantos 22-28). Arcita's prayer goes forth to the realm of Mars in the Thracian fields; there, at the temple of polished steel, the prayer meets Ire, Fear, Treason, and Death. The temple is appropriately decorated with histories of grievous plunders and other violent matters. Mars hears the prayer, and signs are granted to Arcita that his prayer has been heard (Cantos 29-40).

In the meantime, Palamone prays to Cytheraea, saying that only she can transform his misery to joy. Significantly, he says that he does not pray for victory in the lists but only for Emilia's hand. In return, he promises to honor the goddess' temples as long as he lives (Cantos 42-48). Palamone's prayer goes to Cytheraea's temple on Mount Cithaeron, where it sees a beautiful garden with an elaborate temple decorated with the stories of the famous lovers of history; in one of its secret rooms the prayer finds the beautiful Venus lying naked on a couch. Palamone's prayer is granted (Cantos 50-66). At this, a great quarrel arises between Venus and Mars, since they have both promised to grant the apparently contradictory prayers of Palamone and Arcita. They find a means of granting both prayers, but how this is to be done is not disclosed at the time (Cantos 66-67).

While Arcita and Palamone pray to Mars and Venus, Emilia prays to Diana (Canto 70). Emphasizing her virgin state and her consequent right to petition Diana, Emilia says she is more likely to be a good huntress than a loving wife. She asks Diana to calm the desires of the two Thebans, but since she realizes she must have one of them, she prays that it be the one who desires her the most. She then begs Diana to tell her which one is to win her. Diana's followers tell Emilia that the gods have made their decision, but it is necessarily hidden from humans. Hearing the sound of arrows from Diana's quiver, Emilia realizes that her prayers have been heard. She knows the prayer in which she asked that the one who loves her most be allowed to win her has been granted because the two fires she has lit behave peculiarly. One goes out but is magically relighted; the other turns the color of blood and disappears entirely (Cantos 72-92). The remaining cantos of Book VII from which Chaucer borrows material for Book III of *The Knight's Tale* embody the description of the theater, of which only the details in lines 1887-94 of the Knight's eloquent account are found in the *Teseida* (Cantos 108-10).

It is clear that while Chaucer relied heavily upon the *Teseida* for much of his material in Book III, its effects in *The Knight's Tale* are very different from those in Books VI and VII of the Boccaccio poem. In my opinion, two principal factors account for this. Chaucer completely reorganized his source material in terms of the order of events and descriptions, and he emphasized Theseus as the central character. He also, through the Knight's narrative role, so blended his original contributions with the borrowed material as to arrive at a very different state of affairs by the end of Book III than obtains in the *Teseida* by the end of its Book VII. This is hardly surprising in view of the very different treatment of the material in Books I and II of *The Knight's Tale* in comparison to related sections of the Boccaccio. It is significant, however, that even in this portion of *The Knight's Tale*, the artistic effects of the two poems are in no important way comparable.

Chaucer's Knight, then, radically departs from the Boccaccio in the sequence of his descriptions and in his assertions that the magnificent theater and the temples indigenous to it are constructed by Theseus solely for the contest over Emelye. Whereas Boccaccio begins this portion of the *Teseida* with an account of the two Thebans' luxurious year in Athens, Chaucer concentrates all the lavish entertainment in Theseus' authoritative person. Boccaccio launches into his pageantry with the long, epic account of the procession of legendary heroes, proceeds with their entertainment, makes his public announcement in the theater, continues with the prayers of his three principals, and, only as the lists are about to begin, describes the great theater. Thus in the *Teseida* the description of the theater is almost a minor, routine matter— it is incidental, and we take it for granted that the ruler of Athens would have such a grand, permanent arena for all contests at arms.

But in Chaucer, because the theater is custom-built for the occasion and because its imposing description comes at the very beginning of the "epic" part of *The Knight's Tale*, it is the most impressive part of all the pageantry in Book III. Nothing could be more effective in shifting the emphasis from the "poca di cosa" characterization of the love affair in the *Teseida* to that of a conflict of emotions apparently powerful enough—at least in the Knight's view—to warrant all these epic preparations. By integrating the temples with the theater, Chaucer's Knight imputes even greater significance to Arcite's and Palamon's quarrel over the reluctant Emelye. Further, having established the three temples as integral parts of the theater (1902-13), the Knight informs his audience that he forgot to describe other matters:

> But yet hadde I foryeten to devyse
> The noble kervyng and the portreitures,
> The shap, the contenaunce, and the figures,
> That weren in thise oratories thre.   (1914-17)

The doughty narrator then proceeds to regale his listeners with the minutely detailed descriptions of the interiors of the temples. He waxes enthusiastic—the while protesting he is really being concise—and prolongs his account for some 170 lines.

In the *Teseida*, of course, the pictures, carvings, and so on that the Knight describes are not in the temples at all but are in the actual dwellings of Mars, Venus, and Diana. These awe-inspiring decorations are seen by the prayers rendered by Arcita, Palamone, and Emilia, after the prayers arrive at the distant residences of the deities concerned. Thus Chaucer has in fact portrayed Theseus' theater as an edifice of even vaster grandeur than that in Boccaccio, despite the latter's epic paraphernalia.

The Knight's guileless protests that he is really being concise in his seemingly endless catalogue of the wonders of the pagan oratories play a delightfully humorous role from the standpoint of the artistic ambivalence of *The Knight's Tale*. If interpreted literally, they merely heighten the awesome complexity of these mighty preparations in honor of the supposed ideals of courtly love. As humor and satire they remind us in yet another way of the essential absurdity of such preparations for a contest between championing forces, led by two naïve young men who misunderstand every pertinent facet of their situations and who are striving to win a woman who has protested (however hollowly) that she desires neither of them at any price. Thus Chaucer employs a novel version of the *occupatio* device as the Knight says that all the circumstances of love he has mentioned and will mention "By ordre weren peynted on the wal,/ And mo than I kan make of mencioun" (1934-35). He then goes on to cite no less than eight examples, with copious supporting detail, of the victims of love, ending this part of his recital abruptly with: "Suffiseth heere en-

samples oon or two,/ And though I koude rekene a thousand mo"
(1953-54).

Having recounted at length the fabulous decorations in Venus'
temple, the Knight poses a rhetorical question:

> Why sholde I noght as wel eek telle yow al
> The portreiture that was upon the wal
> Withinne the temple of myghty Mars the rede? (1967-69)

He then proceeds with an even longer account of the harrowing
decor of Mars' oratory. Having dwelt in gruesome detail upon the
battle scenes, the Knight sums them up with this ominous redundancy: "A thousand slayn, and nat of qualm ystorve" (2014).
The last part of his description of Mars' victims is concerned with
three historical assassinations, and the catalogue is brought to a
sudden halt with a use of *occupatio*, similar to that in lines 1953-
54: "Suffiseth oon ensample in stories olde;/ I may nat rekene hem
alle though I wolde" (2039-40). These two instances of Chaucer's
flexible adaptation of the *occupatio* device to the Knight's narrative style have the effect of going beyond rhetorical conventions.
As Chaucer employs them here, they result in actual contradictions of what the Knight has said. They therefore subtly echo the
properties of humor and satire shared by the contradictions in
Book II, considered in Chapter V.

After ending his long account of Mars' temple with a description
of the god's statue, the Knight indefatigably turns to a treatment
of the third temple in the theater:

> Now to the temple of Dyane the chaste,
> As shortly as I kan, I wol me haste,
> To telle yow al the descripsioun.   (2051-53)

In fact Chaucer devotes much less space to Diana's oratory than
to that of either Venus or Mars; in keeping with the rest of his
character, the Knight does not seem entirely at ease with the depictions of the goddess of chastity's militant acts: "Ther saugh I
many another wonder storie,/ The which me list nat drawen to
memorie" (2073-74). This, of course, contradicts his introduction
quoted immediately above and is also an example of a device in
the Knight's narrative technique which is entirely confined to
Book III. It amounts to a concentrated form of the reportage
which results from the Knight's first and second narrative devices,

considered in detail in Chapter III. Thus throughout the description of the three temples, the Knight himself partly enters into his tale in the first person with his "saugh I" assertions (lines 1995, 2011, 2017, 2028, 2062, 2065, 2067, and 2073). Chaucer's idealistic narrator, then, says he has seen the very theater he is describing as part of the setting of his tale! His audience cannot doubt the word of a man of honor reporting the testimony of his own eyes. However long ago Arcite and Palamon may have taken part in their contest, since the Knight says he has seen Theseus' theater, we must accept his description of it as matter-of-fact.

This, however, does not alter any of the other matters in the poem with respect to their degree of reasonableness. It merely emphasizes again the supposed importance and deadly seriousness—from the Knight's point of view—of this contest for the hand of the illusory Emelye. This section of the poem ends with the final, unmistakable reiteration that Theseus made all these preparations solely for the approaching battle:

> Now been thise lystes maad, and Theseus,
> That at his grete cost arrayed thus
> The temples and the theatre every deel,
> Whan it was doon, hym lyked wonder weel.
> But stynte I wole of Theseus a lite,
> And speke of Palamon and Arcite.   (2089-94)

Chaucer now has the Knight turn to the flamboyant pageantry of the processions of Arcite's and Palamon's supporters as the great day approaches. First reviewing the condition of Theseus' agreement that each royal Theban bring with him a hundred knights, he launches into a general introduction to this section. Here, as Chaucer makes extensive use of the Knight's third narrative device, the motives of all concerned are once again interpreted for us:

> And sikerly ther trowed many a man
> That nevere, sithen that the world bigan,
> As for to speke of knyghthod of hir hond,
> As fer as God hath maked see or lond,
> Nas of so fewe so noble a compaignye.
> For every wight that lovede chivalrye,
> And wolde, his thankes, han a passant name,
> Hath preyed that he myghte been of that game;

And wel was hym that therto chosen was.
For if ther fille tomorwe swich a cas,
Ye knowen wel that every lusty knyght
That loveth paramours and hath his myght,
Were it in Engelond or elleswhere,
They wolde, hir thankes, wilnen to be there, —
To fighte for a lady, *benedicitee*!
It were a lusty sighte for to see.   (2101-16)

In these sixteen lines we have the very essence of the Knight's views and attitudes concerning chivalry in general, together with his obvious opinion that the events, characters, and setting of his tale are illustrative of the highest principles of chivalry. As a matter of fact, line 2115 is at the very least deceptive. These assembled chivalric warriors are not fighting for a lady in the usual chivalric sense; Emelye neither needs nor desires knightly assistance of any kind. She is being fought *over*, not *for*, and insists she would much prefer that the issue be forgotten.

Chaucer's technique in describing the various members of the procession is very different from that of Boccaccio. While Boccaccio fills forty-four cantos with somewhat stereotyped epic accounts of a host of heroes of antiquity, Chaucer's treatment of this material is confined to seventy-three lines. Besides creating factual changes, Chaucer applies his realistic style to the personal minutiae of the two figures he concerns himself with as compared with the impersonality of Boccaccio's vast catalogue. Thus in *The Knight's Tale*, Lygurge is not Arcite's man, but Palamon's; Chaucer borrows some details from Boccaccio's descriptions of other heroes and ascribes them to Lygurge together with still other details which are not in the *Teseida*. The extravagant splendor of Chaucer's Lygurge is so well known as to make further comment upon it here redundant, but the Knight's introduction to it —which applies to the entire procession—is a delightfully naïve appeal to his audience: "Ther maistow seen, comynge with Palamoun,/ Lygurge hymself, the grete kyng of Trace" (2128-29). Chaucer's literal-minded narrator apparently has become so absorbed in these matters of chivalry which are so dear to his heart that he confuses his tale with external reality, at least for a time. As a result of this he appeals to his listeners also to do away with all aesthetic distance, thus inviting them to share his own literal belief in the material he is relating.

Chaucer disposes of the rest of Arcite's forces by a mere two lines at the end of Emetreus' description: "An hundred lordes hadde he in his route,/ Armed ful wel, with hertes stierne and stoute" (2153-54). Closing the account of the procession with the depiction of Emetreus' followers, the Knight reiterates the marvelous spirit of chivalry he insists lies behind this grand display:

> An hundred lordes hadde he with hym there,
> Al armed, save hir heddes, in al hir gere,
> Ful richely in alle maner thynges.
> For trusteth wel that dukes, erles, kynges
> Were gadered in this noble compaignye,
> For love and for encrees of chivalrye.   (2179-84)

Still another example of the Knight's third narrative device immediately follows, as Chaucer ascribes to Theseus much of the lavish entertainment which in the *Teseida* was divided among Arcita, Palamone, and Teseo; this passage is another illustration of the same form of the *occupatio* rhetorical device discussed earlier:

> This Theseus, this duc, this worthy knyght,
> Whan he had broght hem into his citee,
> And inned hem, everich at his degree,
> He festeth hem, and dooth so greet labour
> To esen hem and doon hem al honour,
> That yet men wenen that no mannes wit
> Of noon estaat ne koude amenden it.
> The mynstralcye, the service at the feeste,
> The grete yiftes to the meeste and leeste,
> The riche array of Theseus paleys,
> Ne who sat first ne last upon the deys,
> What ladyes fairest been or best daunsynge,
> Or which of hem kan dauncen best and synge,
> Ne who moost felyngly speketh of love;
> What haukes sitten on the perche above,
> What houndes liggen on the floor adoun,—
> Of al this make I now no mencioun,
> But al th'effect, that thynketh me the beste.
> Now cometh the point, and herkneth if yow leste.
>   (2190-2208)

Here again the *occupatio* device as Chaucer has modified it has the same contradictory effect as in the similar instances considered above and the same implications of humor and satire. This passage marks the end of the most detailed exposition of chivalric ideals of any portion of *The Knight's Tale*. The Knight's misunderstanding of the significance of his own material in Books I and II is indeed thorough, but nowhere in the poem is it more obvious than in these first 327 lines of Book III.

The "point" the Knight refers to in line 2208 never does become precisely clear—at least not to me. As I read it, he may be referring to Saturn's equivocal statement to Venus at the end of Book III or even to the account of the lists and their final results. In one way or another, the Knight tells us throughout Book III that he is aware of the fact that his descriptions are really digressions, but we are never in any doubt that, for him, these digressions are the very heart and soul of his tale. In the last analysis, it perhaps does not really matter if the idealistic narrator fails to distinguish between the forest and the trees, since the trees are so important from his point of view.

While Chaucer relied heavily upon the *Teseida* as a basic source for much of the material in the three prayers, his manipulation of it results in a very different effect from that in the Boccaccio. The most striking of Chaucer's departures seem to me to be his placing the descriptions of the temples with that of the theater and his changing the order of the three prayers. In the Boccaccio, of course, the descriptions of the temples are linked with the prayers, logically enough, and Arcita's is the first of them, then Palamone's, and, finally, Emilia's. In the Boccaccio any possible dramatic climax which might be attained by Emilia's prayer occupying the final place in the series fails to materialize because her prayer is too obviously a mere convention. Throughout the rest of the *Teseida* she is anything but indifferent to the feelings she has aroused in Palamone and Arcita. The brief allusion in the *Teseida* to the settlement of Mars' and Venus' contradictory commitments is too ambiguous to be genuinely dramatic. A very different state of affairs, however, results from Chaucer's treatment of these same matters in *The Knight's Tale*.

The Knight first recounts Palamon's entreaty to Venus. The entire account of the travels of Palamon's prayer to the dwelling place of Venus, on which Boccaccio lavishes so much detail, Chaucer ignores; the description of the temple which Boccaccio dwells upon at this point Chaucer has already treated at length as a part of the great theater. This, of course, applies also to the prayers of Emelye and Arcite as well as to the descriptions of Diana's and Mars' temples. Hence, as we might expect, this section of Book III of *The Knight's Tale* is much briefer than its counterpart in the *Teseida*. The Knight tells us that Palamon started out for Venus' temple in high spirits, yet no sooner does Palamon kneel to pray than the Knight contradicts himself:

> Whan Palamon the larke herde synge,
> (Although it nere nat day by houres two,
> Yet song the larke) and Palamon right tho
> With hooly herte and with an heigh corage,
> He roos to wenden on his pilgrymage
> Unto the blisful Citherea benigne,—
> I mene Venus, honurable and digne.
> And in hir houre he walketh forth a pas
> Unto the lystes ther hire temple was,
> And doun he kneleth, and with humble cheere
> And herte soor, he seyde as ye shal heere: (2210-20)

Thus at this most incongruous hour for the lark—the harbinger of sunrise—to burst into song, the Knight tells us its voice is heard and Palamon's as well. We are entitled to hope that Palamon's song is more in keeping with the lovely lark's than Arcite's shouted doggerel was with the lovely May morning described in Book II! Palamon is in the most buoyant of spirits, but within five lines the Knight contradicts this carefully established state of affairs. The "humble cheere" of line 2219 is reasonable enough, but that Palamon's heart should suddenly become "soor" as he is about to pray for what would supposedly bring him the brightest joys of his life is certainly both incongruous in this context and inappropriate to the entire situation. The prayer enlarges upon his present misery, thereby emphasizing the contradiction. The last appearance of Palamon and Arcite was at the very end of Book II, when they were overjoyed at Theseus' solution to their problem and wended their way homeward to Thebes "with good hope and with herte blithe" (1878). This direct contradiction obviously shares the humorous and satiric properties of those of Book II, considered in detail in Chapter IV.

In line 2236, Palamon promises that if Venus grants his prayer, among other things he will in the future wage "werre alwey with chastitee." This may be another of the Knight's guileless misunderstandings of his material. What is conveyed here is that Palamon will make the tremendous sacrifice of remaining sexually true to Emelye even when he goes to war, if Venus will but grant him her hand. From what Chaucer has shown us of the Knight's idealistic views of such matters so far, it is highly probable that the significance of this line wholly escapes him. In other respects, Palamon's prayer is substantially the same as in the *Teseida*.

As the Knight relates the details of Emelye's preparations in the temple, he becomes embarrassed, in keeping with his somewhat prissy gentility:

> Smokynge the temple, ful of clothes faire,
> This Emelye, with herte debonaire,
> Hir body wessh with water of a welle.
> But hou she dide hir ryte I dar nat telle,
> But it be any thing in general;
> And yet it were a game to heeren al.
> To hym that meneth wel it were no charge;
> But it is good a man been at his large.   (2281-88)

Chaucer accordingly omits Boccaccio's detailed account of Emelye's rites (Book VII, Cantos 73-76). Professor Robinson points out various possible reasons for the Knight's reticence,[1] but in my opinion the Knight is simply being naïvely modest in keeping with what we already know of his character. Obviously chastity is the proper condition, in his view, of maids of chivalry, and even a description of the goddess of chastity's temple apparently seems to him somewhat immodest.

As a professional military man, Christian or not, Chaucer's Knight is clearly more comfortable and far more enthusiastic in dealing with Mars. Since more space is devoted to material involving the god of war than to the others, and since this material is placed in especially advantageous positions from a dramatic standpoint throughout Book III, Chaucer conveys the idea that the Knight feels the military aspect of the situation the most important of all. Certainly we have ample evidence of this elsewhere—the characterization of Theseus and the interpretation of chivalry discussed in this chapter, for example. But intimate matters pertaining to the ladies embarrass him. He describes Venus as she is depicted in her temple as being carefully covered below the waist by the waves in the picture, while in the *Teseida* she lies totally naked

on a couch (Book VII, Canto 64); he naïvely misses the point of
Palamon's promise to Venus to wage war with chastity if Emelye's
hand is granted to him. Moreover, throughout the poem Emelye
is kept by the Knight a vague, chaste, vision-like image of beauty,
in such descriptive lines as the priceless bathos of "Up roos the
soone, and up roos Emelye" (2273). Such a characterization could
not bear the "humanization" invariably conveyed when Chaucer
exercises his gift for descripton of intimate personal details and
acts.

The "at his large" of line 2288 appears to me to refer to and
corroborate the "any thing in general" of line 2285. While the most
common meaning of "at his large" in Chaucer's time was "to be
free," which this passage is usually interpreted as conveying, I
think "large" is used in another sense here. The *OED* cites a use of
"large" as conveying "in a general way; in a general sense;
without particularizing." The earliest reference is from Bacon's
essay *Of Studies* (1625): "And Studies themselves do give forth
Directions too much at Large, except they be bounded in by
experience." However, the *OED* cites the adverbial form "largely"
as being used in this sense by Wyclif about 1380. Hence the final
line of the passage quoted should be interpreted, in my opinion, as
"But it is a good thing for one to [speak of such things only] in
general terms." Chaucer's Knight is well aware of his audience,
and in such matters as these the Miller and the Reeve could
scarcely be included in the Knight's classification of "hym that
meneth wel." It is barely possible, in line 2308, that Chaucer has
had the Knight innocuously commit a linguistic faux pas on the
same general subject, as Emelye says in her prayer to Diana: "I
am, thou woost, yet of thy compaignye,/ A mayde, and love
huntynge and venerye" (2307-8). "Venerye" may be a pun, although it is dubious and undemonstrable; according to the *OED*
it was in legal usage as early as 1497 in the sense of indulgence
of sexual desire. In any case, the Knight is certainly not consciously
using the word in this sense here.

The remainder of Emelye's prayer corresponds very closely to its
counterpart in the *Teseida*, except for the very end. In the *Teseida*,
as soon as Emilia receives the sign from Diana and realizes she
is to have one or the other of the lovers for her husband, she goes
home and spends a worrisome night—but only because she wonders
which lover it is to be (Book VII, Canto 93). In *The Knight's Tale*,

however, Emelye obviously feels the goddess has failed her in her
hour of need:

> For which this Emelye astoned was,
> And seyde, "What amounteth this, allas?
> I putte me in thy proteccioun,
> Dyane, and in thy disposicioun."   (2361-64)

It is the "allas," of course, which reflects Emelye's supposed hor-
ror at her fate of having to wed one of her lovers. This, then, is
the final attitude of the prize of love over whom Arcite and Palamon, aided by two hundred fierce assistants, are to do mortal
battle on the following day.

With two conspicuous exceptions, Arcite's prayer to Mars in *The
Knight's Tale* corresponds very closely to its *Teseida* source. The
first exception is Chaucer's significantly different treatment of
Arcite's reference to Mars' disappointments in love. The corresponding passage from the *Teseida* is:

> Se per alto valor la mia etade,
>> E le mie forze meritan che io
>> De'tuoi sia detto, per quella pietade
>> Ch'ebbe Nettuno, allor che con disio
>> Di Citerea usavi la beltade,
>> Rinchiuso da Vulcano, ad ogni Iddio
>> Fatto palese; umilmente ti prego
>> Che alli miei preghi te non facci niego. (Canto 25)*

Thus Boccaccio's Arcita merely makes a pertinent reference to
Mars' longing for a loved one who belongs to another, a situation
made known to all the gods by the injured Vulcan when he
trapped the guilty pair. But the circumstantial details in *The
Knight's Tale* are totally unwarranted by the four-line general
reference to Mars' affair in the *Teseida*:

> For thilke peyne, and thilke hoote fir
> In which thow whilom brendest for desir,

---

*If, because of my great valour, my age
And my strength deserve that I
Be called one of yours, in the name of that pity
That Neptune had [for you], when [filled] with desire
You used the beauty of Venus,
Locked up by Vulcano, to all gods
Made known; humbly I pray you
That you may not deny my prayers.

> Whan that thow usedest the beautee
> Of faire, yonge, fresshe Venus free,
> And haddest hire in armes at thy wille—
> Although thee ones on a tyme mysfille,
> Whan Vulcanus hadde caught thee in his las,
> And foond thee liggynge by his wyf, allas! —
> For thilke sorwe that was in thyn herte,
> Have routhe as wel upon my peynes smerte. (2383-92)

Obviously Arcite believes he is presenting perfectly logical grounds for Mars' help on the basis of this analogy between their two situations. In the Boccaccio the analogy is more or less logical, since it rests upon Neptune's pity for Mars and Mars' pity for Arcita. Chaucer's added details have the effect of shifting the base of the analogy to a comparison of Mars' discomfiture upon being found out in his illicit love affair and Arcite's sufferings over his love for Emelye. The "thilke sorwe" of line 2391 can refer only to Mars' misadventure recounted in lines 2388-90, since up to this point Mars' flames of desire are obviously being quenched by the beauteous Venus. The analogy is a false one, then, and shares the humorous and satiric properties of the Knight's account of the disposition of Arcite's soul, the brief passage from the prologue to *The Miller's Tale*, and the structural aspects of the Monk's and Friar's descriptions, analyzed in detail in Chapter II (classifications 1, 2, and 3). It is far-fetched, not to say fatuous, to suppose that Mars would be moved to bestow favor on one who supports his appeal by such an insistent and graphically detailed reminder of what must have been one of the most embarrassing episodes of the god's immortal life!

The second significant change from Boccaccio's version of Arcite's prayer also consists of new material added by Chaucer:

> For she that dooth me al this wo endure
> Ne reccheth nevere wher I synke or fleete. (2396-97)

This seems as obvious an example of the same kind of humor and satire as Arcite's realistic appraisal of the two Thebans' situation in the "dog-and-bone" analogy of Book I.

Book III of *The Knight's Tale* ends with Chaucer's treatment of the turmoil "in the hevene above" caused by Venus' and Mars' mutually contradictory commitments to grant both Palamon and

Arcite their respective desires. Of the forty lines devoted to this material by Chaucer, only these six are found in the *Teseida*:

> ... perchè allora fur sentite
> Diverse cose in la casa sagrata,
> E sì ne nacque in ciel novella lite
> In tra Venere e Marte: ma trovata
> Da lor fu via con maestrevel arte
> Di far contenti i preghi d'ogni parte.
> (Book VII: Canto 67, lines 3-8)*

Chaucer's Knight brings Saturn to the fore as the all powerful problem-solver. In the later books of the *Teseida* Mars at least tacitly consents to Arcita's injury, but perhaps because the Knight seems to reflect an attitude of respect for the mighty god of war, Chaucer has Saturn arrange for the downfall of Mars' faithful servant. Also, since Saturn is Venus' father and he does favor her side of the quarrel, Arcite is indirectly "vanquished by love." The Philostrate pseudonym is accordingly consistent with Chaucer's departures from the *Teseida* here. But the additional material in *The Knight's Tale* consists chiefly of Saturn's ominous account of his power and the harrowing manifestations thereof. Finally he reassures Venus,

> Now weep namoore, I shal doon diligence
> That Palamon, that is thyn owene knyght,
> Shal have his lady, as thou hast him hight.
> Though Mars shal helpe his knyght, yet nathelees
> Bitwixe yow ther moot be som tyme pees,
> Al be ye noght of o compleccioun,
> That causeth al day swich divisioun.
> I am thyn aiel, redy at thy wille;
> Weep now namoore, I wol thy lust fulfille."   (2470-78)

If Palamon is to "have his lady," the future would appear to bode very ill indeed for Arcite despite Mars' help, in view of Saturn's methods of arranging "pleyn correccioun."

---

*. . . because then there were heard
Diverse things in the holy abode
And a new quarrel was born thereof
Between Venus and Mars: but found
By them was a way, with masterful art,
To satisfy the prayers of all sides.

In effect the Knight has revealed the essential outcome of his tale in these lines. This is in direct contrast to the corresponding brief passage from the *Teseida* quoted above, which leaves the outcome of the poem in doubt by its ambiguous statement that a way to please all sides will be found. This is, I think, another indication of the Knight's preoccupation with the chivalric, military aspects of his tale. The supposedly noble motives and the knightly acts resulting therefrom are his chief concern. The account of the coming battle is far more important for its own sake than the foretelling of who is to win the lady for whom it is fought!

Book III ends with the Knight's perfectly open admission that in effect the entire book amounts to a digression:

> Now wol I stynten of the goddes above,
> Of Mars, and of Venus, goddesse of love,
> And telle yow as pleynly as I kan
> The grete effect, for which that I bygan.   (2479-82)

Throughout its course we have had the Knight's own word, conveyed in one way or another, that he will get to his point, and we are now informed with the literal clarity of his first and second narrative devices that the "grete effect" is still to come. Yet in this long series of digressions that Chaucer's Knight obviously finds so fascinating, fully two-fifths of all the material Chaucer borrowed from the *Teseida* may be discovered. Even though it is clear that Chaucer's changes as well as his manipulation of material directly borrowed from the Boccaccio result in very different effects from those of comparable passages in the Italian poem, Book III is inconsistent with the remainder of *The Knight's Tale* in terms of genre. If the *Teseida*'s poetic substance fails to warrant the epic genre, it may be said that *The Knight's Tale* is still less capable of bearing the epic paraphernalia of Book III. Chaucer consistently omitted essentially every epic characteristic of whatever material he borrowed from the *Teseida*, except in this book. Here it is very obvious that he has far exceeded the epic grandeur of the Boccaccio poem, with the resultant artistic ambivalence discussed above.

Despite the different effects derived from Book III of *The Knight's Tale* in comparison with those of corresponding passages of the *Teseida*, Chaucer relied more heavily on the Boccaccio source in this book than in any other. Since this portion is also more inconsistent with the poem as a whole than any other book, it is interesting to discover that this state of affairs is also reflected in an arithmetical representation of the degree of Chaucer's literal reliance on the *Teseida* material in the remainder of *The Knight's Tale*. Thus if we subtract the number of lines in Book III traceable to Boccaccio from the total number of lines in *The Knight's Tale*, we arrive at a remainder of some 1,966 lines; of these some four-fifths in no way correspond to any lines in the *Teseida*, while only about one-twentieth amount to direct translation from the *Teseida*. We may therefore conclude that while this arithmetical evidence is by itself of no real significance in assessing Chaucer's *artistic* debts to the Boccaccio poem, when it is considered together with the extensive evidence of more appropriate kinds so far accumulated, Chaucer's poem is a very different artistic work indeed from that of Boccaccio.

VII

book four

HILE BOOK IV of *The Knight's Tale* contains nearly as many lines which may be traced to the *Teseida* as Book III, the proportions of Chaucer's indebtedness are less dramatic. The 264 lines in Book IV which bear varying degrees of resemblance to Boccaccio's poem comprise slightly more than two-fifths of the total of 622 lines. As was the case with Book III, Chaucer borrowed most freely from the Italian poem in matters of epic pageantry and ceremony for his final book.

The events from the latter part of Book VII through Book XII in the *Teseida* correspond approximately to those in Chaucer's Book IV. In Canto 96 of Book VII, Boccaccio describes with conventional elegance the lovely dawn of the great day. Teseo's grand palace is filled with people of all kinds who enthusiastically discuss the coming battle and the merits of the various contestants (Cantos 97-99). Finally Teseo appears in magnificent array, and then Arcita and Palamone. All three are greeted by the shouts of the assembled personages (Cantos 100-101). Teseo then takes both Arcita and Palamone to Mars' temple, where the two Thebans make sacrifices; when they all return, Arcita and Palamone each join their chosen hundred knights and begin the procession toward the theater (Cantos 102-4). The procession itself is extremely impressive, and all wonder which side will win the fearsome struggle (105-7). Only now does Boccaccio describe the theater in detail;

it is essentially the same as the Knight's description in Book III of *The Knight's Tale*. The theater is a mile in diameter, has marble walls and two impressive entrances with intricately wrought gates (Cantos 108-9). For the populace there are more than five hundred stone tiers, so constructed that everyone can see without blocking anyone else's view (Canto 110). As the huge procession arrives at the theater, Teseo appears first in all his royal glory, flanked by Egeo. Next come the Greeks (presumably as spectators), all without armor, followed by many Thebans (Cantos 111-12). At the end of the procession of spectators are Ippolita and the beautiful Emilia (Canto 113). Finally, the two groups of armed knights enter the theater with their awesome array of armor and weapons (Cantos 114-21). As Arcita sees Emilia, he murmurs to himself a florid entreaty to her not to disdain his great love (Cantos 122-27). When Palamone catches sight of Emilia, he says much the same thing to himself, and the first trumpet call to battle then sounds (Canto 128).

In a relatively brief speech Teseo orders that those who are taken are to leave their arms. The victor will be granted the lady and, as he informed Palamone and Arcita earlier, the loser is to abide by Emilia's decision as to his future (Cantos 130-32). Significantly, there is nothing in his speech in the *Teseida* which corresponds to the "destruccioun of gentil blood" passage in Chaucer's Book IV. Boccaccio brings his Book VII to a close as Teseo has the second call to battle sounded, and the two young Thebans each address their comrades with words of encouragement for the coming battle (Cantos 133-45).

Book VIII of the *Teseida* is almost entirely unrepresented in Chaucer's poem—only four lines of Book IV of *The Knight's Tale* correspond to this portion of the Italian poem. But part of this material omitted by Chaucer is not mere epic detail; indeed, it is central to the *Teseida* as a whole. Thus some of Chaucer's omissions here emphasize once again that the *Teseida* and *The Knight's Tale* are radically different works of art. Since Chaucer's significant neglect of virtually all of Boccaccio's Book VIII gives rise to the same kind of result brought about by the omission of most of Boccaccio's Book I (discussed in Chapter III), it is necessary to consider pertinent passages in considerable detail.

Boccaccio's Book VIII opens with the third and final call to battle; the poet invokes the Muse to help him describe the events.

Arcita's and Palamone's forces fall upon each other fiercely and swiftly (Cantos 1-7). Since they are so nearly equal in strength and valor, they repel each other. The fighting is furious and long, the ground becomes wet with blood, and many on both sides are slain, wounded, bruised, and taken captive. Palamone and Arcita fight even harder than the rest, but Arcita is the most terrible battler of all and performs marvels of knightly combat. Yet Palamone performs similar marvels. While Arcita is taking a short rest he happens to catch a glimpse of Emilia, and thereafter he terrifies all the others (except for Palamone, presumably). Teseo watches the deeds of combat with great interest, and the captured combatants join him to enjoy the awesome spectacle (Cantos 8-92).

In the *Teseida*, the ladies make no bones at all about their deep interest in the course of the battle. Ippolita watches avidly and would dearly love to fight herself:

> Ippolita con animo virile
>   La doppia turba attenta rimirava;
>   Nè già fra sè ne teneva alcun vile,
>   Anzi d'alta prodezza gli lodava;
>   E s'egli avesse il suo Teseo gentile
>   Voluto, arme portarvi disiava,
>   Tanto sentiva ancora di valore
>   Di quella donna il magnifico core.   (Canto 93)*

Emilia's thoughts, however, are far from those of her Amazonian sister. On the one hand she is horrified at all this violence and death:

> Emilia rimirava similmente
>   E conosceva ben fra gli altri Arcita,
>   E Palemone ancora combattente;
>   Ed attonita quasi ed ismarrita
>   Fiso mirava quella marzial gente:
>   E quante volte vedea dar ferita

*Ippolita, with manly courage
Attentively regarded the double crowd;
Nor yet did she consider any of them a coward,
But gave them praise as most valorous;
And if her noble Theseus had so wished,
She would have desired to bear arms for (or against) them,
So much valour still held
That woman's magnificent heart.

A nullo, o che e' fosse in terra miso,
Tante color cangiava il chiaro viso: (Canto 94)*

She wishes that Arcita and Palamone had continued their individual battle in the grove so that this mass bloodshed might have
been averted, and she believes the souls of the dead combatants
will return to haunt her. She bemoans the hard lot love has
brought her. She has not herself burned with desire, yet only she
is fought over by so many. Worst of all, both Palamone and
Arcita are so exceedingly handsome and noble that she cannot
decide which she would prefer. For all this, "Amore" is to blame
(Cantos 95-109).

On the other hand, when Arcita achieves his victory, Emilia no
longer suffers these pangs of conscience, and her love doubts are
quickly resolved. As the combatants become tired, Mars (in the
form of Theseus) asks Arcita if cowardice is holding him back.
Arcita redoubles his efforts, one of the knight's horses bites Palamone in the arm thus unhorsing him, and Arcita manages to
disarm and capture his beloved cousin (Cantos 111-22). Palamone
is grief-stricken, but Emilia is at once in love with Arcita and no
longer cares about Palamone at all (Cantos 123-24). Thus, Boccaccio tells us, he who was loved before is now abandoned—
whereas before Arcita's victory both the royal Thebans appeared
equal to her, now she admires only Arcita. She already joyously
considers herself married to him (Cantos 125-27). His forces quickly
capture the rest of the field, and Book VIII closes as he circles
the battle theater with his men, overjoyed at his great victory
(Cantos 129-31).

Book IX of the *Teseida* opens as Venus and Mars witness
Arcita's triumph. Venus reminds Mars that his part is finished,
and he in turn tells her that she may now do as she wishes
(Cantos 2-3). Venus causes Erinis to pass in front of Arcita's
horse, which rears high in the air and falls backward on top of
Arcita. Arcita's chest is horribly crushed, and his entire body seems

*Emilia similarly observed
And well recognized among the others Arcita
And Palamone still fighting;
And as one astonished and lost
Stared fixedly at the martial crowd;
And as often as she saw someone wounded
Or fallen to the ground
So often would her fair face discolour:

to be one great wound (Cantos 4-9). Emilia becomes deathly pale and mourns to herself the brevity of her ecstasy (Cantos 10-11). Arcita's armor is removed and his face bathed, but he is still unable to speak. Emilia curses the love which has brought this terrible tragedy to Arcita. Palamone grieves deeply for Arcita as well as for his own sad lot (Cantos 13-21).

Teseo disperses the crowd and summons physicians to care for Arcita. Arcita is told he has won Emilia; he asks to hear her voice and wishes nothing better than to die in her arms. Teseo tells Emilia to comfort Arcita, and she tenderly addresses Arcita as her husband, telling him she can hardly bear his pain:

> O signor mio, se vale il mio pregare,
> Confortati, che 'l tuo mal si mi grava,
> Che appena il posso, lassa, comportare:
> I' son sempre con teco, o dolce sposo,
> Oggi stato per me vittorïoso.   (Canto 27, lines 4-8)*

Having lovingly promised him she will always be with him, Emilia accompanies Arcita in his triumphal car around the arena at the head of a glorious procession. After leaving the theater, Arcita has his arms offered to Mars (Cantos 32-35). When they all arrive at Teseo's palace, Arcita is put to bed and the unhappy Palamone and his men are addressed by Teseo. He points out that the fates cannot be resisted and that they should all approve of the gods' pleasure. All the knights are free except Palamone who must remain as Emilia's prisoner (Cantos 48-60).

Palamone falls on his knees in front of Emilia, saying he is her prisoner:

> . . . Madonna, i' son vostro prigione,
> E sono stato continovamente
> Poich'io vi vidi; fate che vi piace
> Di me, che mai non spero sentir pace.
> (Canto 63, lines 5-8)†

*O my lord, if my prayer has any value,
Comfort yourself, for your pain wounds me so,
That I, miserable me, am barely able to stand it:
I am always with you, o sweet husband,
Who was victorious for me today.

†. . . Madam, I am your prisoner,
And have always been
Since I first saw you; do what you wish
With me, for I never hope to be at peace again.

Emilia gently replies to this woebegone submission that she would have loved him, but unfortunately the gods permitted her to have but one. Telling him the Greek cities are full of beautiful ladies, she gives Palamone a ring and insists he is free. But Palamone ardently insists he can love only her (Cantos 66-78). Arcita asks Teseo's permission to marry Emilia, and Teseo replies that it is his will that the marriage take place. Book IX closes with an account of the wedding (Cantos 81-83).

The early part of Book X of the *Teseida* is chiefly concerned with the aftermath of the great battle. That very night instructions are issued for the burning of the dead. All the appropriate preparations are made in the theater, the bodies are burned, and the ashes taken to Mars' temple. Every wounded man recovers except Arcita whose life is despaired of by the most learned physicians (Cantos 1-14). Realizing he is becoming worse, Arcita informs Teseo that he is dying and that his love for Emilia is unconsummated; he feels he has been greatly honored by the victory and asks Teseo to give Emilia to Palamone. Teseo tries to convince Arcita that he will be cured and urges him to take comfort in the possession of Emilia, but Arcita will not be comforted (Cantos 16-34).

Arcita calls for Palamone, telling him that although he (Arcita) is hardly married, he must die. He begs Palamone to perform his funeral rites and insists that it is his earnest desire that Palamone accept Emilia. Palamone tries to convince Arcita that he will live, but Arcita knows this cannot be true. Ippolita and Emilia arrive at his bedside, and Arcita asks Palamone what Emilia is to do if he dies (Cantos 37-59). Arcita's reply to his own question is significant; not only is his dear cousin Palamone more worthy to wed than he—Arcita can hardly praise his former rival enough:

> Ed io che tu sii sua me ne contento
>   Più che d'altrui, poich 'esser non puoi mia:
> Ferma in lui il tuo intendimento,
> E quel pensa di far ch'egli disia;
> Ed io son certo ch'ogni piacimento
> Di te per lui sempre operato fia:
> Egli è gentile, bello e grazïoso,
> Con lui avrai e diletto e riposo.   (Canto 62)*

*And I am happier that you be his
Rather than anyone else's, since you cannot be mine:

Arcita goes on to say that for these reasons he should like to have Emilia belong to Palamone rather than another. Feeling the coldness of death surrounding his heart, he commends his soul to Emilia and asks her to kiss him (Cantos 63-66).

Emilia is grief-stricken and says it is she with whom the gods are angry and not her husband, who is dearer to her than her very life:

> O caro sposo a me più che la vita,
> Non verso te son crucciati gl'Iddii:
> Io sola son cagion di tua partita;
> Io nocevole sono a'tuoi disii. (Canto 67, lines 1-4)*

She laments further that Cytheraea, who took her betrothed Acate from her, now robs her of Arcita as well. She wishes she were never born—now, at last, she understands Diana's signs to her. She will die in grief, and if she outlives Arcita, she will ever remain a virgin, a true follower of Diana. If Palamone wishes to marry, he must find someone else. After kissing Arcita, she will never kiss another. As she kisses the dying man, everyone weeps copiously (Cantos 68-86).

Arcita lingers on and after nine days desires to make sacrifices to Mercury; this is done on the tenth day, and he prays that his soul may be carried away gently to the Elysian fields (Cantos 89-94). All Arcita's intimates come to his chamber, and he tells them his life is failing; death is cruel to him, his strength has fled, and without his Emilia he will always be filled with grief. He does not know where his soul is going, leaving all his dear ones behind. He looks at Emilia, as death, beginning at his feet, approaches his breast. His last words are "Addio Emilia!" (Cantos 95-112). It is significant that the dreadful physical detail Chaucer lavished upon Arcita's death scene is not found in the *Teseida*. Boccaccio confined himself to the gradual progression of the coldness of

---

Fix your resolves in him,
And think of doing what he wishes;
And I feel sure that all your wishes
Forever will he fulfill:
He is gentle, beautiful and gracious,
With him you shall find delight and repose.
*O husband dear to me more than my life
Not against you are the gods enraged:
I alone am the cause of your departure (death);
I am the obstacle to your desires.

death through Arcita's body, and the last words—barely murmered
—as life departed:

> La quale in ciascun membro era venuta
>> Da' piedi in su, venendo verso'l petto,
>> Ed ancor nelle braccia era perduta
>> La vital forza; sol nello intelletto
>> E nel cuore era ancora sostenuta
>> La poca vita, ma già sì ristretto
>> Eragli 'l tristo cor di mortal gelo,
>> Che agli occhi fe' subitamente velo.
>
> Ma poi ch'egli ebbe perduto il vedere,
>> Con seco cominciò a mormorare,
>> Ognor mancando più del suo podere;
>> Nè troppo fece in sè lungo durare;
>> Ma il mormorio trasportato in vere
>> Parole, con assai basso parlare,
>> Addio Emilia, e più oltre non disse,
>> Chè l'anima convenne si partisse. (Cantos 111, 112)*

Arcita's death scene ends Boccaccio's Book X.

Book XI begins with the journey of Arcita's soul into its pagan
afterlife. Boccaccio accords this matter a conspicuously different
treatment than Chaucer, but I strongly suspect the humor in
Chaucer's version to have been inspired by the *Teseida* passage.
According to Boccaccio, Arcita's soul travels toward the concavity
of the eighth heaven and looks down upon the earth where he left
his body (Cantos 1-2). He laughs to himself at the doleful laments
of the throng (just as Chaucer's Troilus does) and joyously de-

---

*Which into each member had come
From the feet up, creeping toward the chest,
And in the arms, too, was lost
His vital strength; only in the mind
And in the heart was still sustained
The little (remainder of) life, but already so gripped
Was his sad heart with mortal cold,
That suddenly it veiled his eyes.
And when he had lost his sight,
He began to murmur to himself,
More and more losing his powers;
Nor did they last very long;
But having transformed the murmur into real
Words, with very low voice,
"Goodbye Emilia," and no more said he,
Because his soul was forced to depart.

parts to the place Mercury has assigned him (Canto 3). All hear the distant laughter and weep at Arcita's death; Emilia addresses him, asking his whereabouts, for she would join him. But all realize that his spirit had changed houses; while Palamone weeps bitterly, Arcita's eyes, nose, and mouth are closed. All weep loudly, and Teseo is inconsolable (Cantos 4-11).

Funeral preparations begin at once; Teseo orders an entire forest to be cut and decides to have the funeral held in the grove where Arcita was wont to sing his love complaints (Cantos 13-14). The bier is furnished with cloth of gold, and Arcita is similarly dressed. He is placed on the bier in the palace, and throughout the city one hears only weeping. All the birds and animals flee the forest as its trees in their many varieties are felled for the pyre. Finally the pyre is finished, its top covered with purple and gold cloth; everyone continues to weep, and the noblest of the Greeks carry the bier from Athens to the grove and set the bier at the top of the pyre. Palamone and Teseo follow the bier, and after them comes Emilia, who carries the funeral torch. She bitterly laments her lot, recalling both her love for Arcita and the fact that she never intended to enter his chambers in such a guise; when she finally sets fire to the pyre, she swoons. Palamone, having cut off his beard and hair, consigns them to the funeral flames, together with his arms and jewels. The account of the funeral continues for many more cantos, embracing all kinds of epic pomp and circumstance. Finally, toward night, the pyre is in ashes and on the following day Arcita's ashes are collected in a golden urn and deposited in Mars' temple. Teseo orders appropriate games in celebration (Cantos 16-66).

Palamone orders a temple to Juno to be built in the grove on the exact site of the pyre, where Arcita's ashes are eventually to be placed. The temple is decorated with all the adventures of Arcita's life, except for his fall from the horse (Cantos 69-91). With this description of the magnificent edifice erected by Palamone in memory of his kinsman, Boccaccio closes Book XI.

Book XII, the final book of the *Teseida*, opens with an account of Emilia's sad condition. She is pale and thin, having wept continuously since Arcita's death (Cantos 1-2). Several days after Arcita's death, Teseo summons Palamone and Emilia, addressing them in words partly assigned to Egeus in Chaucer's Book IV. He points out that all must die, and if one is happy the manner and

place of death really do not matter. Everyone knows that it is wise
to make a virtue of necessity, and the case at hand is no exception.
Accordingly, Arcita has been mourned enough; it is now time to
rejoice. Arcita requested that Emilia be given to Palamone, and,
before any of the assembled guests and combatants depart, Teseo
is determined that Palamone and Emilia's wedding will be celebrated (Cantos 3-19). Palamone demurs rather faintly, believing
his duty should conquer his desire; he fears he would be contradicting his great love for Arcita if he should marry Emilia.
Teseo insists this is not so, and commands Palamone to adhere
to his (Teseo's) will; Palamone silently prays to Jove, Diana,
Cytheraea, and the soul of Arcita for pardon, since he has decided
to obey Teseo's command. Teseo then commands Emilia to comply
with his wish, and Emilia agrees with some misgivings. The state
of her heart is apparently no problem, but she fears Diana will
take vengeance on Palamone as she already has on Acate and
Arcita. Teseo brushes aside her fears, saying that if Diana were
angry, Emilia would be the unhappy recipient of the divine wrath,
not the men in Emilia's life (Cantos 20-43). Everything being
settled, preparations for the wedding proceed, and all Athens
duly rejoices (Cantos 44-45).

Finally the great day of the wedding arrives (Canto 48). Emilia
is radiant, and with all the pageantry of the court the formal
ceremony takes place (Cantos 49-69). The feasting at the palace
goes on for fifteen days, beginning with the day after the wedding. On the wedding night, Emilia enters a chamber with Palamone. After the fifteen days, each of the kings says farewell,
leaving rich gifts behind for the loving couple. Palamone remains
in joy and solace with his lady (Cantos 70-83). Boccaccio ends the
Teseida with a final sonnet to the Muses.

Chaucer begins Book IV of The Knight's Tale with his own account of the last hours before the battle:

> Greet was the feeste in Atthenes that day,
> And eek the lusty seson of that May
> Made every wight to been in swich plesaunce
> That al that Monday justen they and daunce,
> And spenden it in Venus heigh servyse.
> But by the cause that they sholde ryse
> Eerly, for to seen the grete fight,
> Unto hir reste wenten they at nyght.

> And on the morwe, whan that day gan sprynge,
> Of hors and harneys noyse and claterynge
> Ther was in hostelryes al aboute;
> And to the paleys rood ther many a route
> Of lordes upon steedes and palfreys.   (2483-95)

While Boccaccio confined himself to a conventional description of
dawn on the great day and the situation at the palace, Chaucer
sets the scene by his account of the holiday mood of Athens the
day before the battle, followed by the colorful procession through
the city on the great day itself. The procession and the events in
the palace are delightful examples of Chaucer's realistic approach
to material Boccaccio treated merely as the impersonal, formal
impedimenta of his genre. Thus the Knight's naïve enthusiasm
permeates this entire section of Book IV as he describes the
"fomy steedes on the golden brydel," the squires "nailynge the
speres, and helmes bokelynge," the eagerness of the armorers "with
fyle and hamer prikynge to and fro," and "Yemen on foote, and
communes many oon/ With shorte staves, thikke as they may
goon" (2500-2510). Finally come the "Pypes, trompes, nakers, clari-
ounes,/ That in the bataille blowen blody sounes" (2511-12).
Then, without transition, Chaucer's Knight turns to the goings-on
in the palace:

> The paleys ful of peple up and doun,
> Heere thre, ther ten, holdynge hir questioun,
> Dyvynynge of thise Thebane knyghtes two.
> Somme seyden thus, somme seyde "it shal be so";
> Somme helden with hym with the blake berd,
> Somme with the balled, somme with the thikke herd;
> Somme seyde he looked grymme, and he wolde fighte;
> "He hath a sparth of twenty pound of wighte."
> Thus was the halle ful of divynynge,
> Longe after that the sonne gan to sprynge.   (2513-22)

The complex pageantry of the first part of the procession reminds us yet again that the supposedly deadly serious purpose
behind these mighty preparations is a full-scale battle for the hand
of a most reluctant lady. Yet it seems to me that the tone of some
passages—notably those describing the holiday mood of the populace on the preceding day and the "dyvynynge" of the court
circle—is in sharp contrast to and nullifies the effect of the sup-

posed high seriousness. Is not the atmosphere of the city much too merry, and do not the "dyvynynge" nobles reflect an entirely too casual emotional attitude—one amounting to sportive entertainment—toward an event marking the most powerful demonstration of chivalric ideals? It would not be out of keeping with this attitude if Chaucer's gentlemen had proposed a friendly wager or two on the outcome of the battle! In these passages the Knight's interpretations of the events he is relating are conspicuously absent; Chaucer employs the first and second stylistic devices of his narrator. Hence this material seems to me to reflect the same kind of inconsistency as Theseus' flippancy in his long address in Book II. Such lightness of attitude is hardly consistent with the highly serious matters that the Knight tirelessly assures us are at stake throughout his tale.

At this delicate point in Book IV, moreover, it is significant that the Knight's third (interpretive) narrative device reappears simultaneously with Theseus' participation in the events of the long-awaited day:

> The grete Theseus, that of his sleep awaked
> With mynstralcie and noyse that was maked,
> Heeld yet the chambre of his paleys riche,   (2523-25)

After Palamon and Arcite have been brought to the palace with suitable protocol,

> Duc Theseus was at a wyndow set,
> Arrayed right as he were a god in trone.
> The peple preesseth thiderward ful soone
> Hym for to seen, and doon heigh reverence,
> And eek to herkne his heste and his sentence.   (2528-32)

Certainly the description of Theseus in line 2529 is directly related to that in Book I, as Theseus, "in his mooste pride," haughtily deigns to become officially aware of the grieving women. Similarly, lines 2530-32 reflect the same response on the part of Theseus' audience to every appearance and act—regardless of their ethical implications—of Theseus throughout the poem. The "grete Theseus" of line 2523 subtly echoes the Knight's "gentil duc" and "worthy duc" of Book I. Thus the Knight describes him as "this gentil duc" when the great conqueror is moved to pity, not because of what has happened but because it happened to those of noble rank (952-56). Theseus became "this worthy duc" upon committing the two royal Thebans to perpetual, ransomless imprisonment (1022-27).

The transparent artificiality of the Knight's notion of the chivalric ideal is again emphasized in his interpretation of Theseus' motives for minimizing loss of life and limb in the approaching battle, as the herald pompously announces:

> "The lord hath of his heigh discrecioun
> Considered that it were destruccioun
> To *gentil* blood to fighten in the gyse
> Of mortal bataille now in this emprise.
>
>   (2537-40; italics mine)

The herald finishes the address with the details of weapon limitations, and the populace voices its appreciation for Theseus' decision. In the repetition of Theseus' alleged motive, however, the important modifier is—significantly—omitted:

> The voys of peple touchede the hevene,
> So loude cride they with murie stevene,
> "God save swich a lord, that is so good,
> He wilneth no destruccion of blood!"   (2561-64)

This concludes the introductory section of Chaucer's Book IV, except for four transitional lines.

From the standpoint of artistic ambivalence, it is clear that the humorous and satiric effects of these passages are derived in the same manner as in the directly related passages from Book I cited here, which were analyzed in detail in Chapter III. Many of these effects are so subtle in this part of Book IV that their confirmation is almost dependent upon the parallel instances in Book I. By his sweeping reorganization of Boccaccio's material and by his frequent departures from it, Chaucer enables us to derive artistic effects entirely different from those of comparable portions of the *Teseida*. This is further confirmation of the fact that the artistic relationship between the *Teseida* and *The Knight's Tale* may be clearly seen only by placing proper emphasis upon Chaucer's departures from and omissions of many vital portions of the Italian poem.

Previous critical assessments of the dependence of *The Knight's Tale* upon the *Teseida*, cited earlier in this study, have been concerned either with the extent of the literal similarities of the two poems or with the somewhat fragmentary analyses of the nature—but not the significance—of Chaucer's departures from Boccaccio. Since some four-fifths of *The Knight's Tale* fails to correspond to the *Teseida*, it seems obvious that these departures warrant the examination I am presently undertaking. As we have seen, the conclusion drawn from others' research in this area is, in generalized form, that *The Knight's Tale* is essentially an abridgment of the *Teseida*, although Chaucer's manner of telling his tale—the "tone"—is his own. In the present investigation, which by now has embraced most of the poem, it is amply clear that in fact the two poems, in terms of their creative artistry, are entirely different works.

Accordingly, in the section of Book IV presently under consideration, the most radical departure from the *Teseida* is Theseus' sweeping modification of the rules of battle to preclude loss of life. This is in complete harmony with Theseus' characterization throughout the poem, as are the various allusions to those aspects of his personality that may best be described as manifestations of pride. It fully confirms the discussion of his personality in Chapter III; Theseus is a truly fine human being as Chaucer portrays him for us, but he is also a credible one who is by no means exempt from the most universal of all human frailties. In a broader sense, this departure from the Boccaccio results in a profound change in the total situation, which must affect our interpretation of the poem accordingly. The alleged enmity unto death of Arcite and Palamon over the hand of the reluctant Emelye has resulted in the gathering together of the most renowned and accomplished troops of chivalric slayers available to the medieval imagination. This enmity is now to be dissolved by an armed contest in which every precaution against fatal injury is to be taken! It is for this, then, that these enormous preparations have been made. With the presumably tragic certainty of knightly fratricide no longer a factor in the contest, the poem's artistic ambivalence seems more obvious than ever.

Chaucer's Knight brings the introductory section of Book IV to a close with another of his naïve redundancies:

> Up goon the trompes and the melodye,
> And to the lystes rit the compaignye,

> By ordinance, thurghout the citee large,
> Hanged with clooth of gold, and nat with sarge. (2565-68)

Line 2568 is a happier example of this stylistic idiosyncrasy of the
Knight than the one in Book III, wherein we learned that Mars'
temple is charmingly decorated with the grisly depictions of "A
thousand slayn, and nat of qualm ystorve" (2014).

The details of the procession from the palace to the theater
are similar in literal content to those in the *Teseida,* but Chaucer's
superb stylistic realism lends touches of psychological believability which do not emerge from the epic generalities of the Italian
poem. Thus Palamon enters the theater through the east gates
under Venus, "With baner whyt, and hardy chiere and face" (2586).
Also, the Knight insists,

> In al the world, to seken up and doun,
> So evene, withouten variacioun,
> Ther nere swiche compaignyes tweye;   (2587-89)

The battle is also rendered far more believable by Chaucer's
realistic approach. Boccaccio fills the first ninety-two cantos of
Book VIII of the *Teseida* with the involved progress of the contest,
while Chaucer completes his account in less than forty lines which
take us up to the capture of Palamon; none of these lines corresponds to the *Teseida.* The Knight almost revels in the imagined
prospect of the mighty struggle:

> Ther seen men who kan juste and who kan ryde;
> Ther shyveren shaftes upon sheeldes thikke;
> He feeleth thurgh the herte-spoon the prikke.
> Up spryngen speres twenty foot on highte;
> Out goon the swerdes as the silver brighte;
> The helmes they tohewen and toshrede;
> Out brest the blood with stierne stremes rede;
> With myghty maces the bones they tobreste.
> He thurgh the thikkeste of the throng gan threste;
> Ther stomblen steedes stronge, and doun gooth al;
>   (2604-13)

Arcite and Palamon unhorse each other twice. As they meet in
hand-to-hand battle, "The jelous strokes on hir helmes byte;/
Out renneth blood on bothe hir sydes rede" (2634-35).

The circumstances of Palamon's capture differ greatly from those in the *Teseida*. As I have stated, in the Boccaccio Palamone's capture is in part the result of an accident of the battlefield rather than his being overcome by force of arms. I suspect two factors may account for Chaucer's very different treatment of this episode. In the first place, Chaucer's Knight is at great pains to describe fully the fierce prowess of both cousins; for the narrator, both Thebans are glorious to behold on the battlefield. For one of them to lose the battle principally because he was bitten by a horse is scarcely in keeping with the Knight's notion of chivalric heroism. In the *Teseida* such details are easily absorbed in the mass of epic impedimenta which makes consistency in such matters more or less unnecessary. Also, since of all the divinities interested in the battle the Knight naturally feels Mars is the most worthy, we expect Mars' faithful servant to be clearly victorious in the battle. Nonetheless, Palamon puts up an heroic struggle. He is taken only after Emetreus wounds him while he is engaged with Arcite, and even then no less than twenty knights are needed to drag him to the neutral stake:

> The stronge kyng Emetreus gan hente
> This Palamon, as he faught with Arcite,
> And made his swerd depe in his flessh to byte;
> And by the force of twenty is he take
> Unyolden, and ydrawe unto the stake.   (2638-42)

Theseus immediately stops the battle. Significantly, however, he attributes Arcite's victory to "fortune" rather than military superiority:

> He cryde, "Hoo! namoore, for it is doon!
> I wol be trewe juge, and no partie.
> Arcite of Thebes shal have Emelie,
> That by his fortune hath hire faire ywonne."   (2656-59)

The spectators are overjoyed at the result of the battle, but Venus weeps in frustrated shame. Here, again, Chaucer departs markedly from the Boccaccio in having Saturn rather than Venus arrange for Arcite's fatal accident. In any event, Chaucer's Knight obviously assigns no chivalric qualms to the ominous Saturn, who proceeds to comfort Venus:

> Saturnus seyde, "Doghter, hoolde thy pees!
> Mars hath his wille, his knyght hath al his boone,
> And, by myn heed, thow shalt been esed soone." (2668-70)

At this point the Knight once again forgets himself and apparently becomes so enrapt by his narration that he becomes confused. Thus as he tells of the noise of the trumpets and "loude mynstral- cie," and heralds "that ful loude yelle and crie," he says: "But herkneth me, and stynteth noyse a lite,/ Which a myracle ther bifel anon" (2674-75).

In the *Teseida*, at the very instant of Arcita's victory, Emilia fell most extravagantly in love with him. At this point in *The Knight's Tale*, Emelye indulges in what is possibly her second voluntary response to this "hoote fare," the first having been in her prayer to Diana in Book III (as she begged to be relieved of the atten- tions of both lovers). In all her other appearances in the poem she has been only an illusion—even her weeping with the other ladies of the court over Palamon's and Arcite's proposed fates in Book II is mere convention. Thus as Arcite—no doubt flushed with the joys of victory and love—gazes up at her, he receives the fruits of his valor: "And she agayn hym caste a freendlich ye" (2680).

Such is the glorious reward which falls to the lot of this faithful chivalric lover after eight years of frightful suffering and two bloody battles. Undoubtedly, according to the Knight's interpreta- tion of chivalric human nature, Emelye's friendly glance is tanta- mount to an expression of her undying love for Arcite. But accord- ing to her portrayal throughout the poem, she is incapable of genuine human love and, consequently, of any spontaneous ex- pression of it. However, her glance may well be an expression of some form of human feeling for Arcite and hence a voluntary response of a sort to his love. It may also be a purely conventional response arising from the peculiar concept of the chivalric code implicit throughout the poem, or she may be making a voluntary response to worldly success.

If Emelye transcends her role as a personification of convention anywhere else in the poem, it is in her prayer to Diana. In the *Teseida*, Emilia's prayer is so inconsistent with her character that it is obviously only a convention. In *The Knight's Tale* Emelye's prayer is totally consistent with everything else we know of her. As she insists that she desires to remain a virgin undisturbed by love and wants nothing to do with the company of men, marriage, or pregnancy, she may well be sincere. If so, she betrays a desire not only to avoid sharing her emotions with anyone but also a desire to escape participation in *any* act or association which may either symbolize or be substituted for natural womanly emotions. Yet she also asks Diana, if it should be necessary for her to accept Palamon or Arcite, to send her the one who desires her most!

If the entire prayer is interpreted as part of the Knight's concept of the chivalric code, this passage is both incongruous and inappropriate, with humorous and satiric effects. If we are to take the entire prayer literally, Emelye becomes either a puppet of convention or an extremely selfish woman, depending upon how we interpret her wish that if she must be married let it be to him who desires her the most. If the wish is sincere rather than a conditioned response to convention, she desires to take all and share nothing. Considered from any one or combination of these standpoints, Emelye as the object of the burning emotions and deeds of Palamon and Arcite is farcically ironical.

The last three lines of this passage apparently reflect the view on the part of the Knight that the friendly glance of Emelye shows her to be—like most women—a worldly, opportunistic creature:

> (For wommen, as to speken in comune,
> Thei folwen alle the favour of Fortune)
> And was al his chiere, as in his herte.   (2681-83)

Professor Robinson points out that lines 2681-82 are not present in the best manuscripts and believes Chaucer may have intended to omit them.[1] However this may be, it does not seem to me that we are demanding too much of the Knight's naïveté (not to say gullibility) to assume he believes that while a woman's love is dependent solely upon Fortune's granting the man worldly success, this kind of love is nevertheless the right and proper core of the chivalric ideal. From all we have learned about him, he would be guilelessly unaware of any inconsistency between the two royal Thebans' emotions and Emelye's responses. Since he really considers it improper to know too much about any feminine matter which could be construed as personal, we are scarcely surprised that he finds Emelye a perfectly reasonable heroine. In any case, these two lines have obvious enough implications in terms of humor and satire to make further discussion of them redundant. The exact meaning of line 2683 has not been determined, but it obviously conveys that Arcite's heart is full of gladness as he receives Emelye's friendly glance.

Chaucer's version of Arcite's accident differs considerably from that of Boccaccio, and only one line of the sixteen-line passage contains any reference to the accident's supernatural genesis. Thus Pluto accedes to Saturn's request by causing a "furie infernal" to rise out of the ground, at which Arcite's horse leaps aside and falls. Arcite's injuries and appearance are equally frightful:

> His brest tobrosten with his sadel-bowe.
> As blak he lay as any cole or crowe,
> So was the blood yronnen in his face.   (2691-93)

Chaucer omits the triumphal procession of the *Teseida,* wherein Emilia accompanies Arcita around the theater and his arms are offered to Mars. More significantly, Chaucer also omits the scene on the battlefield in which Emilia comforts Arcita, calling him her sweet husband, and telling him she can scarcely bear his pain but will be with him always. This great difference between the two poems emphasizes once more the entirely different characterizations of Boccaccio's Emilia and Chaucer's Emelye. Emilia's words and actions in this part of the *Teseida,* while performed at Teseo's suggestion, are in harmony with Boccaccio's portrayal of her throughout the poem, while these same words and actions would be completely out of character for Chaucer's Emelye. In *The Knight's Tale* Arcite is taken at once to the palace, cut out of his armor, and put to bed, whereupon he recovers consciousness and is "alwey criynge after Emelye" (2699).

In the Boccaccio, Teseo had the theater cleared of people before the triumphal car began its journey. Chaucer has Theseus return to the palace with the vast train of nobles "With alle blisse and greet solempnitee" (2700-2702), and the wounds and broken bones are attended to. There are no fatalities. No one believes Arcite will die, and Theseus entertains in his usual royal fashion:

> For which this noble duc, as he wel kan,
> Conforteth and honoureth every man,
> And made revel al the longe nyght
> Unto the straunge lordes, as was right.   (2715-18)

The Knight is at pains to make clear, perhaps because it would be unthinkable that Emelye's future husband is not a mighty chivalric battler, that Palamon's valor is respected by all. There is nothing in the *Teseida* that resembles this passage:

> For fallyng nys nat but an aventure,
> Ne to be lad by force unto the stake
> Unyolden, and with twenty knyghtes take,
> O persone allone, withouten mo,
> And haryed forth by arme, foot, and too,
> And eke his steede dryven forth with staves
> With footmen, bothe yemen and eek knaves,—
> It nas arretted hym no vileynye;
> Ther may no man clepen it cowardye.   (2722-30)

Also Theseus' proclamation of the cessation of all rancor and strife is not in the *Teseida*, and his dismissal of all the personages who came to Athens for the lists is a most significant departure from the Italian poem:

> For which anon duc Theseus leet crye,
> To stynten alle rancour and envye,
> The gree as wel of o syde as of oother,
> And eyther syde ylik as ootheres brother;
> And yaf hem yiftes after hir degree,
> And fully heeld a feeste dayes three,
> And conveyed the knyges worthily
> Out of his toun a journee largely.
> And hoom wente every man the righte way.
> Ther was namoore but "Fare wel, have good day!" (2731-40)

The Knight catalogues Arcite's harrowing symptoms in great detail, another significant departure from the *Teseida* which permits, as Professor Baum remarks, an "extraordinary" lapse into facetiousness.[2] The humor is clear enough and is another example of the Knight's ending a seemingly endless series of details with an abrupt line or two, the content of which results in a humorous or satiric effect, or sometimes both. Frequently this results from one of Chaucer's modifications of the *occupatio* rhetorical device. Indeed, perhaps the most striking example of this in the entire poem occurs in the almost interminable account of Arcite's funeral, which follows within a few lines of the death scene. Chaucer shortens the time span of Arcite's death from the several days of the *Teseida* version to a matter of hours, and the Knight makes this graphically clear from the very beginning of the death scene:

> Swelleth the brest of Arcite, and the soore
> Encreesseth at his herte moore and moore.
> The clothered blood, for any lechecraft,
> Corrupteth, and is in his bouk ylaft,
> That neither veyne-blood, ne ventusynge,
> Ne drynke of herbes may ben his helpynge.
> The vertu expulsif, or animal,
> Fro thilke vertu cleped natural
> Ne may the venym voyden ne expelle.
> The pipes of his longes gonne to swelle,
> And every lacerte in his brest adoun
> Is shent with venym and corrupcioun.
> Hym gayneth neither, for to gete his lif,
> Vomyt upward, ne dounward laxatif.
> Al is tobrosten thilke regioun;
> Nature hath now no dominacioun.
> And certeinly, ther Nature wol nat wirche,
> Fare wel phisik! go ber the man to chirche!   (2743-60)

In view of the supposed high seriousness of the entire poem and of this specific passage (both of which must be considered as providing the total context of lines 2759-60), it is difficult to imagine a more incongruous or inappropriate couplet than this plebeian proverb. Its date of origin has not been determined, so far as I know—Chaucer may well have coined it.

Chaucer, of course, omits the marriage of Arcite and Emelye which in the Boccaccio takes place almost immediately after the battle. Otherwise there is a loose correspondence between the two poems from this point in *The Knight's Tale* until Arcite's death (2761-2808). Typically, however, Chaucer changes much of the order of the material, makes many minor departures from it and one or two major ones, and greatly softens the intensity of Arcite's insistence that after his death Emelye should marry his beloved kinsman. In *The Knight's Tale*, Arcite recounts his sorrows and turns to a brief consideration of melancholic philosophy, concluding it with a crashing redundancy:

> What is this world? what asketh men to have?
> Now with his love, now in his colde grave
> Allone, withouten any compaignye.   (2777-79)

Lines 2778-79 seem to me among the most subtly ambivalent in the whole poem. In the immediately preceding lines, Arcite recalls the "peynes stronge" he has suffered so long for Emelye and bemoans the "departynge of oure compaignye" (2771-74). He ends the series with what amounts to at least an emotional paradox: "Allas, myn hertes queene! allas, my wyf!/ Myn hertes lady, endere of my lyf" (2775-76). If this is to be interpreted as tragedy, the literal meaning (with due allowance for the conventions of complaint and of specific courtly love terms) seems clear enough.

In my opinion, however, the case for humor and satire is demonstrably stronger. Arcite's life has hardly been pleasant for these past eight years; if half of the extravagant torments the Knight attributed to the two Thebans throughout the poem had an element of truth in them, death for either one of them would seem to be an anticlimax. When Arcite refers soulfully to the "departynge of our compaignye" (i.e., his and Emelye's), he is in fact referring to something which never existed. Similarly, Emelye is not his "wyf." This has been noted by more than one critic, and Professor Robinson believes it may have been meant here as a term of devotion.[3] While this is quite possible, it is directly and conspicuously contradicted in the next few lines in exactly the same manner as several equally significant matters were contradicted in Book II, which was analyzed in terms of humor and satire in Chapter V.

Finally, the "endere of my lyf" certainly may be interpreted as a double entendre, although this becomes clear only when it is compared to line 2780: "Fare wel, my sweete foo, myn Emelye!" Both phrases—"endere of my lyf" and "my sweete foo"—may at first glance seem to be merely the typical language of medieval love poetry, and Professor Robinson notes that this is the case with "my sweete foo."[4] But the example he cites in Chaucer as substantiation is in fact far more closely related to the "endere of my lyf" phrase. Troilus refers to his stricken state over Criseyde in similar terms immediately after he has fallen in love with her: "O quike deth, O swete harm so queynte" (*Troilus and Criseyde,* Book I, line 411). Obviously, however, Emelye is also literally the cause of Arcite's death from one standpoint: were it not for her, he would not be dying under these circumstances. The redundancy in lines 2278-79 is in its structure and in terms of its relation to its immediate context exactly like the redundancies of the Knight discussed above, the effects of which are clearly either humorous or satiric or both.

Arcite's final wish, as in the *Teseida*, amounts to an attempt to unite Emelye and Palamon. However, in keeping with Chaucer's portrait of Emelye, Arcite's words in *The Knight's Tale* are essentially suggestions, as opposed to the more or less prescriptive tone in the comparable passages of the Italian poem (Book X, Cantos 59-63). In the *Teseida* Arcita assumes Emilia will of course marry someone; obviously it should be Palamone. This is perfectly reasonable in view of Boccaccio's characterization of Emilia throughout the *Teseida*. Chaucer's Arcite can merely make the suggestion. While he does not go so far as to insist Palamon would make a better husband than he, as Boccaccio's Arcita does, he praises Palamon's qualifications as an able servant of love. Furthermore,

> As in this world right now ne knowe I non
> So worthy to ben loved as Palamon,
> That serveth yow, and wol doon al his lyf.
> And if that evere ye shul ben a wyf,
> Foryet nat Palamon, the gentil man."   (2793-97)

Despite the humorous and satirical implications in Arcite's last appearance in the poem, the noble simplicity of lines 2796-97 emphasizes the fundamental human dignity and goodness of a man of high ideals who in his last moments reveals a truly selfless love for those dear to him. From this point on Chaucer borrows the actual death scene almost line for line from Boccaccio, except for Arcite's last words: " 'Mercy, Emelye!' " (2808). If these are to be taken as the dramatic climax of a tragic scene, their relation to the rest of the poem reflects a return to the theme that the "natural" feelings of the noble may be expressed only through the artificial conventions of the chivalric code. From the standpoint of humor and satire, there are two possible meanings of "mercy" here: "clemency" or the French "merci." Arcite surely has no reason either to ask Emelye's mercy now, or to thank her for what has befallen him. Its relationship to the "endere of my lyf" seems inescapably clear.

Considering Arcite's death scene in its entirety, we may say that it is among the most delicately balanced examples of artistic ambivalence in the poem. Perhaps the most significant instances of humor and satire here are the "endere of my lyf" of line 2776; Arcite's self-contradiction in addressing Emelye as "my wyf" in

line 2775, while saying in line 2796 "if that evere ye shul ben a wyf";
the redundancy in line 2779; and "his laste word."

The Knight's discourse on the disposition of Arcite's soul has
been considered in detail in Chapter II. Emelye's alarming condition and Palamon's immediate reaction to Arcite's passing are
priceless. After Emelye swoons and is taken away to weep night
and day, the Knight treats his audience to another of his notions
of womanhood, no doubt speaking "in commune":

> For in swich cas wommen have swich sorwe,
> Whan that hir housbondes ben from hem ago,
> That for the moore part they sorwen so,
> Or ellis fallen in swich maladye,
> That at the laste certeinly they dye.   (2822-26)

It seems obvious that line 2823 echoes Arcite's contradiction. With
this exception, most of the extravagant mourning for Arcite and
the entire account of the funeral is borrowed from the *Teseida*.
Some of it is thoroughly reorganized by Chaucer, and his stylistic
approach to it is everywhere evident.

The oral imagery in line 2817 is echoed elsewhere, and the contrast between the supposed tragedy in high life and the nature of
the imagery the Knight employs here and elsewhere in his description of it is very sharp indeed. Thus Emelye shrieks, which is
at least somewhat inappropriate (the utmost expression of her love
for Arcite she has indulged in until his death is the friendly glance
in the battle theater), while Palamon howls. Later, as Arcite lies on
his bier, the great hall of the castle "roreth" with the crying (2881).
Arcite's face was black "as any cole or crowe" when he was injured
in the theater. Surely this kind of imagery is incongruously and
inappropriately plebeian for the supposed high tragedy of the entire affair. The grieving women of the city are quoted by the
Knight as sharing the sentiments of a folk proverb which is
similarly distinctly out of harmony with the situation: " 'Why
woldestow be deed,' thise wommen crye,/ 'And haddest gold
ynough, and Emelye?' " (2835-36). As the Knight says, "Allas, the
pitee that was ther"!

While according to Boccaccio Teseo is inconsolable immediately
after Arcita's death, the Knight says Theseus' elderly father Egeus
cheers him up. Chaucer assigns to Egeus the same sentiments
Boccaccio assigns to Teseo at this point. In the *Teseida* Teseo

addresses them to Palamone and Emilia to raise their spirits, while in *The Knight's Tale* they serve to "gladen" Theseus himself. In point of fact, Chaucer's Knight communicates, through all three of his narrative devices, that all the extravagant exhibitions of mourning on the part of all concerned are the "natural" conventions of chivalric grief.

Theseus is soon himself again and "with al his bisy cure" is trying to make up his mind where the sepulchre is to be placed. In Book II, as he laid down the rules for the armed contest, Theseus announced it would be held in the grove where he discovered the two Thebans fighting each other. Presumably the theater was built within the grove, although in the involved description of it in Book III the Knight does not mention its location. In any case, Theseus decides to bury Arcite "in that selve grove, swoote and grene,/ Ther as he hadde his amorouse desires," and where he and Palamon first "Hadden for love the bataille hem betwene" (2857-61). The great funeral fire is to symbolize Arcite's complaint and the hot fires of his love.

The funeral proceeds very much as it does in the *Teseida* but with changes in the orders of some of the minor events and occasional exaggerations of even Boccaccio's epic detail. Indeed the most exaggerated use in the entire poem of the *occupatio* rhetorical device (or one of Chaucer's typically modified versions of it) occurs at the end of the account of the funeral. The Knight proceeds to tell his audience what, nearly fifty lines later, he insists he is not going to tell them:

> But how the fyr was maked upon highte,
> Ne eek the names that the trees highte,
> As ook, firre, birch, aspe, alder, holm, popler,
> Wylugh, elm, plane, assh, box, chasteyn, lynde,
>   laurer,
> Mapul, thorn, bech, hasel, ew, whippeltree,—   (2919-23)

Going into similar detail on more than twenty different matters, he promises once more to get to his point:

> I wol nat tellen eek how that they goon
> Hoom til Atthenes, whan the pley is doon;
> But shortly to the point thanne wol I wende,
> And maken of my longe tale an ende.   (2963-66)

From the standpoints of humor and satire, while we have an even more richly detailed catalogue here, this long passage has the same effects as the similar passages cited in Book III. Also, like the "dog-and-bone" analogy in Book I, the point of all this "hoote fare" seems exceedingly small to warrant the excessive detail the Knight devotes to it. In his last grand fling at such matters, the effect is very much like that of most of the material in Book III. The epic paraphernalia is far too cumbersome for the slightness of the underlying emotional motivation in the poem. It is accordingly clear that the verbosity in Books III and IV is in those sections in which Chaucer drew most heavily from the Boccaccio source. In some instances Chaucer has even emphasized the epic character- istics already present in the borrowed material. But for the most part the excessive descriptive detail so many critics have noted is actually not Chaucer's but Boccaccio's, and Chaucer's manipulation of this material fully supports an interpretation of the poem in terms of artistic ambivalence. Who can say that this—or some- thing very much like it—was not a part of Chaucer's artistic in- tention in *The Knight's Tale*?

One of Chaucer's most drastic departures from the *Teseida* is at this point in Book IV, and it affects the interpretation of the poem as a whole. In the Boccaccio poem, Palamone and Emilia were rushed into marriage by Teseo within days after Arcita's death. Teseo was most anxious to have the ceremony before all the noble personages who had taken part in the lists left for their homelands. Chaucer has the Knight pack them off almost im- mediately after the contest and before Arcite's death. The gifts given them by Theseus in *The Knight's Tale* apparently represent a contradiction of the Boccaccio, where the noble guests instead gave gifts to Palamone and Emilia on their wedding day. Similarly, the three-day feast and other farewell entertainments in Chaucer's poem seem to have been substitutes for the fifteen-day wedding festival in the *Teseida*. But Chaucer's Knight tells his audience that many years pass before these happy events, and in the meantime Theseus seems to have acquired a medieval parliament. Signifi- cantly, the political considerations here fully substantiate the analy- sis of Theseus' character and personality in Chapter III:

By processe and by lengthe of certeyn yeres,
Al stynted is the moornynge and the teres

Of Grekes, by oon general assent.
Thanne semed me ther was a parlement
At Atthenes, upon certein pointz and caas;
Among the whiche pointz yspoken was,
To have with certein contrees alliaunce,
And have fully of Thebans obeisaunce.   (2967-74)

While the mourning has gone on for years, it seems, in *The Knight's Tale,* Teseo put an end to it in a matter of days in the *Teseida.* Once again the Knight forgets himself and apparently feels his tale is a comment on current events—as contemporary to him as his interpretation of its characters, events, and motivating forces—as he seems to recollect there was a "parlement." But the most significant matter is the passage of years. By the time the contest of arms was held, some eight years have passed since Arcite and Palamon first fell in love with Emelye. Obviously by medieval standards she was mature enough to marry when they saw her for the first time, and by those same medieval standards, in eight years she would have been at least overripe. In any case, Chaucer's realistic psychological approach makes this matter extremely conspicuous. Moreover, throughout the poem Emelye's youth and beauty are constantly emphasized.

Just possibly one may attribute this glaring inconsistency to Chaucer's use of literary convention up until the time of Arcite's death. But to add still more years of unspecified number to these eight seems to me to massively support an interpretation of artistic ambivalence, with the strongest possible implications for humor and satire. Inescapably, Emelye is by this time past the age and necessary physical attributes for marriage within the very conventions with which Chaucer's Knight permeates the poem.

Theseus' Boethian discourse has been so thoroughly explored by others as to require no further comment here. The last part, wherein he speaks so convincingly and humanely of converting virtue to necessity, of Arcite's honorable death "in his excellence and flour," and the propriety of rejoicing over Jupiter's providence rather than grieving, is an amalgam of Chaucer and Boccaccio. He concludes most movingly, "I rede that we make of sorwes two/ O parfit joye, lastynge everemo" (3071-72). Finally, unlike the Boccaccio, where Teseo in effect instructs Emilia, Theseus appeals to Emelye:

> "Suster," quod he, "this is my fulle assent,
> With al th'avys heere of my parlement,
> That gentil Palamon, youre owene knyght,
> That serveth yow with wille herte, and myght,
> And ever hath doon syn ye first him knewe,
> That ye shul of youre grace upon hym rewe,
> And taken hym for housbonde and for lord.
> Lene me youre hond, for this is oure accord.
> Lat se now of youre wommanly pitee.   (3075-83)

Theseus goes on to speak of Palamon's rank and birth, and concludes with "For gentil mercy oghte to passen right" (3089). He then urges Palamon to take Emelye by the hand, and the bond is then and there agreed upon. At last, "with alle blisse and melodye/ Hath Palamon ywedded Emelye" (3097-98). Emelye utters no word through all this, characteristically enough.

The long account of the wedding celebration in the *Teseida* is omitted by Chaucer, and the Knight contents himself with the hope that God will send Palamon the love he has so dearly bought. This would appear to be the case:

> And Emelye hym loveth so tendrely,
> And he hire serveth al so gentilly,
> That nevere was ther no word hem bitwene
> Of jalousie or any oother teene.   (3103-6)

I can think of no better words with which to end this examination of *The Knight's Tale* than those of Chaucer's Knight himself:

> Thus endeth Palamon and Emelye;
> And God save al this faire compaignye! Amen.

VIII

"the sentence of this matere"

IN THE INTRODUCTION I stated that of the valences which are my concerns in this study, the traditional point of view of *The Knight's Tale* is too ably explored and documented elsewhere to warrant extensive treatment of it here. But nothing I have dealt with in this essay has been intended to refute or fundamentally disagree with such an interpretation as *one* dimension—a most important one—of the poem. It is therefore not surprising that an analysis of satire and humor in the tale brings into focus those elements of balance and unity which help define both its serious and humorous dimensions and reveal anew Chaucer's superb structural artistry.

The most obvious of the unifying elements, perhaps, are the series of processions. With the possible exception of the formal hunting party in Book II, Theseus' travels are always in the form of colorful display and pageantry. We find him at the very beginning of the poem returning in triumph to Athens and later in Book I, having conquered Thebes and passed the sentence of ransomless imprisonment, "He took his hoost, and hoom he rit anon/ With laurer crowned as a conquerour." If Theseus' direct participation in Arcite's funeral procession of Book IV is obscure, his active organization of its every detail conveys his complete dominance over this brilliant parade of death. The funeral procession is an ironic dramatic parallel to the inordinate grandeur of the arrival in

Athens of Arcite's and Palamon's champions, again a result of Theseus' organization of the tournament. Uniting the whole series of processions, of course, is the consistent theme of triumph which reaches its apparent apex in the excessive pageantry of the champions. But the final victor is death, and the true apex of the theme of triumph as it is reflected in the processions is Arcite's funeral procession. For only after this, the ultimate triumph, can the accordingly anticlimactic marriage of Palamon and Emelye take place "with alle blisse and melodye."

Theseus' "L'etat c'est moi" dispositions in Book I are balanced in one form or another later in the poem. Obviously the decision to make war on Thebes and the ransomless imprisonment sentence of Book I are echoed in the hasty death sentence in Book II. Its swift reversal, partly as a kindly sop to the women's grief for all its marked flippancy of attitude, is in turn paralleled by the final moving humanitarianism of Theseus' funeral oration and the superbly effective marriage address to Emelye. The flippant elements of Theseus' address in Book II lie in ironic juxtaposition to his serious application of Boethian philosophy in Book IV to the entire sequence of events and their causes that culminate in Arcite's death.

Of the many references to death in *The Knight's Tale*, the effect of balance by contrast of its physical manifestations is among the most interesting—and, so far as I know, critically unexplored—unifying elements. The treatment accorded the bodies of the slain husbands of the complaining women by Creon and those from which the wounded Arcite and Palamon are torn in Book I reminds us of the very different treatment accorded Arcite's body in Book IV. Just as Theseus is responsible for the return of the mistreated corpses of their husbands to the grieving women for proper funerals, so does he supervise the royal rites for Arcite.

Other matters which may be said to be balanced by contrast include Emelye's garden scene in Book I and Arcite's deceptively similar grove scene in Book II. Both involve singing and an unseen audience whose presence is unsuspected by the singers, and both are part of the love complex of the tale. There are also the paradoxical changes in outlook of Arcite and Palamon following their argument in Book I. Early in Book II Palamon adopts Arcite's former point of view as expressed in the argument, while Arcite adopts Palamon's. By the end of Book II they have returned to at least portions of their original attitudes in their argument, but in

Arcite's death scene their mutual feelings become moving examples of the knightly brotherhood that we may assume marked their relationship at the beginning of the poem.

More consistency is reflected in the parallels of Arcite's and Palamon's characterizations in Book I and Book IV. For despite their changes in attitude and the evidence some critics have cited to assign mutually contradictory character traits to them, in one centrally important respect they remain steadfast in belief and deed. Arcite is the more argumentative and aggressive in Book I and later prays to and is favored by Mars to whose service he remains true to the end. Similarly Palamon, who allegedly mistakes Emelye for Venus the moment he sees her, then and there offers up a prayer to her. Later the unity is complete when he offers up his prayer to the goddess herself and is rewarded accordingly for his loyalty.

The great descriptions are unbalanced; the excessive display of the parade of Arcite's and Palamon's champions is equaled, perhaps, by the excessive description of the kinds of wood in Arcite's pyre and by other instances of Chaucer's use of *occupatio*. But they are so unrelated to one another that attempts to compare and contrast them in terms of unity and balance become mere sophistry. Finally, there is no balance in the love complex. Whatever we may choose to believe Emelye's true motivation to be, nothing available to us justifies the equating of her emotional involvement to that of Palamon and Arcite.

Although Theseus is the most apparent unifying force, what really brings "order out of chaos" in the poem is the awesome reality of death, the final triumphant resolution of both human and divine will. The futility of man's earth-bound notions of greatness vanish before the supreme grandeur of death, the final awakening of man to eternal life. The Christian significance of Arcite's death (despite the Knight's pseudo-pagan account of the disposition of Arcite's soul) we may assume was not unperceived by a medieval audience, nor can it fail to reach out to us today. Indeed, it transcends the boundaries of all doctrines to the very limits of man's conception of his relationship to the universe and to whatever he may seek to understand in it.

The most obvious result of this examination of *The Knight's Tale* is that the hypotheses formulated in the Introduction and in the first chapter have been confirmed by the evidence accumulated in subsequent chapters. We may accordingly conclude that despite the presence of some external characteristics of the metrical romance and courtly allegory, *The Knight's Tale* is not only fundamentally atypical of these genre but also is permeated with Chaucer's humor and satire. Moreover, since so much of this pervasive humor and satire in effect treats the external characteristics of these literary forms as expressions of the consequences of human folly, we may also conclude that the artistic ambivalence in the poem has been decisively demonstrated.

If we accept the literal-minded view of the characters, events, and emotional motivation emphasized throughout *The Knight's Tale* by the Knight himself, the poem is—as critics have long believed it to be—a metrical romance embracing some aspects of courtly love. Equally implicit in the poem, however, is the de-lightfully humorous satire that, for the perceptive reader, effectively exposes the Knight's exaggerated, naïvely serious interpretation of his material for what it is. From such a point of view, the poem has been demonstrated to be a superb satire of the conventions of the chivalric code as they are displayed by Arcite, Palamon, and Emelye, and the events their emotional involvements give rise to.

The conclusions arrived at in Chapters VI and VII are, first, that Chaucer exaggerated the epic characteristics of the material from the *Teseida,* an effect achieved through the kinds of selections he made as well as his manipulation of these selections. Second, if the epic paraphernalia of the *Teseida* is unwarranted by the slightness of the events, characters, and emotions of that poem, it is even more unwarranted in *The Knight's Tale* in view of Chaucer's careful omission of virtually all the epic impedimenta of those sections of the *Teseida* that approximately correspond to Books I and II. Finally, these relationships between *The Knight's Tale* and the *Teseida* reveal once and for all that Chaucer's deviations from his source are of vastly greater importance in understanding his poem than the borrowings. In Books III and IV, the depar-tures from the Boccaccio enable us to form a clearer perception of the sustained satire and delightful humor implicit in the entire poem.

Much of the humor and satire in *The Knight's Tale* evolves from the basic inconsistencies between the alleged nature of Arcite's and Palamon's love for Emelye and the actual expression of their love in thoughts, acts, and deeds. Ostensibly, the two Thebans are experiencing the idealistic suffering "natural" to courtly love. Yet, while this thesis is steadfastly shared by the Knight, Arcite, and Palamon, Chaucer concentrates so heavily upon detailed, realistic accounts of motivation, character, and action that major inconsistencies cannot be ignored unless we are willfully subjective. We are entitled to seek reasonable explanations simply because the "idealists" in the poem themselves regularly insist that their feelings and actions have reasonable or logical bases. The evidence accumulated here demonstrates conclusively, however, that neither Palamon's and Arcite's actions nor the reasons given for them reflect in any important way the alleged *nature* of their love, as Chaucer's Knight naïvely "interprets" it for us.

Adherents to the traditional point of view have certainly found convincing evidence of external characteristics of both the courtly love code and the metrical romance genre in the poem, and it would surely be a mistake not to take this into account. Our conclusion must be that the significance of this material has been misunderstood. Arcite, Palamon, the Knight, and the pallid Emelye are supposedly figures straight out of the metrical romances or courtly allegories, yet we find that they are in fact atypical of their ostensible literary relatives in every major respect. I submit that this is the result of Chaucer's psychological realism. Thus so long as such heroes and heroines remain shrouded in the vagueness of the superhuman ideals and feats of the romance and allegory of yesteryear, our critical faculties adjust themselves accordingly. But when Chaucer mixes earth-bound human motivation and reason with the ideals and actions peculiar to the literary knights and damsels of medieval romance and allegory, we can scarcely expect the artistic product to share fundamental characteristics with either genre.

I agree with Lewis that Chaucer's satire and humor should not be interpreted as mere mockery.[1] As I remarked earlier, I do not believe Chaucer ever mocked any genuine human ideal. But the most important effect of the satire in *The Knight's Tale* is surely the humorous exposure of society's interpretation of those fundamentally noble ideals which were supposed to have found their expression in the medieval romance and courtly allegory. We have no more grounds for believing that Chaucer was deliberately satirizing the ideals of love in *The Knight's Tale* than we have for believing that he was satirizing the ideals of the Church in the Monk's and Friar's descriptions in the *Prologue*. Clearly, the object of the satire is the human folly that Chaucer seems to imply is the inevitable concomitant of man's interpretation of so many of his highest ideals. Thus in *The Knight's Tale* it is not the ideals of love that are so treated as to convey effective satire and humor, but man's interpretation of them through the social edifices of courtly love and the chivalric code. We must conclude that man-created convention has been so successfully superimposed upon Arcite's and Palamon's genuine feelings—to say nothing of Emelye's —and the humanitarian ideals of their society that the ideals and feelings themselves become ridiculously distorted.

Yet whether Chaucer intended to convey it or not, all concerned, including the Knight, guilelessly believe that the dictates of sometimes fatuously artificial convention are inviolable "natural" laws and involuntary expressions of the sublime instincts peculiar to those of noble birth. The kind of love Palamon and Arcite feel for Emelye we have no reason to suppose is any different than that of any other men for a lovely girl. In the *Teseida*, Boccaccio makes it clear that the two Thebans first fall in love in the springtime; Arcita is released in October, presumably to pine away for Emilia during his travels even as Palamone will pine away in the luxurious palace. The significance of the seasons is obvious. In *The Knight's Tale*, too, it is in the springtime that the two young men's fancies turn to love, which we may easily derive from the description of Emelye in the garden. What could be more natural? It remains for the supposedly rigid discipline of chivalric convention to infallibly guide Arcite, Palamon, the Knight, and Emelye to the public misinterpretations of their intensely personal emotions. Thereby we are shown in the poem that the concept of courtly love, which is shared by everyone except Theseus, in fact is not a kind of emotion at all, but the imposition of man's stilted convention upon what should be the most spontaneous of all feelings. This convention, together with other equally unrealistic aspects of the chivalric code to which it is linked in *The Knight's Tale*, is the center of the humor and satire in all four books.

We should certainly bear in mind that the interpretation of the chivalric age vouchsafed us by the Knight was available to Chaucer's audience almost solely through the literature of romance and allegory. The ideals of chivalry in terms very similar to those of the Knight exist for us today in much the same way, that is, in popular sentimental or "historical" romantic novels or by the current tireless producers of chivalric soap operas. The formulae are the same in every age and may be summed up in the magic word with which the Knight begins his tale: "Whilom." Thus chivalric interpretations of human ideals for Chaucer's audience and for us rest upon literary authority rather than real-life observation and experience; all the noble tales are spun from the gossamer of "used-to-be." Chaucer's realistic stylistic approach to his material throughout *The Knight's Tale* enables us to realize that life was never really like this. Accordingly, the chivalric conventions that are so humorously satirized are derived from the metrical romance and courtly allegory, which is precisely why the external characteristics of *The Knight's Tale* are practically identical with those of romance and allegory. From one point of view Chaucer's treatment of them results in effective satire of the literary forms themselves, as well as of the interpretation of human ideals that make up the chivalric code implicit in these "romances of prys."

There are, in my opinion, broad implications in the results of this study for future work in Chaucerian studies. My findings should at least give pause to those who insist Chaucer respected and believed in the courtly love code, on the basis of his treatment of it in his "serious" works. I strongly suspect, for instance, that an examination of *Troilus and Criseyde* which embodied the same methodology I have employed here would reveal the same kind of artistic ambivalence in that superb poem. Similarly, we might well find the patient Griselde of *The Clerk's Tale* too saintly to be taken seriously, the courtly sentiments in *The Parliament of Fowls* in fact treated in a far less elevated manner than most critics suppose, and *The Legend of Good Women* also a rich mine of Chaucer's delightful humor and satire, to cite but three more specific possibilities.

In spite of the warnings of many traditional Chaucerians, these and related possibilities should not be thought of as iconoclastic, for it cannot be claimed that they substantially refute or replace the more traditional views of Chaucer's poetry. But if such examinations were successful, a most important new dimension would be added to our appreciation of some of Chaucer's finest work. To consider Chaucer a mocker is to belittle and thoroughly misunderstand his literary art. We must realize that his humor and satire as we have perceived them in *The Knight's Tale* are not directed at genuine human ideals but at man's interpretation of ideals which are ultimately, perhaps, divine in their origin. Thus Chaucer's humor and satire portray a far-reaching view of humanity, revealing truths which are no less profound for the delightful manner of their revelation. This, then, is the nature of the new dimension of appreciation for *The Knight's Tale* made avilable to us by the evidence accumulated in this investigation. It seems to me obvious that similar investigations of much of Chaucer's art would be very likely to furnish us with the same kind of new dimension of appreciation for other monuments of his poetic genius.

notes

CHAPTER I

1. John Dryden, *Fables, Ancient and Modern, Translated into Verse from Homer, Ovid, Boccace and Chaucer: with Original Poems*, in Carolyn F. E. Spurgeon (ed.), *Five Hundred Years of Chaucer Criticism and Allusion, 1357-1900*, I, 284. Complete information for references in footnotes may be found in the Bibliography.

2. Sir Walter Scott, *Works of John Dryden*, XI, 245, in Spurgeon, II, 40.

3. William Hazlitt, *Lectures on the English Poets, Collected Works of William Hazlitt*, ed. Waller and Glover, 1902-1906, V, 30, in Spurgeon, II, 102.

4. Paull F. Baum, *Chaucer: A Critical Appreciation*, p. 90.

5. *The Canterbury Tales*, ed. John Matthews Manly, p. 540.

6. Albert H. Marckwardt, *Characterization in Chaucer's Knight's Tale*, p. 9; Hoxie Neale Fairchild, "Active Arcite, Contemplative Palamon."

7. R. M. Lumiansky, "Chaucer's Philosophical Knight."

8. Robert Kilburn Root, *The Poetry of Chaucer*, pp. 169, 171.

9. William George Dodd, *Courtly Love in Chaucer and Gower*, p. 245.

10. George Gordon Coulton, *Chaucer and His England*, pp. 222, 230.

11. George Lyman Kittredge, *Chaucer and his Poetry*, p. 167.

12. Root, p. 102.

13. Dodd, p. 5; C. S. Lewis, *The Allegory of Love*, pp. 35-36.

14. Root, p. 104.

15. Percy Van Dyke Shelly, *The Living Chaucer*, pp. 229, 234, 236.

16. John Speirs, *Chaucer the Maker*, pp. 121, 122.

17. D. S. Brewer, *Chaucer*, pp. 89-90.

18. For instance, Raymond Preston, *Chaucer*, p. 188, and William P. Ker, *Form and Style in Poetry*, p. 74.

19. Walter Hoyt French and Charles Brockway Hale (eds.), *Middle English Metrical Romances*, p. 741, lines 637-58.

20. J. R. R. Tolkien and E. V. Gordon (eds.), *Sir Gawain and the Green Knight*, pp. 13-14, lines 423-36.

21. A. J. Bliss (ed.), *Sir Orfeo*, p. 12, lines 120-26.

22. Charles Muscatine, "Form, Texture, and Meaning in Chaucer's *Knight's Tale*," pp. 913-14.

23. Dale Underwood, "The First of the Canterbury Tales."

24. Baum, "Characterization in the *Knight's Tale*," pp. 302, 303n2.

25. Howard Rollin Patch, *On Rereading Chaucer*, pp. 201-2, 203.

26. Baum, *Chaucer*, pp. 102, 103, 104.

27. J. S. P. Tatlock, *The Mind and Art of Chaucer*, pp. 94-95, 96.

28. *The Works of Geoffrey Chaucer*, ed. F. N. Robinson, p. 4.

29. Baum, "Characterization in the *Knight's Tale*," pp. 302, 303n2.

30. Tatlock, *The Development and Chronology of Chaucer's Works*, pp. 232-33.

31. J. R. Hulbert, "What was Chaucer's Aim in the Knight's Tale?" p. 385.

CHAPTER II

1. Robinson, pp. 34-35. All citations from Chaucer's text carry line numbers from this edition.

2. *Ibid.*, p. 676.

3. *Ibid.*, p. 890.

4. John Peter, *Complaint and Satire in Early English Literature*, pp. 6-7.

5. Robinson, p. 682.

6. Patch, pp. 226-28.

7. D. W. Robertson, Jr., *Preface to Chaucer*, pp. 386-87.

8. Patch, pp. 226-28.

9. Preston, pp. 51-52.

10. *Ibid.*

11. Wilhelm Ewald, *Der Humor in Chaucers Canterbury Tales*, p. 97.

12. *Ibid.*, p. 7.

13. *Ibid.*, p. 62.

14. *Ibid.*, pp. 78-79.

15. Preston, pp. 240-48.

CHAPTER III

1. Speirs, *loc. cit.*

2. Baum, *Chaucer*, p. 104.

3. Henry J. Webb, "A Reinterpretation of Chaucer's Theseus."

4. William Frost, "An Interpretation of Chaucer's Knight's Tale."

5. J. S. P. Tatlock and Arthur G. Kennedy, *A Concordance to the Complete Works of Chaucer and to the Romaunt of the Rose.*

6. Coulton, *Medieval Panorama*, pp. 239, 241-43, 247.

7. Willard Van Orman Quine, *Methods of Logic*, p. 477.

8. Robinson, pp. 669-70.

9. Robert Armstrong Pratt, "The Knight's Tale."

10. Robinson, p. 669.

11. Italics mine. Pratt, "Chaucer's Use of the Teseida."

12. Stuart Robertson, "Elements of Realism in the Knight's Tale."

13. Hubertis M. Cummings, *The Indebtedness of Chaucer's Works to the Italian Works of Boccaccio.*

14. Pratt, "The Knight's Tale," p. 82.

Chapter IV

1. Lewis, esp. pp. 171-72, 236-37.
2. Amy Kelly, "Eleanor of Aquitaine and her Courts of Love."
3. Robinson, p. 737.
4. Christien de Troyes *et al.*, "Sir Perceval of Galles." All references to the text are from this edition.
5. John M. Manly, "Sir Thopas: A Satire."
6. de Troyes *et al.*, p. xv.
7. Robinson, p. 740.
8. William H. Schofield, *Studies on the Libeaus Desconus*. All references are from this work.
9. *King Horn*, in French and Hale, pp. 25-70. The editors used the Hall edition, and all references to the poem are from it.
10. F. Hall (ed.), *King Horn*, pp. 179 ff.
11. Boris Ford (ed.), *The Age of Chaucer*, p. 37.
12. Eugen Kölbing (ed.), *The Romance of Sir Beves of Hamtoun*. All references are from this edition.
13. General Julius Zupitza, *The Romance of Guy of Warwick. The First or 14th-century Version*. All references are from this edition.
14. See D. W. Robertson, Jr., "Chrétien's Cligés and the Ovidian Spirit."
15. Robinson, p. 565.
16. Robertson, *Preface to Chaucer*.
17. *Ibid.*, pp. 430 ff.
18. *Ibid.*, p. 469.
19. Lewis, pp. 2-43. See also the comments of Professors Root and Dodd cited in Chapter I.

Chapter V

1. Robinson, p. 673.

Chapter VI

1. Robinson, p. 679.

Chapter VII

1. Robinson, p. 681.
2. Baum, *Chaucer*, p. 90.
3. Robinson, p. 681.
4. *Ibid.*

Chapter VIII

1. Lewis, p. 163.

BIBLIOGRAPhy

Aristotle. *The Rhetoric and Poetics of Aristotle*. Translated by W. Rhys Roberts
and Ingram Bywater, notes and intro. Friedrich Solmsen. New York, 1954.
Baugh, Albert C. "The Original Teller of the Merchant's Tale," *MP*, 35
(1937), 16-26.
Baum, Paull F. "Characterization in the *Knight's Tale*," *MLN*, XLVI (1931),
302-4.
————. *Chaucer: A Critical Appreciation*. Durham, North Carolina, 1958.
Birney, Earle. "Is Chaucer's Irony a Modern Discovery?" *JEGP*, 41 (1942),
303-19.
Bliss, A. J. (ed.). *Sir Orfeo*. Oxford, 1954.
Boccaccio, Giovanni. *La Teseida*, ed. S. Battaglia. Firenze, 1938.
————. *La Teseida*, ed. Ignazio Noutier. Milano, 1837.
Brewer, D. S. *Chaucer*. London, 1953.
Bronson, B. H. *In Search of Chaucer*. New York, 1960.
Brusendorff, Aage. *The Chaucer Tradition*. London, 1925.
Camden, Carroll, Jr. "Chauceriana," *MLN*, 47 (1932), 360-62.
Cazamian, Louis. *The Development of English Humor*. New York, 1930.
Chaucer, Geoffrey. *Canterbury Tales*, ed. John Matthews Manly. New York,
1928.
————. *The Complete Works of Chaucer*, ed. Walter Skeat. Oxford, 1925.
————. *The Works of Geoffrey Chaucer*, ed. F. N. Robinson. 2nd ed. Boston,
1957.
Coghill, Nevill. *Geoffrey Chaucer*. London, 1899.
————. *The Poet Chaucer*. London, 1949.
Cook, Albert S. *The Historical Background of Chaucer's Knight*. New Haven,
1916.
Coulton, George Gordon. *Chaucer and His England*. 8th ed. London, 1952.
————. *Medieval Panorama*. New York, 1955.
Cowling, George H. *Chaucer*. New York, 1927.
Crawford, W. R. *Bibliography of Chaucer*. New York, 1966.

Cummings, Hubertis M. *The Indebtedness of Chaucer's Works to the Italian Works of Boccaccio.* University of Cincinnati Studies, X, Part II, (1916).
Curry, Walter C. *Chaucer and the Mediaeval Sciences.* Oxford, 1926.
D'Arcy, Martin Cyril. *The Mind and the Heart of Love, Lion and Unicorn; A Study in Eros and Agape.* New York, 1947.
Dempster, Germaine. *Dramatic Irony in Chaucer.* Stanford University Publications in Language and Literature, IV (1932).
————. "The Original Teller of the Merchant's Tale," *MP,* 36 (1938), 1-8.
Dodd, William George. *Courtly Love in Chaucer and Gower.* Boston, 1913.
Donaldson, E. T. *Chaucer's Poetry.* New York, 1958.
Ewald, Wilhelm. *Der Humor in Chaucers Canterbury Tales.* Studien zur Englischen Philologie, XLV (1911).
Fairchild, Hoxie Neale. "Active Arcite, Contemplative Palamon," *JEGP,* 26 (1927), 285-93.
Ford, Boris (ed.). *The Age of Chaucer.* London, 1955.
French, Robert Dudley. *A Chaucer Handbook.* 2nd ed. New York, 1947.
French, Walter Hoyt. "The Lovers in the Knight's Tale," *JEGP,* 48 (1949), 320-28.
French, Walter Hoyt, and Charles Brockway Hale (eds.). *Middle English Metrical Romances.* New York, 1930.
Frost, William. "An Interpretation of Chaucer's Knight's Tale," *Review of English Studies,* XXV (1949), 289-304.
Gerould, Gordon Hall. *Chaucerian Essays.* Princeton, 1952.
Giffin, Mary. *Studies on Chaucer and his Audience.* Quebec, 1956.
Griffith, Dudley David. *Bibliography of Chaucer 1908-1953.* Seattle, 1955.
Hall, F. (ed.). *King Horn.* Oxford, 1901.
Hazlitt, William. *Lectures on the English Comic Writers.* London, 1900.
Highet, Gilbert. *Classical Tradition: Greek and Roman Influences on Western Literature.* Oxford, 1949.
Hulbert, J. R. "The Canterbury Tales and Their Narrators," *SP,* 45 (1948), 565-77.
————. "What was Chaucer's Aim in the Knight's Tale?" *SP,* XXVI (1929), 375-85.
Kaluza, Max (ed.). *The Romaunt of the Rose.* London, 1891.
Kelly, Amy. "Eleanor of Aquitaine and her Courts of Love," *Speculum,* XII (1937), 3-19.
Ker, William P. *Form and Style in Poetry,* ed. R. W. Chambers. London, 1928.
————. *English Literature: Medieval.* New York, 1912.
Kernan, Alvin. *The Cankered Muse.* New Haven, 1959.
Kittredge, George Lyman. *Chaucer and his Poetry.* Cambridge, Mass., 1920.
Kölbing, Eugen (ed.). *The Romance of Sir Beves of Hamtoun.* London, 1894.
Lawrence, W. W. *Chaucer and the Canterbury Tales.* New York, 1950.
Lewis, C. S. *The Allegory of Love.* Oxford, 1958.
Little, W. W., W. H. Wilson, and W. Edgar Moore. *Applied Logic.* Boston, 1955.
Loomis, Laura Hibbard. "Chaucer and the Breton Lays of the Auchinleck MS," *SP,* 38 (1941), 14-33.
Lowes, John L. "Chaucer and the Seven Deadly Sins," *PMLA,* 30 (1915), 237-371.
————. *Geoffrey Chaucer.* Bloomington, Ind., 1958.
Lüdeke, H. *Die Funktionem des Erzählers in Chaucers epischer Dichtung.* Studien zur Englischen Philologie, LXXII (1928).

Lumiansky, R. M. "Chaucer's Philosophical Knight," *Tulane Studies in English*, No. 3 (1952).

———. *Of Sondry Folk*. Austin, Texas, 1955.

McNabb, Vincent Joseph. *Geoffrey Chaucer, a Study in Genius and Ethics*. London, 1934.

Malone, Kemp. *Chapters on Chaucer*. Baltimore, 1951.

Manly, John Mathews. *Chaucer and the Rhetoricians*. Warton Lecture on English Poetry, XVII. London, 1926.

———. "Sir Thopas: A Satire," *Essays and Studies*, collected by Caroline F. E. Spurgeon, XIII, 52-73. London, 1928.

———. *Some New Light on Chaucer: Lectures Delivered at the Lowell Institute*. New York, 1926.

Marckwardt, Albert H. *Characterization in Chaucer's Knight's Tale*. University of Michigan Contributions in Modern Philology, No. 5, 185-93. Ann Arbor, 1947.

Meyer, Emil. *Die Charakterzeichnung bei Chaucer*. Studien zur Englischen Philologie, XLVIII (1913).

Mixon, William E. "Italian Influence on Chaucer," *Chaucer Memorial Lectures*, Royal Society of Literature of the United Kingdom. London, 1900.

Muscatine, Charles. *Chaucer and the French Tradition*. Berkeley, California, 1957.

———. "Form, Texture, and Meaning in Chaucer's *Knight's Tale*," *PMLA*, LXV (1950), 911-29.

Neilson, William Allen. *The Origins and Sources of the Court of Love*. Boston, 1899.

Patch, Howard Rollin. *On Rereading Chaucer*. Cambridge, Mass., 1939.

Peter, John. *Complaint and Satire in Early English Literature*. Oxford, 1956.

Pratt, Robert Armstrong. "Chaucer's Use of the Teseida," *PMLA*, LXII (1947), 598-621.

———. "Conjectures Regarding Chaucer's Manuscript of the Teseida," *SP*, XLII (1945), 745-63.

———. "The Knight's Tale," *Sources and Analogues of Chaucer's Canterbury Tales*, ed. William Frank Bryan and Germaine Dempster, 82-105. Chicago, 1941.

Preston, Raymond. *Chaucer*. London, 1952.

Quine, Willard Van Orman. *Methods of Logic*. New York, 1950.

Robertson, D. W., Jr. *Preface to Chaucer*. Princeton, 1962.

———. "Chrétien's Cligés and the Ovidian Spirit," *Comp. Lit.*, VII (1935), 35-42.

Robertson, Stuart. "Elements of Realism in the Knight's Tale," *JEGP*, XIV (1915), 226-55.

Root, Robert Kilburn. *The Poetry of Chaucer*. Cambridge, Mass., 1922.

Salter, Elizabeth. *The Clerk's Tale and The Knight's Tale (A Critical Study)*, in Barron's Educational Series, ed. David Daiches. 1963.

Schlauch, Margaret. "Chaucer's Merchant's Tale and Courtly Love," *ELH*, Schoeck, Richard J., and Jerome Taylor (eds.). *Chaucer Criticism*, 2 vols. 4 (1937), 201-12.

Notre Dame, Ind., 1960.

Schofield, William H. *Studies on the Libeaus Desconus. Harvard Studies and Notes in Philology and Literature*, IV. Boston, 1895.

Shelly, Percy Van Dyke. *The Living Chaucer*. Philadelphia, 1940.

Skeat, Walter W. *The Student's Chaucer*. Oxford, 1929.

Slaughter, Eugene E. *Love and the Virtues and Vices in Chaucer.* Nashville, Tenn., 1946.

Speirs, John. *Chaucer the Maker.* London, 1951.

Spurgeon, Carolyn F. E. (ed.). *Five Hundred Years of Chaucer Criticism and Allusion, 1357-1900.* 3 vols. Cambridge, Eng., 1925.

Swift, Jonathan. "A Modest Proposal," *Eighteenth Century Poetry and Prose,* ed. Louis I. Bredvold, Alan McKillop, and Lois Whitney, pp. 242-47. New York, 1939.

Tatlock, J. S. P. *The Development and Chronology of Chaucer's Works.* 2nd ser. London, 1907.

————. *The Mind and Art of Chaucer.* Syracuse, 1950.

Tatlock, J. S. P., and Arthur G. Kennedy. *A Concordance to the Complete Works of Chaucer and to the Romaunt of the Rose.* Washington, D.C., 1927.

Ten Brink, Bernhard. *Chaucers Sprache und Verskunst.* dritte Auflage, bearbeitet von Ed. Eckhardt. Tauchnitz, 1920.

Tolkien, J. R. R., and E. V. Gordon (eds.). *Sir Gawain and the Green Knight.* Oxford, 1930.

de Troyes, Christien, *et al.* "Sir Perceval of Galles," *The Thornton Romances,* ed. James Orchard Halliwell, pp. 1-87. London, 1844.

Tupper, Frederick. "Chaucer and the Seven Deadly Sins," *PMLA,* 29 (1914), 93-128.

————. "Chaucer's Sinners and Sins," *JEGP,* 15 (1916), 56-106.

Underwood, Dale. "The First of the Canterbury Tales," *ELH,* XVII, 455-69.

Wagenknecht, Edward Charles (ed.). *Chaucer: Modern Essays in Criticism.* New York, 1959.

Webb, Henry J. "A Reinterpretation of Chaucer's Theseus," *Review of English Studies,* XXIII (1947), 289-96.

Weese, Walter E. "Vengeance and Pleyn Correccioun," *MLY,* 63 (1948), 331-33.

Williams, George Guion. *A New View of Chaucer.* Durham, N. C., 1965.

Zupitza, General Julius (ed.). *The Romance of Guy of Warwick. The First or 14th-century Version.* London: Early English Text Society, 1883, 1887, 1891.